THE ORDNANCE SURVEY GUIDE TO
GUIDE TO
GARDENS
IN BRITAIN

Edited by

Robert Pearson, Susanne Mitchell
and Candida Hunt

ORDNANCE SURVEY
NEWNES

COUNTRY LIFE BOOKS

Contributors

Edward Fawcett Events Organiser for the National Trust, with a wide knowledge of British gardens and garden history.

Kenneth Lemmon Editor of *The Northern Gardener*, the journal of the Northern Horticultural Society, and a much respected gardening historian.

Robert Pearson Gardening Correspondent of the *Sunday Telegraph*; until recently Publisher of Collingridge Books, with a long career in garden publishing and journalism; member of the Council of the Royal National Rose Society.

Eric Robson Gardens Adviser to the National Trust for Scotland, immensely knowledgeable on gardens and gardening in Scotland.

Mark Rumary A talented landscape designer, director of a landscaping company within the East-Anglian Notcutt group.

F. W. Shepherd N.D.H. (Hons.), F.I.Biol., V.M.H. Past director of the Rosewarne Experimental Horticultural Station at Cambourne, Cornwall, and afterwards Senior Horticultural Adviser of the Government's National Agricultural Advisory Service; member of the Royal Horticultural Society's Examinations Board.

Anne Stevens An amateur gardener with a detailed knowledge of West Country gardens, on which she lectures; contributor to *Amateur Gardening*.

Tom Wright B.Sc. (Hort.) Senior Lecturer in Landscape and Amenity Horticulture at Wye College, University of London, with a deep knowledge of British gardens.

First published 1986 by
Ordnance Survey   and   Country Life Books
Romsey Road   an imprint of Newnes Books
Maybush   a division of The Hamlyn Publishing Group Limited
Southampton   Bridge House, 69 London Road
SO9 4DH   Twickenham, Middlesex TW1 3SB, England

Maps Crown Copyright © 1986

Copyright © in text Newnes Books 1986

Photographs by Michael Warren and Edward Gabriel/Photos Horticultural © Newnes Books 1986

Regional maps on pages 14-15, 72-73, 120-121, 153, 189, 227, 261 by Thames Cartographic Services, © Newnes Books and Ordnance Survey 1986

Newnes   Ordnance Survey
ISBN 0 600 36885 8 (softback)   ISBN 0 319 00070 2 (softback)
ISBN 0 600 36859 9 (cased)   ISBN 0 319 00069 9 (cased)

Printed in Great Britain

Contents

How to use this guide

This guide is arranged regionally; a key map showing the area covered by each region is given on the opposite page. Within each region, the gardens are listed alphabetically by county.

A detailed description is given of how to find the way to each garden from the nearest town, together with the sheet number of the Ordnance Survey Landranger Map which covers the area and the National Grid reference of the garden site. Sections of Ordnance Survey maps are also included for over 60 of the gardens.

The National Grid reference given for each garden consists of two letters and four numbers. This pinpoints the location to within 1 kilometre on Ordnance Survey maps. The following example identifies how these references are constructed:

Furzey Gardens, Hampshire has a grid reference SU2711

SU This identifies the 100 kilometre grid square in which the garden lies and can be ignored from the point of view of locating the gardens in this book.

27 Can be found in the top and bottom margins of the relevant Ordnance Survey Landranger map sheet (identified at the start of each garden description). It is the reference number for one of the grid lines running North/South on the map.

11 Can be found in the left and right hand margins of the relevant Ordnance Survey Landranger map sheet. It is the reference number for one of the grid lines running East/West across the map.

These numbers together locate the bottom left hand corner of the 1 kilometre grid square in which Furzey Gardens appear.

When planning routes or driving to the areas of the gardens included in this guide, the *Ordnance Survey Motoring Atlas of Great Britain* at 3 miles to 1 inch scale and the *Ordnance Survey Road Atlas of Great Britain* at 1:250,000 (approximately 4 miles to 1 inch) are ideal. For pinpointing the site once in the area use Ordnance Survey Landranger (1:50,000) or Pathfinder (1:25,000) maps. For London gardens, the Ordnance Survey *ABC London Street Atlas* is a useful location guide.

Key to symbols

P Car park	**A** Picnic area
WC Toilets	**⚜** Plant sales
⊖ Public transport	**✿** Guide book on sale
⌂ Parties acceptable	**★** Shop
D Dogs acceptable	**⌂** House open to public
☞ Refreshments available	**⌇** Nature trail

M: Monday   T: Tuesday   W: Wednesday   Th: Thursday
F: Friday   S: Saturday   Su: Sunday

NGS: reference should be made to the National Garden Scheme's publication *Gardens Open to the Public* and to *Scotland's Gardens*, a guide to gardens open under Scotland's Gardens scheme.

4

Map to regions

HIGHLAND

GRAMPIAN

Scotland

TAYSIDE

CENTRAL

FIFE

LOTHIAN

STRATHCLYDE

BORDERS

DUMFRIES
AND
GALLOWAY

NORTHUMBERLAND

1 TYNE AND WEAR
2 CLEVELAND
3 WEST YORKSHIRE
4 SOUTH YORKSHIRE
5 GREATER MANCHESTER
6 MERSEYSIDE
7 WEST MIDLANDS
8 BEDFORDSHIRE
9 BERKSHIRE
10 WEST GLAMORGAN
11 MID GLAMORGAN
12 SOUTH GLAMORGAN

DURHAM

CUMBRIA

The North

NORTH YORKSHIRE

LANCASHIRE

HUMBERSIDE

GWYNEDD

CLWYD

CHESHIRE

DERBY-
SHIRE

NOTTINGHAM-
SHIRE

LINCOLNSHIRE

STAFFORD-
SHIRE

LEICESTERSHIRE

NORFOLK

SHROPSHIRE

Wales and
Western Counties

Central
England

Eastern Counties

POWYS

HEREFORD
AND
WORCESTER

WARWICK-
SHIRE

NORTHAMPTON-
SHIRE

CAMBRIDGE-
SHIRE

SUFFOLK

DYFED

GLOUCESTER-
SHIRE

OXFORD-
SHIRE

BUCKINGHAM-
SHIRE

HERTFORD-
SHIRE

ESSEX

GWENT

GREATER
LONDON

AVON

WILTSHIRE

London and
Southern England

SURREY

KENT

SOMERSET

HAMPSHIRE

WEST
SUSSEX

EAST
SUSSEX

The West Country

DEVON

DORSET

ISLE OF
WIGHT

CORNWALL

5

Introduction

Gardening as an art follows in the footsteps of civilisation. In this country its development can be traced back to the Romans. Before their arrival the ancient Britons, never safe from feuds, invading neighbours and tribal warfare, limited their efforts to primitive agricultural needs – growing leeks, onions and carrots to supplement their diet. The Romans introduced at least 38 new species of vegetables, herbs, fruits, trees and shrubs, and flowers. The Roman villa garden in Britain was a replica of the Italian gardens they had left behind: theatrical, formal, but a garden of some luxury and taste. Excavations at the villa of Fishbourne, near Chichester, for example, have revealed that there were large rectangular lawns between gravelled or sanded paths, edged with regular matching patterns of box in which statues and busts would almost certainly have been placed. There would have been roses on lattice work and colonnading round the greenery, fanciful topiary work and wall frescoes, fountains and fountain basins. This high standard of garden making was not to be matched for a thousand years.

There is no gardening without peace, and there was little of that during the Dark Ages, as warring hordes of Jutes, Anglo-Saxons, Picts, Scots and Danes all took their turn in ravaging the land. The advent of Christianity and the spread of monasteries was to prove the turning-point in gardening history. In peaceful seclusion, vegetables and herbs could be grown by the monks to supplement their often meatless diet, to provide simples and medicines, to put fruit on the table and flowers on the altar. These gardens were necessarily small. Most of our present-day herbs were grown, and the flowers included lilies, roses, wallflowers and irises, and shrubs such as rosemary, sweet bay and laurel. After the Norman Conquest in 1066 there was a greater interchange with the Continent, which led to the introduction of new plants and the reintroduction of others that had been lost.

The medieval secular gardens belonged to the monastic garden genre: small, enclosed, private, though they were slightly more ornamental in layout. No illustrations of medieval gardens in this country exist earlier than the 13th century; but there are many after 1450. The typical garden was a regular four-square design, often with four raised beds centred by a fountain or pool. An arbour was frequently made by vines tumbling over trellis work.

With the settled period that came with the establishment of the Tudors, the nobility began to build stately homes instead of castles. The feeling for luxurious living and expanding horizons was reflected in their garden surrounds. The Renaissance was beginning to influence both architecture and garden layout. Under Henry VIII, and particularly in the reign of Elizabeth I, the garden was used for pleasure and aesthetic satisfaction. More flowers were to be seen, and layouts became increasingly elaborate – a trend exemplified by the knot garden, with its complicated geometric patterns within low box hedges. Knots were first illustrated in 1499, and their popularity was long-lasting. By the end of the 17th century parterres imported from France had become the vogue. These were less intricate and more free-flowing, incorporating box scroll work or arabesques cut in turf, or both, and with the spaces often filled with coloured gravels and brick dust so that the graceful shapes could the better be seen. The maze was also popular as a garden ornament at this time.

One of a series of enclosed 'garden rooms' at Sissinghurst, Kent.

A significant change to the English garden landscape was brought by Charles II after the Restoration in 1660. He introduced French-influenced water canals, statues and fountains. His gardens at Hampton Court were imitated by stately home owners on whatever scale they could afford. Avenues, too, continued to be popular into the 18th century, in spite of William and Mary's introduction of the fussy, compartmented Dutch style. Topiary, introduced by the Romans, had its heyday during their reign. The 17th-century influences can still be seen at Badminton, with its avenue $2\frac{1}{2}$ miles (4 km) long, the geometric gardens of Longleat, Wrest, Ragley, Chatsworth and others. In these great gardens during the 17th century a greenhouse culture grew up: buildings of glass and stone with opaque roofing were built to overwinter evergreens and that most fashionable of fruit, the orange. As the 18th century progressed, the orangeries became increasingly ornamental, their architecture often matching that of the mansion. Greenhouses were confined to the kitchen garden, as they continued to be during the 19th century and indeed still are today. The orangery became more and more the repository for the wealth of ornamental plants introduced from all over the world during the 18th and early 19th centuries. The Victorians liked their conservatories attached to the house, adjoining a main room so that it was possible to look out onto a lush jungle or a display of highly coloured exotics at all times of the year.

The 18th century was an important one in the history of gardening. It gave the *Jardin anglais* to the world. Art and literature played a considerable part in the storming of the formal-garden barricades; Alexander Pope, for example, heavily satirised the topiary figures in gardens, and ridiculed formality in his verse. There was a gradual change in attitude. Charles Bridgman, who laid out the Serpentine in London's Hyde Park, was the early landscape designer to advance towards the new informal style. At Castle Howard John Vanbrugh opened the garden to the countryside. But it was William Kent, with Lord Burlington (who brought in the Palladian style of architecture) as his patron, who carried out the literary, poetical and pictorial ideas of the rich estate owners. Kent claimed that nature abhorred a straight line, and worked on Pope's philosophy to 'consult the genius of the place'. Horace Walpole summed up his work thus: 'Kent leapt the fence and saw all nature was a garden'. An almost original Kent landscape can still be seen at Rousham in Oxfordshire; at Stourhead, Stowe and Chiswick the classical basis of the new gardening is also much in evidence. Architectural features were also in vogue at this time.

Into this landscape came Lancelot (Capability) Brown, a working gardener who began his landscaping career in 1751. He had worked with Kent, but had a completely different outlook. He was a man of common sense without the advantage of a classical education, of travel or of training in the arts of painting or architecture – a no-nonsense gardener.

It was Brown who broke the rules and kicked over the classical traces, who brought the greensward to the very doorways of the mansions, banished terraces and parterre gardens, turned streams into lakes, demolished the long avenues and worked to bring into being smooth, undulating parklands decorated with clumps of trees, and bordering the green picture with encircling lines of trees on the skyline. 'Clumping and belting' his detractors called it, but at Harewood, Bowood, Blenheim, Nuneham Courtney and scores of other great gardens, it worked.

In the latter part of the 18th century, the 'age of reason', the Romantic movement urged the owners of the great Palladian mansions to adopt a different approach. This was the age of Chinoiserie, grottoes, medieval barns, the Gothic revival, of ruins, arches and mock castles, follies and willow pattern bridges. The Picturesque movement extended the feeling of the Romantic – rough rocks were needed to look wild in a landscape, and shaggy horses and cows were regarded as preferable to smooth-coated ones. This was a glorious time for trying out different features. Another view was expressed in his writings by Humphry Repton, who felt that gardens 'should show a full sense of general utility'. One result of his approach was that terraces and flower beds near the house were introduced again.

In the early gardens there were few ornamental shrubs and evergreens, but in the 18th and 19th centuries a flood of new plants was brought into the country. By the end of the 18th century 5500 new plant species had been introduced; during the 19th century almost 9000 more arrived. Garden makers had a wealth of new forms and colours to use from among the floral treasures of China and Japan, the Himalayas, South America and the American Pacific coast, and the contents of many gardens were completely altered. The number and diversity of exotic trees made possible the creation of the arboretum and the pinetum. Both became very popular during the 19th century. Another different look resulted from the activities of plant hunters, with their diverse introductions of flowering shrubs, for example many cherries as well as the richly coloured rhododendrons. To house the more tender newcomers the great glasshouses and conservatories of the 19th century were built, as at Chatsworth, Syon Park, Kew and Somerleyton, as well as extensive ranges of greenhouses in mansion gardens.

During the 19th century 'gardener's gardens' became fashionable. Thousands of half-hardy annuals would be raised each year to create the eye-catching bedding schemes that can still be seen in many public parks. In later Victorian times and during the Edwardian period the rose became a much favoured plant, used for the first time for itself alone instead of as part of a mixed border, and featured in rose gardens and rose pergolas. Hybrid teas were introduced in 1867, though it was not until 1924 that the first floribundas became available.

The labour-intensive approach to gardens possible in Victorian days could not be sustained in the 20th century, as the First World War caused shortages of men and of money. It had in any case been superseded by those such as William Robinson and Gertrude Jekyll, who encouraged the use of native plants in mixed herbaceous borders and in the wild garden, and preached restful, well-ordered colour schemes instead of mosaics of brash colours. In both grand and more modest gardens today, the trend is towards the labour-saving grace of the hundreds of flowering shrubs available, underplanted with ground-cover subjects and interspersed with flowering plants and accompanied by trees. Gardens are planned to be colourful, convenient and pleasing to look at: gardens for pleasure as well as for pride.

What to see and where

There can be no other country in the world that can show its centuries of garden history and evolution on the ground in such detail, or display in its gardens such an immense variety of alien plants brought from every continent.

The climate Britain's place in the northern temperate zone makes our gardens the congenial home of some 12,000 species of hardy plants. If the many great palm houses and conservatories of the botanic gardens are also taken into account, visiting British gardens is almost a botanical tour of the world. To the weather should be added the benign influence of the Gulf Stream, which gives Devon and Cornwall and the western coast of Scotland conditions in which rhododendrons of the high Himalayas and of the peaks of Tibet and China, the camellias of Japan, the magnolias of both China and Japan, and remarkable Australian inhabitants such as tree ferns and bottle brushes, can flourish. Such gardens are to be found in Scotland at Inverewe, Brodick Castle, the Younger Botanic Gardens, Logan, and the Edinburgh Botanic Garden; and in England, among many other gardens, at Heaselands, Exbury, the Isabella and Waterhouse Plantations in Richmond and Bushy Park, the Savill and Valley Gardens at Windsor, Cragside, Leonardslee and Wakehurst Place. In Cornwall and Devon Lanhydrock, Trelissick, Trengwainton, Knightshayes Court and Bodnant, and in Wales Plas Newydd, all spring to mind.

Roses These best-loved flowers have a special place in some gardens as a feature, and in some botanical gardens are planted to show the long history and evolution of the flower. These visual lessons can be seen at Oxford, at Ness (the University of Liverpool Botanic Gardens) in the Wirral and at the Gardens of the Rose, St Albans, the Royal National Rose Society's gardens and trial grounds. At Mottisfont Abbey in Hampshire the National Trust has brought together all the old-fashioned and shrub roses still in cultivation in this country; there are rose gardens at Castle Howard, Sissinghurst, Nymans, Hardwick Hall, Tintinhull, Queen Mary's Rose Garden in Regent's Park, at Wisley and at Kew. Large rose nurseries such as Mattocks at Nuneham Courtenay near Oxford and Harkness's at Hitchin, Hertfordshire are also open to view.

Many arboreta are most rewarding in the autumn; Westonbirt is no exception.

left *A profusion of roses at the RNRS's Gardens of the Rose at St Albans.*

Tree collections Although most of our wild native woodland and forests have gone, Britain can boast some of the finest collections of both native and colourful exotic trees in arboreta and pinetums. These are to be found at Bedgebury, Bicton Park, Bressingham, Sheffield Park, Thorp Perrow, Killerton, Batsford Park, Winkworth, Westonbirt, the Edinburgh Botanic Garden, Hergest Croft, Wakehurst Place and Kew.

Rock gardens A Victorian innovation, rock gardens and alpine plants have increased in popularity. Some of the best displays are at Killerton, Ness and Wisley, the Edinburgh Botanic Garden and Kew. They are also to be seen at the Cambridge Botanic Garden, Bicton and Harlow Car, Aberdeen University, Luton Hoo, Threave, Alton Towers, Wakehurst and Ascott.

A display of alpines in the rock garden at the RHS Garden, Wisley.

Water is an increasingly popular feature in gardens of all types and sizes.

Topiary Best fitted to the style and feeling of formal gardens, there are still many fine specimens of the topiarist's art to be seen – at Levens Hall, Ascott, Hidcote, Arley Hall, Antony House, Tyninghame, Packwood, Hever Castle, Dartington Hall, Great Dixter, Crathes, Blickling Hall and Newburgh Priory.

Japanese gardens In design completely alien to the traditions of British landscape gardening, Japanese gardens were popular in the early years of this century. One of the best is at Tatton Park, and there are others at Compton Acres, Cliveden and Newstead Abbey.

Formal gardens Through conservation and reconstruction, examples can be seen of period gardens ranging back to medieval times. Oxford and Cambridge colleges are typical, as is the reconstructed Monk's Garden at Ashridge, and Newstead Abbey with its medieval fish pond. Hampton Court gives a useful picture of Tudor gardening. Other examples include Kirkby Hall, Erddig, Moseley Old Hall, Edzell Castle, Pitmedden, Little Moreton Hall, Drummond Castle, Holker Hall and Dunham Massey. The Queen's Garden at Kew is a replica of a 17th-century layout, and Melbourne Hall has retained its original layout dating from the same century; an idea of the Dutch garden influenced by William and Mary can be seen in the white garden at Hidcote, and at Bramham Park there are still great 'French' avenues.

Ornamental buildings These formed an important part in the design of 18th-century landscape gardening. One of the earliest classically ornamented gardens can be seen at Rousham near Oxford; other examples are at Stowe, Stourhead, Studley Royal, Chatsworth, Claremont, Melbourne and Culzean Castle. At Castle Howard an approach to an Elysian landscape was made in the early 1700s; at West Wycombe Park there is a mixture of classical and romantic ornamentation; Kew retains some of its many buildings; there are ruins at Shugborough; Wroxton Abbey displays well both the picturesque and the Gothic revival.

Herb gardens At Hardwick Hall, Hatfield House and Scotney Castle the herb gardens are in strict keeping with the period, as they also are at Moseley Old Hall and the Queen's Garden at Kew. Among many others, herb gardens can also be found at Sissinghurst, Gunby Hall and Little Moreton Hall.

Terrace gardens Three rare 17th-century terrace gardens are at Duncombe Park, Rievaulx and Farnborough Hall. Because of the elevated position of the house, terracing is also well illustrated at Powis Castle.

Water features A notable water garden at Burnby Hall holds one of the largest collections of water-lilies in Europe. Blenheim Palace, with its water parterre and Brown's lake, is memorable. Some of the best examples of water in formal gardens can be seen at Westbury Court, Wrest Park and Lochinch Castle. Other good water gardens are those at Sheffield Park, Savill Gardens, Wakehurst Place, Harlow Car, Hodnet Hall, Newburgh Priory, Bramham Park, Chatsworth and Studley Royal.

Landscape gardens There are many living illustrations of the landscape revolution that swept this country in the late 17th century: at Stowe, Claremont, Rousham, Harewood House, Chatsworth, Bowood, Blenheim, Audley End and Petworth. Landscapes by Repton can be seen at Sheringham, Antony House, Tatton and Plas Newydd.

The 19th-century parterre work is best seen at Broughton Hall, Trentham, the terrace at Harewood House, the Syon Vista and the Broad Walk at Kew. The Jekyll and Lutyens collaboration is well displayed at Gledstone Hall.

The landscaping of the campus of York University by the late Frank Clark is modern landscaping at its best. Russell Page's work can be seen at Tyninghame and Percy Cane's at Dartington.

London and Southern England

Ipswich

ORDSHIRE

E S S E X

Harlow

A T E R

Regent's Park

Kensington Gardens
Hyde Park
Chelsea Physic
Garden

Greenwich
Park

Southend

N D O N

Canterbury

Sandling
Park

Great
Comp

Eyhorne Manor

Goodnestone
Park

Maidstone

K E N T

Northbourne
Court Garden

Hever
Castle

Hall
Place

Crittenden
House

Withersdane
Gardens

Y

Sissinghurst
Castle Garden

Coldham

Dover

Penshurst
Place

Ladham
House

Crawley

Waystrode
Manor

Standen

Scotney
Castle

Bedgebury Pinetum

e High
eeches

Wakehurst
Place

Cobblers

Nymans

Borde
Hill

E A S T

Great Dixter

selands

Sheffield
Park

S U S S E X

Hastings

Brighton

The Old Rectory BERKSHIRE

Mr and Mrs R. Merton, Burghfield, nr Reading.
tel. Burghfield Common (073 529) 2206

A most ingeniously designed and planted garden of about 6 acres (2.5ha), full of surprises and many different features, and still comparatively young since, apart from the 18th-century house and the mature trees, the remainder has been created over the past 30 years. A border beneath the house windows is planted in themes of blue, yellow and white with irises, sages, lavenders, and eryngiums. The paved south terrace is gay with beautifully planted pots and containers, a special feature of the garden. On the warm walls are sun-loving climbers. On the east side is a sheltered south-west facing border with two notable specimens – a fine 20-year-old *Magnolia grandiflora* 'Exmouth' and the August-flowering golden rain tree, *Koelreuteria*. Lilies, roses and geraniums thrive everywhere. Next to the lean-to conservatory is a small intimate paved 'French garden' with pots of hibiscus, citrus, oleanders, and scented pelargoniums. The main vista from the south terrace is the double herbaceous border backed by mature yew hedges. Beyond this is a wild or spring garden which leads to a large natural pool where massed azaleas and rhododendrons give colour and backing. A cool, shaded church walk passes beneath mature oaks and yews. There are other notable features here, where old-fashioned plants and colour themes are the special characters beloved by the owners.

5 m SW of Reading turn W off A33 and W to Burghfield

SU 6668 (OS 175)

Open Feb to Oct last W in month (exc Aug) 1100-1600; last 2 Su in year 1400-1800; other times by appt.

P ⊖ ⊟ D (guide dogs only) ☕ (limited opening) ★ (limited opening)

Old Rectory Cottage BERKSHIRE

A. W. A. Baker Esq., Tidmarsh, Reading.
tel. Pangbourne (073 57) 3241

This is a 2-acre (0.8ha) plantsman's paradise, remarkable for its rare and unusual plants and the fact that it has been created by the owners from a cottage garden jungle. The Bakers were attracted by the capabilities of the site when they arrived in the late 1950s. Two quite different kinds of garden have evolved after 25 years, each merging imperceptibly with the other. Round the house, an informal cottage-garden style is characterised by grass paths, island beds and an abundance of plants carefully chosen for shape, texture, and colour contrasts. Concealed boundaries of the garden are a backcloth of gold, purple, grey and variegated trees and shrubs. Every wall is covered with a climber or wall shrub. The rock garden is a delight in May and June. Very different in character is the wild garden: cool, shaded paths wander among willows, poplars and old apple trees to the lake and the delightful river. Spring bulbs, primulas, hellebores, ferns and hostas, festoons of roses over the trees, lilies of many species and varieties, and bold foliage and waterside plants are all to be discovered here. Sawdust, horse manure and old hay mulches have been liberally used on the chalky clay soils throughout this garden to give wonderful fertility and growth.

½ m S of Pangbourne
turn E off A340 and left
at T-junction

SU 6375   (OS 175)

Open frequently Feb to
Sept by appt and on
several Su under NGS

Peak months Mar-Apr;
June July

🚻 (gardening societies
only) 🐕 (occasional)

Savill Gardens and Valley Gardens

BERKSHIRE

Crown Estate Commissioners, The Great Park, Windsor.
tel. Windsor (95) 60222

These large-scale Royal gardens are set in the magnificence of Windsor Great Park, its 4,500 acres (1,821ha) of planned and planted woodlands and vistas including the ancient royal hunting forests. The Savill Garden was laid out first, from the mid-1930s, by Eric Savill, the then Deputy Surveyor, who combined a keen eye for landscape and a great horticultural knowledge with a drive and persuasive persistence that impressed the Royal Family. He created 35 acres (14ha) of vistas, glades and ponds, creating a rich adornment of acid soil-loving rhododendrons, azaleas and countless other trees and shrubs.

The Valley Gardens, lying to the south of the Savill Gardens, were also laid out by Eric Savill, who from 1947 created 400 acres (162ha) of superb woodland gardens exploiting a series of valleys lying along the north bank of Virginia Water, the attractive, very large 18th-century artificial lake. Bold planting was again practised in groups of four to nine trees or shrubs, with spectacular massing as in the famous Punch Bowl of evergreen azaleas, at its best in late May. There are 50 acres (20ha) of rhododendrons, azaleas, camellias, maples, hydrangeas, etc., and autumn colour is also outstanding.

4 m S of Windsor on A328 take 1st turn W after junction with A30

SU 9770   (OS 175)

Open Savill Gardens: Mar to late Dec daily 1000-1800; Valley Gardens: daily dawn to dusk

🅿 WC ♿ (1½ m walk) 🚻
D (Valley Gardens only)
🛍 (Savill Gardens)
🅰 (Savill Gardens)
🏵 (Savill Gardens)
✿ (Savill Gardens)
★ (Savill Gardens)

Exbury Gardens HAMPSHIRE

E. D. de Rothschild, Esq., Southampton.
tel. Fawley (0703) 891203

These world-famous gardens are synonymous with the names of Rothschild and of rhododendrons, since it was here that Lionel de Rothschild created nearly 200 acres (81ha) of woodland gardens, and over 1,000 new hybrids of rhododendrons and azaleas have been bred in the 70 years or so since the work began. The large porticoed 20th-century house rebuilt in the 1960s in Regency style with its attendant cedars, looks out across a great expanse of lawn. An area of the former New Forest was the basis for the gardens that came into being in the early 1920s. For ten years 150 men worked to complete the garden that included miles of walks, thousands of trees and shrubs, ponds, bridges and a great rock garden. The design is completely informal, and the scale such that a day can easily be spent here, and without the plan available at the gate one could get lost. From March to late June the spectacular sequence of colour displays unfolds. First the early daffodils, the magnolias and species rhododendrons and then a great blaze of azaleas and May- and June-flowering rhododendrons, so many raised here by the Rothschild family. There are also many other fine things: Japanese maples, conifers, camellias, wisterias, and round the ponds, candelabra primulas and exotic foliage plants. Perhaps the most spectacular feature in late May is Lady Chamberlain's Walk, devoted to the orange-salmon waxy bell-flowered rhododendron of that name.

2 m S of Dibden Purlieu
turn S off B3054

SU 4200   (OS 196)

Open early Mar to mid
June daily 1000-1730;
reduced rates for
parties of 15 or over

Peak month May

🅿 WC ♿ D 🍽 ⛱ ⛽
🌿 ★

Greatham Mill HAMPSHIRE

Mrs Frances M. Pumphrey, Greatham, Liss.
tel. Blackmoor (042 07) 219/294

A really superb 'cottage type' garden developed around a charming old mill (built in 1694) and its river valley setting. Frances Pumphrey and her husband came here in 1949 to find no real garden, an old orchard and 1½ acres (0.6ha) of land along the river. With no previous knowledge or experience she began making the garden with the valuable help of her gardener, Jim Collins. A water garden was the first very successful feature to be made, using the mill tail race that flows between stone retaining walls across the front garden to the river. A charming and intimate front garden is bounded on one side by the parapet wall of this water garden where one can look down on a luxuriant association of hostas, royal ferns, rodgersias and giant gunneras and many more. The rest of the garden lies beside and behind the house following the course of the river, itself quite small, melodious and full of character. Paths lead to many carefully designed features inviting one ever onwards. There is a golden foliage corner, a purple and red border, a most effective and attractive rock outcrop and dry garden; massed shrub roses and yet another water garden made from the mill tail gate with attractive brick arch. At the furthest point is an arboretum and wild garden, and on higher ground an old tennis court site has been made into a long dry wall feature. Good plants are everywhere.

7 m SE of Alton on B3006 turn off at Hawkley

SU 7630 (OS 186)

Open early Apr to late Sept Su and Bank Hols 1400-1900; nursery garden weekdays by appt

Peak months May to JUly

P WC 🖳 (by appt) 🎋 🐕

Houghton Lodge HAMPSHIRE

Capt. and Mrs Martin Busk, Stockbridge.
tel. Stockbridge (026 481) 0502

Houghton Lodge is a seductively pretty 'cottage orne' in a lovely setting, its smooth lawns sloping gently down to the River Test with its peaceful pastures and willow-fringed banks and passing swans. Created in the Humphry Repton style in the early 19th century, this ornamental house is cleverly sited above the river, and its 4 acres (1.6ha) of grounds are essentially fairly simple. A bold sweep of mature trees and shrubberies clothe a ridge behind the lawns where a perimeter walk beneath some fine planes, oaks and horse chestnuts gives tempting glimpses of the river below. In spring snowdrops abound here, and in earlier times snowdrop parties were held combined with an elegant lunch. Later in the spring massed daffodils are a great feature. A unique flint folly in the form of a turretted postern gate once carried a bridle path into the grounds from the south-west. There are young autumn-colouring trees near the river, especially Indian gums and maples. A fine walled garden is linked with farm buildings as the productive elements of Houghton Lodge. Inside the tiled strong 10-ft (3-m) walls can be found a well-maintained, very productive garden. The glasshouses have been restored, with vines, cucumber and decorative plants, labelled espalier fruit trees line the paths, and the central dipping well still survives with its bucket and chain intact. A new formal garden is proposed to link the house with the garden on the south side.

On W edge of
Stockbridge turn S
to North Houghton

SU 3433   (OS 185)

Open Mar to end July
W and Easter Su and M
1400-1700

Peak season spring

P WC ⊖ ⊟ ● (Easter
only) ⊛ ☎ (by appt)

Jenkyn Place HAMPSHIRE

Mr and Mrs Gerald Coke, Bentley.
tel. Bentley (0420) 23118

One of the finest private gardens in the country could well be described as an outstanding plantsman's formal garden, developed continually over the past 30 years or so on the Hidcote/Sissinghurst principle of a number of enclosed gardens each with its own very specialised character and planting theme. The late 17th-century house overlooks the garden, which falls away steadily to the south east towards the River Wey, the fertile upper greensand soils and warm slope playing an important part in the range and the rarity of the plants to be found here. Connected by beautifully detailed and designed gates, arches, steps, and paths, there are many exciting gardens to explore. Near the house a charming intimate Dutch garden concentrates on scented plants around a delightful fountain. A sundial garden leads to an elegant rose garden with elongated pool, rose beds and many fine and rare plants on the walls. Dominating a terrace on the next level are two superb herbaceous borders, deliberately designed to provide maximum colour and effect in high season. An Italian garden, a herb garden and a sunken garden are also to be discovered here, and new gardens are still in the making. Rare plants abound, beautifully grown and maintained, and the setting of the house and many old mature trees add to the sense of combined maturity and development created by a husband and wife team with their gardeners since the Second World War.

4 m SW of Farnham on
A31 turn N to Bentley

SU 7844   (OS 186)

Open May to end Aug
Su 1400-1800; parties at
other times by appt

⊖ (limited) 🚻 (by appt;
not Su) ♿ ✿

Mottisfont Abbey HAMPSHIRE

The National Trust, nr Romsey.
tel. Lockerley (0794) 40757

The Augustinian Priors chose this beautiful sequestered place beside the River Test (still a fine trout river) for the abbey, and the 'font' or spring from which its name derives still wells up clear water in a shaded dell near the old house. On the Dissolution the buildings were embodied into a large gabled country house by William Sandys, Chamberlain to Henry VIII, and later enlarged in the 19th century and surrounded by magnificent trees, lawns and parkland, with walled kitchen gardens away to the west. The National Trust acquired Mottisfont in 1957 and in 1972 created in the walled kitchen garden the superb rose gardens for which this place is now internationally famous. The emphasis is on old shrub roses and climbers, many richly scented and many now rare in cultivation diligently collected by the great expert Graham Stuart Thomas, who also designed the garden. A visit in June and July is quite magical. Association of spring and summer herbaceous plants extend the season and provide contrast. A further rose garden is being developed in a second walled garden to house shrub roses of mainly German and Continental origins. In complete contrast, the extensive parkland and shady walks around the old house enable one to admire the magnificent trees. A pleasant paved walk and lime avenue, and a paved octagon with enclosing yew hedges can also be found.

4½ m NW of Romsey on A3057 turn W

SU 3227   (OS 185)

Open Apr to end Sept W-Su (exc Good Fri) 1400-1800; parties at other times by appt

Peak months June and July

P WC ⊖ (1 m walk)
🍴 (by appt) ⚹ ★
🏛 (limited opening)

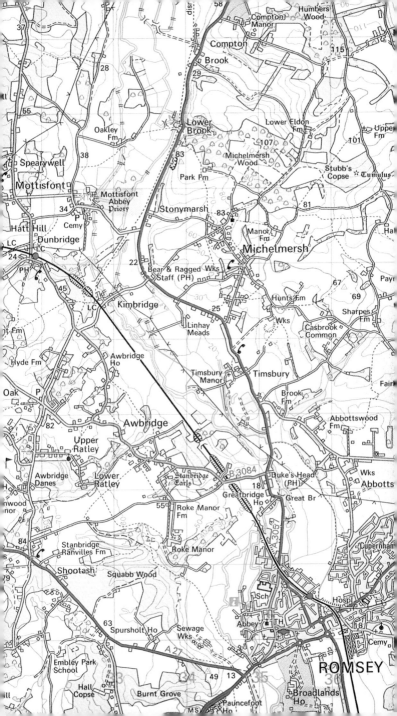

Spinners HAMPSHIRE

Mr and Mrs P. G. G. Chappell, Boldre, Lymington.
tel. Lymington (0590) 73347

This is a remarkable plantsman's garden *par excellence*, created and developed by Mr and Mrs Peter Chappell over the past 25 years, around a small retreat of a house that they found hidden away in a neglected oak wood when they arrived here in 1960. On this wooded slope high above Lymington River, with its acidic gravelly soils and patches of deep clay and humus, they made the gardens, removing scrub and thinning the tree canopy with great care and foresight so as to retain the spirit and atmosphere of the adjacent New Forest. Paths wander up and down between fascinating groups and masses of many distinctive plants. In spring the forest floor is rich with cyclamen, trilliums, erythroniums, hellebores, the unusual bloodroot (*Sanguinaria*) to mention only a few, while above and around are magnolias, followed by species and hybrids of rhododendrons selected for cream and apricot, scarlet and blue flowers and for foliage and texture. Lower down the paths open out, and the trees give way to open clearings. Deeper soils favour massed beds of geraniums, hostas, irises, meconopsis, primulas and many ferns and unusual grasses all carefully and beautifully combined. On the grassy slopes are fine specimen trees. Mulching and leafmould dressings are a key to the healthy appearance of all these plants. Most tempting of all to enthusiasts is the nursery here, a plant-hunter's paradise, including many rare and unusual plants.

2 m N of Lymington on A337 turn E to Pilley for 1 m

SZ 3298   (OS 196)

Open mid Apr to end Aug daily (exc M) 1400-1800; other times by appt

The Vyne HAMPSHIRE

The National Trust, Sherborne St John, Basingstoke.
tel. Basingstoke (0256) 881337

The parkland setting, the beautiful, mellow brick house and the lake are perhaps the most immediately appealing features of the Vyne, since extensive formal gardens are not to be found here, nor elaborate flower gardens for the colour seekers. The original old house was built by the same Lord Sandys of Mottisfont, and then enlarged in the 17th century by the Chute family with a handsome portico and two corner blocks of red brick. This can all be seen to perfection from the far side of the lake in reflections too, on a still day, and here the 18th-century landscape influence can be seen in the lake created by damming a small stream, and the groups of fine trees, and the wild garden, where once a Chinese Gothic bridge spanned the enlarged stream. Near the house yew hedges enclose carefully planned herbaceous borders and two rose borders frame the entrance door planted with the old and trusty variety 'Gruss an Aachen'. Away to the north, beyond the kitchen garden (private), stands a charming brick garden pavilion of Inigo Jones mould. Notable trees are oaks, limes, beeches, cedars, a fine lime avenue leading to the nursery and the grey willows beside the lake. Massed Himalayan roses tumble on the stable blocks and tea rooms. The Vyne is a perfect place for peaceful relaxation and meditation.

4 m N of Basingstoke on A340 turn E at Sherborne St John, 1½ m on Bramley road

SU 6356 (OS 175)

Open Apr to late Oct daily exc M and F but inc Bank Hol M (closed following T) 1400-1800 (Bank Hol 1100-1800), Oct 1400-1730; parties on other days by appt; reduced rates for parties on T, W, Th

Peak months summer

P WC ⊖ 🚻 D 🍴 (limited opening) ✿ ★ 🏠

Bedgebury Pinetum KENT

The Forestry Commission, Goudhurst, Cranbrook.
tel. Goudhurst (0580) 211392

Scarcely a garden in the accepted sense, this unique place has been included in this book because it has probably the largest single collection of conifers in Europe and was designed from the outset to be a place of great landscape attraction. It has been developed over the past 50 years or so by the Royal Botanic Gardens, Kew and more recently the Forestry Commission, using part of the former grounds of nearby Bedgebury Park (now a girls' school). A well-wooded setting of valleys, streams and a lake proved an ideal place to establish the Pinetum although the soils are exceptionally acid, and frosts actually occur here every month of the year! In the original design by W. Dallimore of Kew, conifers are mostly grouped in genera, but interspersed with deciduous trees, many being fine old oaks once part of the ancient Wealden Forest. He also laid out rides and vistas now reaching fine maturity. Particular features are the unusual Brewers' weeping spruces in the Spruce Valley, the Lawson cypress collection of over 30 different cultivars, gold, silver, blue, weeping, dwarf and tall – a remarkable sight. The wellingtonia grove is still growing rapidly after 50 years and may reach impressive heights in the next century or so. A comparatively new addition is the dwarf conifer collection near the information centre, nicely labelled and laid out.

7 m E of Tunbridge Wells on A21 turn N onto B2079 for 1 m

TQ 7233 (OS 188)

Open daily 1000-dusk

Peak months May and June

P WC 🚻 D 🍴 (limited opening) 🏕 🚭 ★

Eyhorne Manor KENT

Mr and Mrs Derek Simmons, Hollingbourne.
tel. Hollingbourne (062 780) 514

A truly delightful and unique cottage garden wonderfully reflecting the character and charm of an old manor house, and equally the personality and instinctive tastes of the owners. Eyhorne Manor is a small historic hall or yeoman's house, oak timbered and tiled roof, which has been completely and carefully restored. It now combines a comfortable family house with a museum of country life providing a wealth of things to see. The garden was, like the house, in a sad state when the Simmons family came here in 1952 – disused chicken runs, vegetable patches, rubbish tips, 'privies' and an old apple tree. Old hedges were tidied up and retained and gradually the garden took shape. The design is apparently informal, but within little more than an acre (0.4ha), quite different intimate spaces have been created, with narrow pathed walks, tiny lawns and everywhere massed associations of old-fashioned plants. From spring to midsummer this garden is an aromatic and nostalgic dream. Violets, purple honesty, pheasant-eye narcissus, lilacs, sweet rocket, old double crimson peonies, herbs of every description are followed in early summer by masses of old scented roses, of which there are over 100 different kinds in the garden. There are different levels too, to add interest, with sunken paths between rock walls richly planted with a host of small and attractive plant associations.

5 m E of Maidstone just
N of A20 on B2163

TQ 8355 (OS 188)

Open May to July S,
Su; Aug T, W, Th, S, Su
and Bank Hol M 1400-
1800; parties at other
times by appt

Peak month June

P (limited) WC (limited)

Goodnestone Park KENT

The Lord and Lady FitzWalter, nr Wingham, Canterbury.

A secluded, privately owned park and garden answering to the local pronunciation of 'Gunston'. There are really three main periods of garden styles and planting to detect at Goodnestone. The first and the oldest, dating back to the 18th century, comprises the extensive parkland and its fine trees, the old cedars near the house, and, of course, the porticoed house itself linked in that century with Jane Austen (her brother married a daughter of the Bridges family who built it) and the series of fine old walled gardens. The second period is after the First World War, when an enthusiastic gardening aunt of the present Lord FitzWalter planted unusual trees such as the cut-leaved alder near the front of the house, and laid out the woodland, shrubbery and rock garden with its walks and more trees, especially a large southern beech (*Nothofagus*). The final period brings us up to the present time with the series of delightful gardens made over the past fifteen years or so by the present Lady FitzWalter using the walled gardens and areas around the house for old world plant associations, scent, colour and contrasts. There are massed groups of old roses, lavenders, pinks, border plants and climbers on the wall, all done with the aid of one full-time gardener, and some part-time and family help.

5 m E of Canterbury on A257 turn S onto B2046, after 1 m turn E

TR 2554 (OS 179)

Open Apr to early July M-Th, also Su in June and few other Su under NGS

Peak months Apr to June

P WC 🚻 ☕ (Su only) 🚻 ⚘ (occasional) 🌿

Great Comp KENT

Great Comp Charitable Trust, Borough Green, Sevenoaks.
tel. Borough Green (0732) 882669

A remarkable garden developed over the past 30 years by two people, Mr and Mrs Cameron, who until quite recently were entirely responsible for its development and maintenance. When they bought the property in 1957 they found a sturdy 17th-century house, mature lime trees, and an Edwardian-style garden and some woodland and a paddock and to this they added two more acres (0.8ha) of market garden land, transforming the whole 7 acres (3ha) into the present mature and interesting garden. Thoughtful advance tree planting of fast-growing pines, birches and evergreens soon gave shelter and the woodland glade effect they wanted. A natural and informal style was favoured, with vistas and glades using unusual trees and shrubs of great variety and association, underplanted with carefully selected ground cover using heathers, conifers, brooms and other maquis-forming shrubs. In the more shaded woodland areas are hostas, hardy geraniums, ferns and naturalised bulbs. An excellent printed guide lists in detail the 3,000 or more plants to be found in this garden. More formal terraces and enclosures around the house are sensitively planted, lavenders, roses and many other plants providing fragrance and summer colour for the visitors enjoying the delicious home-made teas, or attending performances in the delightful barn theatre the Camerons skilfully converted.

Between Maidstone and Sevenoaks, turn S off A25 onto B2016 at Wrotham Heath and ½ m W at first crossroads

TQ 6357 (OS 188)

Open Apr to end Oct daily 1100-1800

🅿 WC ♿ (1½ m walk) 🚻 (by appt) 🍽 (limited opening, parties by appt) 🐕 ⚘

Ladham House KENT

Betty, Lady Jessel, Goudhurst.
tel. Goudhurst (0580) 211203

The Kentish Weald is the setting for these fine gardens, set on a small plateau 200ft (61m) above sea level with distant views of the fruit orchards and hop gardens. The gardens are well protected by fine mature belts and groups of forest trees, especially oaks and beeches. Some of the specimen trees on the front lawn are over 80ft (24m) high. The 19th-century Georgian-style house acts as a division between the two contrasting styles of gardens at Ladham, a more natural, flowing design of massed trees and shrubs on sloping ground to the north-east, and the enclosed, more formal flower and walled gardens to the south-west. The late Sir George Jessel and Betty, Lady Jessel, developed these gardens over the past 40 years. The acidic clay loams are ideal for the bold groups of rhododendrons, azaleas, heathers, flowering dogwoods, many fine conifers, and other unusual trees and shrubs for foliage contrast. These informal areas are especially colourful in May and June and again with autumn colours in October. A small sunken dell of moisture-loving plants should also be discovered, and the rather mysterious rock garden. The walled gardens on the warmer side of the house have fine wall plants, mixed borders, specimen magnolias and camellias, and many other plants. The kitchen gardens, like the rest of the gardens at Ladham, are all beautifully maintained.

11 m E of Tunbridge Wells on A262 turn N at Goudhurst to Curtisden Green

TQ 7338 (OS 188)

Open few times each year under NGS and at other times by appt

Peak months May and July

🅿 WC ⊖ ⊟ (by appt) D
※ (occasional)

Northbourne Court KENT

The Lord Northbourne, Northbourne, Deal.
tel. Sandwich (0304) 360813

A series of intimate, enclosed gardens protected by high brick walls is the especial feature of Northbourne, and everywhere is a profusion of plants carefully selected for colour, fragrance and individuality, reflecting the personality and sensitive artistry of the late Lord Northbourne, who largely developed the gardens. Northbourne Court has Saxon origins but the main structure of the garden is Jacobean, with the tiers of terracing inside several acres of high brick walls, acting as raised walks or prospects, that once faced across to the long-vanished house in the time of James I. The present house dates from the 18th and 19th centuries. Its great historic barn, farm buildings and massed old evergreen oaks provide atmosphere and valuable protection to the gardens from the cold north-east winds that can blow across this rather exposed part of East Kent. The well-drained soils and the maritime climate – the sea is only a few miles away – and the warm walls offer homes for many interesting plants with emphasis on late spring, summer and early autumn effects. The smaller courts around the house are richly clothed with plants, on the walls especially, while the brick or paved 'floors' are a mosaic of massed pinks, junipers, grey-foliaged plants, and many more. Great copper urns and old pots spill over in summer with fuchsias and blends of foliage and colour.

On A258 to W of Deal take road to Great Mongeham and Northbourne

TR 3352 (OS 179)

Open end May to Aug; several Su 1400-1800 and W 1400-1700 under NGS

Peak months June and July

P WC ⌂ (by appt) D
⋔ (in car park) ⌘ ✿

Estate

Blue
Pigeons LC

*2

Saxon Shore Way

Royal Cinque Ports Golf Links

Mary Bax's
Stone

PH
P

Worth

Upton
Ho

MS

A 258

13

L Y D D E N   V A L L E Y

North Stream

Chequers
(PH)

3

THE

SMALL D

+

Hacklinge

Tenants
Hills

CH

PH   MS

Foulmead
Fm

Sandhills

Sandown Castle
(remains of)

ham

PH   5

Conveyor

Cottington Court
Fm

CG Sta

teshanger
Colliery

MS

LC

LC

Sholden

Mus

TH & Mus

Pier

DEAL

P

Northbourne Court

PH

Northbourne

Sholden
Downs

PH

18

Upper
Deal

Hosp

Castle

44

Great
Mongeham

P

Little
Mongeham

Sch

Cemy

Bks

Lifeboat & IRB

Mill Hill

34

3

36

WALMER STA

Walmer

38

utton Hill

Sutton Vale
Ho

PH

27

Ripple

Coldblow
Fm

LC

39

Castle

6

on

Ripple
Fm

55

A 258

Hawkshill
Down

44

Ripple
Court

Knights
Bottom

47

Winkland
Oaks Fm

Kingsdown

45

B 2057

P

PH

Penshurst Place KENT

The Viscount De L'Isle, VC, KG, Penshurst, Tonbridge.
tel. Penshurst (0892) 870307

Undoubtedly one of the finest and best preserved heritage houses in the country, standing in parkland and surrounded by its old walled gardens whose outline has changed little since the Elizabethan period. The excellent guide to Penshurst tells the story of the great house, its zenith at the time of Sir Philip Sydney and visits by royalty, its long period of neglect and the great revival during the last century. Penshurst lies in the River Medway valley close to the charming village and church. Within the boundary walls are a series of gardens, some still being developed by the present Lord De L'Isle. The greatest open space is the Italian garden, a large sunken parterre laid out with geometric patterns of box and a dwarf red variety of polyantha rose round a central oval pool. Axial walks lead away past the great south front of the house where boldly planted attractive borders are colourful in summer with old roses, grey, yellow and pink shrubs and perennials. Two wide borders leading from the entrance gate are backed with fine old apple trees, carefully retained, since much of this area was once an orchard. The rose garden is a simple, effective design of mainly pink and red roses underplanted with grey-blue herbs. A magnolia garden, nut garden and grey garden are also here, while beyond the great lime avenue is an interesting farm exhibition area and an adventure centre for children.

3 m N of Tunbridge
Wells road on A26 turn
W onto B2176 for 3 m

TQ 5244 (OS 188)

Open Apr to early Oct
daily exc M but inc Bank
Hol M 1230-1800;
reduced rates for
parties

Peak months June, July

WC ⊖ 🚻 🍴 🏕 ⚹ ★ 🏛 🚶

Sandling Park KENT

Major A. E. Hardy, Hythe.

A large and spectacular 30-acre (12-ha) woodland garden on rich acidic soils, where rhododendrons and magnolias and many other plants flourish as well as they do in the great Sussex and West Country gardens. The original 19th-century mansion was destroyed in the Second World War, but its great walled garden and terraces are still here, and the woodland garden that mostly came into being in the late 19th century. A winding figure-of-eight path leads down a steadily descending slope through glades of fine beeches, oaks and other trees. Everywhere are rhododendrons of all ages and kinds, including many different species and hybrids. The collection here is now one of the most comprehensive in the country. In late May and early June there are massed Japanese and deciduous azaleas rich with scent and lighting up the woodland glades. Magnolias, camellias, viburnums and many Japanese maples are also a feature here. Another delight is the rich undercarpet of woodland flowers, especially lily of the valley and bluebells, while the many streamlets are flowering meads of candelabra primulas, ferns and bog plants. Among the great trees in the wood is the tallest alder in Europe, about 90ft (27m) high. Nearer the house is a great weeping beech and huge pines and cedars, and the more formal enclosed gardens and a large kitchen garden.

2 m N of Maidstone on
A229 turn E at Sandling

TQ 7558 (OS 188)

Open few days each
year under NGS

Peak months May, early
June

P WC ⊖ 무 ㅈ ✿

Scotney Castle KENT

The National Trust, Lamberhurst, Tunbridge Wells.
tel. Lamberhurst (0892) 890651

A perfect example of the picturesque period of landscape gardening, created using the ancient ruined castle in its lily-studded moat as the romantic feature among rambling wooded walks and rocky paths. The De Scotene family once possessed the castle, but it was the Hussey family who in the 18th and 19th centuries created the Scotney we see today, building a large 'Gothic' house on a commanding terrace well above the lake, and turning the old castle into a picturesque ruin. There are really no formal or flower gardens at Scotney, the essential features being the framework of magnificent trees, beeches, oaks and limes and some cedars and other evergreens of great size and character, and informal walks down the quite steep-sided valley in whose floor lies the old castle and its lake. The rich, acidic clay soils are fine for rhododendrons, azaleas, kalmias, magnolias and other May- and June-flowering shrubs. Autumn effects are also spectacular here. An old, secluded quarry, from which stone was taken to build the house, was made into a large rock garden, with steep, mysterious paths crossing the rocky outcrops. The old castle with its walls and courtyards have been attractively planted, using herbs and fragrant plants. The moat is colourful with water-lilies, and its margins attractive with natural waterside associations.

6 m E of Tunbridge Wells on A21 SE of Lamberhurst

TQ 6835 (OS 188)

Open Apr to Oct W-F (exc Good Fri) 1100-1800; S, Su and Bank Hol M 1400-1800 (or dusk if earlier); reduced rates for parties on weekdays by appt

P WC 🚻 ♿ ⚘ ★

Sissinghurst Castle Garden KENT

The National Trust, Sissinghurst, nr Cranbrook.
tel. Cranbrook (0580) 712850

These world-famous gardens attract over 100,000 visitors each year creating problems for those who keep up the remarkable standards notwithstanding. To enjoy a reasonably peaceful visit to Sissinghurst, choose a week day or a weekend early or late in the season or go early, or late in the afternoon. Once an important seat in the 16th and 17th centuries with a hunting park and royal visitors, a long decline in its fortunes ended with only fragments of the original great buildings remaining by the early 20th century, notably the fine gate house and red brick tower. Harold Nicolson and Vita Sackville-West bought the ruins in 1930 and during the next 20 years or so created the fascinating garden we can enjoy today. The story is dramatically told in Nigel Nicolson's guide to the gardens. The magic of Sissinghurst is that in a relatively small enclosure of 6 acres (2.4ha) a series of garden rooms has been made, each one furnished quite differently with rich collections of plants, and linked by vistas, walks and hedged paths so that the garden seems much larger than it really is. The old walls have been beautifully planted, and there are themes throughout the seasons, a red border, white garden, spring walk and an old orchard massed with bulbs of many kinds. A unique experience is the bird's eye view of the garden from the tower.

7 m NW of Tenterden off A262

TQ 8038 (OS 188)

Open Apr to mid Oct T-F 1300-1830 (exc Good Fri 1000-1830) S, Su 1000-1830; reduced rates for parties on weekdays by appt

P WC ⊖ 🚌 🍽 ♨ ★ ⏬

Withersdane Gardens KENT

University of London, Wye, Ashford.
tel. Wye (0233) 812401

The main gardens of about 5 acres (2ha) were created in the grounds of Withersdane Hall, a mid-Victorian country house purchased by the University of London in 1946 as part of Wye College. They were laid out from 1948 onwards for teaching, demonstration and aesthetic purposes using many plants suited to the rather chalky soils of this part of Kent. The most intimate and concentrated plantings are in the series of gardens made within the former kitchen garden by dividing up the rather large space with yew hedges and using an old mulberry tree as the focal feature. A long, wide south-facing border, once devoted entirely to flag irises, is now a luxurious association of sun-loving shrubs, grasses and ground-cover plants. Noteworthy here are pittosporum, trumpet vines and New Zealand flax. A sundial garden is mainly used for foliage plants, and a herb garden and pool garden are at their best in early summer. The rose garden, main borders and summer gardens are intended for mid-summer to late summer displays. A wellingtonia dates from the late Victorian era, and the parkland south of the house has been planted with groups of specimen trees that should provide continuity and shelter. A paulownia tree planted in 1952 is now probably one of the largest in the country. The very severe winter of 1984–85 killed many mature trees and shrubs here; a replanting programme is planned.

3 m NE of Ashford on A28 turn E to Wye

TR 0646 (OS 179)

Open several Su for charity, some under NGS and at other times by appt

Peak months June to Sept

 WC ⊖ ☕ ⚕

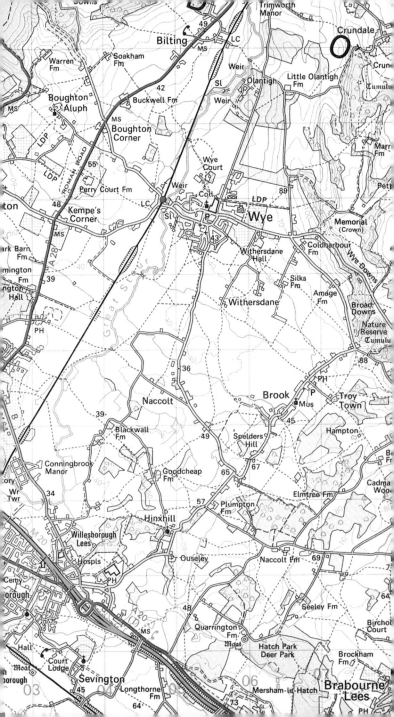

Chelsea Physic Garden GREATER LONDON

Trustees of the Chelsea Physic Garden, 66 Royal Hospital Road, SW3.
tel. (01) 352 5646

Three hundred years of accumulated history and plant lore assume almost
tangible proportions in this famous garden – 3.8 acres (1.5ha) of notable and
interesting trees, shrubs, perennials and other plants representing some 6,000
species. It would be difficult to overestimate the garden's influence on the
progress of botany and gardening, especially during the 18th century when it
was instrumental in introducing here so many plants from the Americas and
the Near and Far East. Plants and seeds have been exchanged with other
botanical gardens throughout the world since 1683. Founded in 1673 as the
Apothecaries' Garden, it is a living monument to great men like Sir Hans
Sloane, who acquired the freehold in 1712, and Philip Miller whom he
appointed head gardener in 1722. Successively the garden passed from the
Apothecaries to the Charity Commissioners in 1893, the Trustees of the City
Parochial Foundation in 1899 and to new trustees in 1983, who are committed
to the advancement of this historic garden as a centre for horticultural study
and research. For the visitor the garden is deeply rewarding. Among much of
great interest are 126 different species of trees – large and venerable mulberries,
a large olive, a superb golden rain tree, *Koelreuteria paniculata*, and a cork oak,
Quercus suber, to mention but a few.

Between Royal Hospital
Road (B302), Swan
Walk and Chelsea
Embankment (A3212)

TQ 2777 (OS 176)

Open Apr to Oct W, Su
1400-1700; also during
Chelsea Flower Show

WC

Greenwich Park GREATER LONDON

Dept. of the Environment, Superintendent's Office, Blackheath Gate, Blackheath, SE3.
tel. (01) 858 2608

For those who would make the journey, by boat, road or rail, historic Greenwich Park has much to offer. Undoubtedly the best and most enjoyable form of transport from central London is by boat down the River Thames. The park rises from river level to over 400ft (122m), at which level is sited the Woolf Statue. Two main garden features, the observatory gardens and the flower gardens, are completely different in character. The first occupy steeply rising ground with peat walls and serpentine paths and plantings of mainly bulbous and ericaceous plants. They are at their most decorative in spring. The flower gardens are a bedding plant enthusiast's paradise, for numerous beds are set in large expanses of grass with borders round the perimeter. These beds and borders are, of course, for summer display. While mature trees are a feature of this park, Dutch elm disease has denuded it of many of its oldest and finest specimens. Replacement planting has been carried out but it will, of course, be many years before the new trees reach sizeable proportions. Part of the park, known as the Wilderness, has been set aside for a small herd of deer. This area is not open to the public but there are views into it.

¼ m E of Greenwich station, at junction of A206, A2211 and A200

TQ 3977 (OS 177)

Open daily throughout the year dawn to dusk

Peak months May to Sept

WC ⊖ D ● ⌂
☎ (observatory)

Hampton Court Palace Gardens
GREATER LONDON

Dept. of the Environment, East Molesey, Surrey.
tel. (01) 977 1328

The gardens which surround the Tudor palace at Hampton Court have a grandeur and historical importance which immediately impresses itself on the visitor, and most of all when surveying the scene from the Broad Walk, over the Great Fountain to the tree-lined Long Water which forms the central axis of the goose-foot pattern of lime trees. The clipped yews in the foreground of this view lead the eye onwards to one of the most noble garden prospects in Britain. Gardening enthusiasts, moreover, find delights at every turn, from the grand herbaceous border and the superb bedding to the proliferation of fine climbing and wall plants which beguile the eye and, of course, the features for which Hampton Court is famous: the Privy Garden with its colourful parterre, the pond gardens and the knot garden, the rose garden, the famous maze and the vinery with its equally famous Black Hamburgh grape vine. This was planted in 1769, has a branch spread Of well over 100ft (30m) and regularly produces over 500 bunches of grapes each year. Roughly triangular in shape and embraced on two sides by a loop in the River Thames, the many features of Hampton Court Gardens are interlinked by paths and driveways.

On A308 at junction with A309

TQ 1668 (OS 176)

Open daily throughout the year

Peak months Apr to Dec

🅿 WC ⊖ 🎌 🍽 ⛲ ♨ ★ 🏛

Isabella and Waterhouse Plantations

GREATER LONDON

Dept. of the Environment, Richmond Park and Bushy Park.
tel. (01) 948 3209

For lovers of beautiful woodland gardens nothing could be more satisfying than a visit to the Isabella and Waterhouse Plantations at the height of their beauty in May and June, a perfectly feasible proposition on the same day, if so desired, for they are only a few miles apart – the Isabella Plantation in Richmond Park, the Waterhouse Plantations (for there are two) in Bushy Park, adjoining Hampton Court. Both rely for their effectiveness on mass planting of such colourful shrubs as rhododendrons, azaleas and camellias which delight in the dappled shade that high-branched trees provide. In the Isabella Plantation a meandering stream provides the ideal conditions for moisture-loving plants like primulas and hostas, while the presence in the Waterhouse Plantations of the man-made Longford River provides the opportunity to use water as a feature in its own right in a dramatic way. But if these gardens have a late spring peak, nobody should be discouraged from visiting them at other times, for they are always rewarding.

Isabella: in Richmond
Park, off A307, A205,
A306 and A3.
Waterhouse: in Bushy
Park, off A308

TQ 1971; TQ 1668
(OS 176)

Isabella open daily
0700-dusk
Peak months May to
June

Waterhouse open daily
0900-dusk
Peak months Apr to
June

P WC ⊖ ⊟ (by permit)
D ⋒ (in park)

Regent's Park GREATER LONDON

Dept. of the Environment, The Store Yard, Inner Circle, Regent's Park, NW1.
tel. (01) 486 7905

Some 470 acres (190ha) of loveliness might well be a fitting description of this much-appreciated park – a park known not only for Queen Mary's Rose Garden but also for the bedding which is carried out in the Broad Walk. The park is still much the same as it was when it was designed for the Prince Regent in the early 19th century, with the well-known inner and outer circles being central to the layout. Queen Mary's Rose Garden is considered one of the finest of its type in this country and probably in the whole of Europe, including more than 60,000 roses both modern and old-fashioned. Also within the boundary of the rose garden is the begonia garden, which is also a great summer attraction. The flower walk – also part of the original concept – is a series of beds planted with a wide range of bedding plants. Again, trees are one of this park's great assets. A small and little-known garden where peace and quiet rules is situated near the entrance to St John's Lodge. Three circular beds form the design with each bed smaller than the last, as approached from the gate. A large lake is used for boating – except round Heron Island – but it is not fished, although fish are present. Heron Island is so named because a few years ago a family of herons decided to nest there and rear their young.

Within the Outer Circle off Marylebone Road, Park Road, Prince Albert Road, Albany Street

TQ 2882 (OS 176)

Open daily throughout year

🅿 (from 1100) WC ♿ 🚻
🍴 ⛱ (additional facilities: art gallery)

Royal Botanic Gardens, Kew

GREATER LONDON

Kew Road, Richmond, Surrey.
tel. (01) 940 1171

A landscaped garden of over 300 acres (121ha) evolved from 18th-century Royal pleasure gardens overlaid by formal 19th-century features with modern additions and a reproduced 17th-century garden. Historic buildings include Kew Palace and Queen Charlotte's Cottage, Pagoda, Orangery, Temples, Ruined Arch, Botanical Museums and the Marianne North Art Gallery. Extensive botanical collections (c. 50,000 different types of plants) from around the world are housed in greenhouses, arboretum and herbarium. Collections under glass range from the giant Amazon water-lily to minute Arctic alpines with comprehensive display collections of aroids, bromeliads, cycads, carnivorous plants, ferns, orchids, palms, succulents, and regional plantings such as for plants from Australasia, the Canary Islands and Southern Africa. The extensive herbaceous collections are displayed in the Natural Order Beds, Grass Garden, Duke's and Queen's Gardens and the large arboretum includes a great variety of trees with many historic or rare specimens, collections of magnolias, oaks, pines, etc., lake and ponds, and special features such as berberis and rhododendron dells, azalea, bamboo, heath and rose gardens. The Queen's Cottage grounds form a natural bluebell wood and are kept as a nature reserve planted with native trees and shrubs.

On A307 (Kew Road) S of Kew Bridge ¼ m W of Kew Gardens station

TQ 1876 (OS 176)

Open daily exc 25 Dec and 1 Jan 1000, closing times vary from 1600 to 2000 according to season

WC ♿ 🚻 D (guide dogs only)🐕 (limited opening) 🏛 ⚘ ★ 🎁

Claremont Landscape Garden SURREY

The National Trust, Esher.

This is included as a remarkable example of a recently restored early 18th-century landscape garden. The grand concept at Claremont was commissioned by the Duke of Newcastle in the 18th century when Vanbrugh built a strategically placed Belvedere on the hilly terrain that is such a feature of this part of Surrey, from which the Duke could survey several counties as well as the ponds and wooded grounds of his park. Then followed Charles Bridgeman's great 3-acre (1.2-ha) amphitheatre. William Kent in the 1730s enlarged the lake and made an island and pavilion and then in the 1770s Capability Brown was employed by the new owner, Lord Clive of India, to build a new mansion and extensively plant the estate. He altered the line of the main London/Portsmouth road, the better to improve the viewpoints! In 1975 work was started to restore the gardens to the 1750 period. The most spectacular success was the uncovering of Bridgeman's unique amphitheatre, the terraces remarkably well preserved beneath a jungle of rhododendrons, laurels and also several massive cedars. The lake was dredged, the pavilion on the island restored, and the grotto rebuilt. Merrist Wood College provided valuable help to the National Trust in this programme. Do not expect flowers and sophisticated gardening at Claremont. Rather enjoy the sort of informal, yet designed pictorial landscape for which the 18th century in England became world famous.

On S outskirts of Esher
E of A307

TQ 1263 (OS 187)

Open daily exc 25 Dec and 1 Jan; Apr to Oct 0900-1900 (sunset if earlier); Nov to Mar 0900-1600

P WC ⊖ D (limited opening)

Polesden Lacey SURREY

The National Trust, nr Dorking.
tel. Bookham (31) 58203/52048

The present elegant house was built in the 1820s by Joseph Bonsor who also enlarged the estate and planted more than 20,000 trees. He had purchased the estate and an older house from the playwright Richard Sheridan, whose 25 years of ownership saw the making of one of the finest features of Polesden, the long grass promenade named after him. Early in this century Captain and Mrs Greville bought Polesden and developed most of the garden as it exists today. The whole estate was left to the National Trust in 1942. The Trust has produced an excellent plan and guide to the gardens detailing all the main trees, shrubs and roses and other garden features. After the long beech and lime avenues comes the marvellous surprise of the house set below the brow of the hill, with its thyme-studded lawns, and colourful flower beds. There are lovely views from here and the pinetum and Sheridan's walk to the left. To the right lie the enclosed gardens all linked to the house by interconnecting walks and vistas. There the dominant feature is the rose garden with its many pergolas covered in mostly Edwardian rambling roses, a splendid central Venetian well-head and fine mixed borders. There is also a rather original lavender garden, an iris garden, and outside the walls an informal winter garden and a thatched bridge. A rock and shrub bank exhibits high mature ground cover at its best, with a more informal area of grass and shrubs below.

2 m SW of Leatherhead on A246 turn S at Great Bookham onto road to Westhumble

TQ 1352 (OS 187)

Open daily 1100-sunset; reduced rates for parties T-Th by appt

▓ WC ⊟ D ● (limited opening) ⊓ ⋇
★ (limited opening)
✿ (limited opening)

Sutton Place SURREY

Sutton Place Heritage Trust, nr Guildford.
tel. Guildford (0483) 504455

A visit here is a unique experience to see the gardens now taking shape as part of one of the grandest new garden projects seen in this country since the Second World War. The American Stanley J. Seegar purchased the Tudor house and grounds in 1980. In so doing he wished to realise his dream of creating a cultural and arts centre 'to recapture the logic and spirit of the 16th century'. Major restoration work in the house has been matched by ambitious developments in the gardens masterminded by the famous landscape architect Sir Geoffrey Jellicoe. There are a number of new and somewhat controversial features, the most impressive being a completely walled Paradise Garden which is full of excitement with fountains, water spouts, trellises, arbours, regular and irregular paths, and massed plants chosen for colour, texture and scent. A gate leads to the Moss or Secret Garden and from a new octagonal pavilion one can look down into this garden or across the grand prospect of the park. An Edwardian topiary yew walk leads from the house to a wild garden above the River Wey. The old walled gardens have become new gardens with such fanciful names as the Miro Pool Garden, and the Surreal Garden, still in the early stages of development. Modern sculpture finds a place here, while away to the north of the house a great fish-shaped lake graces the park-like landscape.

On N outskirts of Guildford on A320 turn E to Jacobs Well and Sutton Green

TQ 0153 (OS 186)

Open frequently throughout the year (W to S by appt)

Peak months Apr, June to Aug

P WC ⊖ (limited)
⊟ (by appt) ⛱ ⚘
📷 ⚹

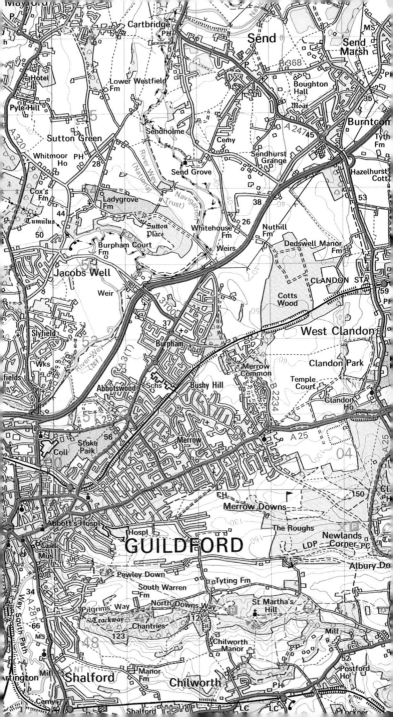

Winkworth Arboretum SURREY

The National Trust, nr Hascombe, Godalming.

The Aboretum dates from 1938 when Dr Wilfred Fox MD, FRCP, an enthusiastic horticulturist, bought 5 acres (2ha) of neglected woodland. Working mainly alone and also helped by friends he cleared and planted the main area of the Arboretum which eventually extended to about 100 acres (40ha). He gave Winkworth to the National Trust in 1952. The original character of the site, a dramatic wooded hillside overlooking two lakes 'a valley quite unspoilt, of pastoral and wooded character' is today one of the great qualities of the Arboretum, the other being the quality and diversity of the plantings, now maturing in the 40 years or more since it all began. Dr Fox's plan was to create really bold groups of species, going for seasonal effects and contrasts. The Trust today offers two trail walks – a spring walk and an autumn walk, highlighting the two seasons when a visit is particularly recommended. In spring there are early magnolias, cherries and malus (ornamental crabs) and in late spring massed azaleas and rhododendrons, while bluebells, wood anemones and wild flowers are everywhere. In autumn, preferably early to mid-October, there are brilliant effects from Japanese maples and cherries, the plum-coloured Indian gum (*Liquidambar*), and along the lakeside the orange and scarlet-leaved tupelo trees (*Nyssa sylvatica*) seen against the steely blue of Atlas cedars. There are many more beautiful trees to find here.

2 m SE of Godalming on B2130 turn E to Thorncombe Street

SU 9941 (OS 186)

Open daily during daylight hours

Peak months May, Oct and Nov

P WC ⊖ (limited) 🚻 (by appt) D ☕ (limited opening)🌳 ★ (limited opening)

Wisley Garden SURREY

The Royal Horticultural Society, Woking.

The outstanding garden of the Royal Horticultural Society, ranking among the finest in Europe for its well labelled, comprehensive collections of hardy plants and many new special demonstration areas aimed at the gardening public. The garden began in the 1870s when Mr G. F. Wilson purchased 60 acres (24ha) of wild, damp oak and birch woods and began to develop the area. In the oak wood near the western boundary he created his famous wild garden and he constructed the ponds and mass planted these with waterside plants. In 1904 the Society moved here from its overcrowded site in Chiswick. The wild garden was largely retained with many of Wilson's specimen trees and shrubs and these still form the bulk of the mature planting in this area today. In 1911 the rock garden was constructed. The alpine house was built in 1926 and the great collections of rhododendrons and azaleas were planted on Battleston Hill from 1937 onwards. The pinetum was created in the early 1900s and considerably extended from 1946 onwards, including the planting in 1948 of the first seedlings of the newly introduced dawn redwood, *Metasequoia glyptostroboides*. Many other additions and improvements have been made between 1946 and the present day, particularly in glasshouses, demonstration gardens, visitor facilities and extensive new trial grounds.

7 m E of Guildford turn W off A3

TQ 0558 (OS 187)

Open daily exc 25 Dec; M-S 1000-1900 (sunset if earlier); Su 1400-1900 (sunset if earlier); reduced rates for parties by appt

P WC ⊖ ⊟ ● (limited opening) 🚏 ⊛ ⚹ ★

Cobblers EAST SUSSEX

Mr and Mrs Martin Furniss, Crowborough.

Perfection in planting and design has always been the aim of Martin Furniss since he began making this remarkable garden over 25 years ago. When Mr and Mrs Furniss bought Cobblers in 1965 there were 2 acres (0.8ha) of land given over to pigsties, an old orchard and much jungle, with a small garden near the house. The design chosen for the garden is what Repton would have described as 'an irregular modern flower garden', a garden that flows in an orderly manner, so that the visitor is led onwards by vistas, tempting features and partially concealed views, offering the prospect of something new and exciting around each bend. Martin Furniss is an architect and the firm but flowing lines of the garden with ribbon-like brick paths, terraces, steps and retaining walls were all built by himself to a very high quality. The plant associations are carefully chosen to provide a succession of colour and interest with the emphasis on May to August. There are many different borders and habitats with over 2,000 species and varieties of plants. These range from the dry, sun-loving rock and alpine types on the terraces round the house, a multitude of mixed borders with shrubs, perennials, roses, bulbs and foliage plants to the moisture-loving bog plants around the upper circular pond, and a superb range of aquatics and marginal plants in the serpentine main pool – one of the most cleverly designed and planted pools seen in any garden. In the coolest, lowest part of the garden is a rhododendron grove.

At Crowborough turn E off A26 onto B2100; turn right at 2nd crossroads into Tollwood Road

TQ 5231 (OS 188)

Open several Su each year under NGS

Peak months May to Aug

Great Dixter EAST SUSSEX

Quentin Lloyd, Esq. (Director), Northiam.
tel. Northiam (079 74) 3160

No garden existed in 1910 when Mr Nathaniel Lloyd bought the neglected old farmhouse and asked Edwin Lutyens to help him restore it and to lay out the gardens. Another local timbered house was grafted on to the original house and Lutyens designed the gardens, incorporating the great oast houses, old barns and buildings into the clever design that largely characterises the gardens today. He skilfully linked the different levels by means of walls, terraces, steps and paths, using as always local material. Nathaniel was responsible for the many yew hedges and topiary. This architectural framework thus became furnished with a rich array of carefully selected plants, originally the genius of Mrs Lloyd but for many years chosen by the plantsman and author, Christopher Lloyd, one of her sons. This is a garden of contrasts and ever–changing seasonal effects. In spring and early summer the old orchards and the meadow garden in front of the house are flowering meads of wild flowers and naturalized bulbs, and from June to October in particular, the famous mixed border is a magnificent blend of shrubs, perennials and annuals. The sunken pool garden, the old rose garden with its many highly scented varieties, and the many walls clad with clematis, roses and many unusual climbers are only a few of the fascinating features to be explored at Dixter.

12 m N of Hastings on
A28 turn W to Northiam

TQ 8125 (OS 188)

Open Apr to mid Oct
T-Su and Bank Hol M
1400-1700; open Su in
July, Aug and Spring
Bank Hol M; reduced
rates for parties by appt

P WC ♿ 🚻 (by appt) 🚗 (in
car park) 🐕 ★ 📷

Sheffield Park EAST SUSSEX

The National Trust, Uckfield.
tel. Danehill (0825) 790655

A great landscaped arboretum originating in the 18th century and richly planted over the succeeding centuries with magnificent groups of contrasting trees, conifers and massed shrubs around a series of extensive lakes. The 'Gothic' house dating from the 1770s and its terraces should really afford the finest views of the landscaped gardens where Capability Brown was asked to assist with the layout, but the house, now under separate ownership, is divided from the gardens by screen planting. Humphry Repton also improved the designs in the late 18th century and added two more lakes to the original lake. A Mr Arthur Soames bought Sheffield Park from the Earl of Sheffield in 1909 and he transformed the gardens and parklands with an immense and imaginative programme of planting, using a great variety of North American trees. The tupelo trees are the finest planting in Great Britain and are brilliant in red and flame colours in mid-October. This is a fine time to see this garden, the tinted maples, swamp cypress, the tupelos contrasting with dark pines and blue cedars and reflected in the mirrors of the lakes on a still fine day. Rhododendrons and azaleas are also colourful in May and June. Under the skilled and effective management of the National Trust new areas are still being opened up in the 80 acres (32ha) or more of woodland and parkland.

10 m N of Lewes on A275

TQ 4124 (OS 198)

Open Apr to mid Nov T-S (exc T after Bank Hol M and Good Fri) 1100-1800; Su and Bank Hol M 1400-1800 (all closing times 1 hour earlier after end of BST); reduced rates for parties

Peak seasons spring and autumn

WC ⌂ ▼ (limited opening) ⌱ (in car park) ⅍ ★

Borde Hill WEST SUSSEX

Borde Hill Garden Ltd., Haywards Heath.
tel. Haywards Heath (0444) 450326

One of the largest Sussex gardens covering 400 acres (162ha) of ornamental gardens, woodland and parkland. The original house dates from the early 1600s but it was considerably enlarged in the last century in the neo-Elizabethan style by the Stephenson Clarke family. Robert Stephenson Clarke began the planting in the 1890s by creating a pinetum and arboretum on the grand scale, including many rare and unusual trees and shrubs, and developing ornamental gardens around the house. Two successive generations have continued his work and the family are members of the Borde Hill Trust which administers the gardens today. The more intensively designed gardens around the house are fascinating and full of interest. Rhododendrons, azaleas, magnolias, and camellias are brilliant, huge, and abundant in May and early June. The collection of rhododendrons alone is enormous. The more intimate, herbaceous borders close to the house are lovely in June, edged with effective alchemilla. Several new and attractive features include the Bride's Pool, the replanted west bank terrace, using more half-hardy summer shrubs and colourful perennials, and the very clever conversion of the roofless old potting sheds to tiny garden rooms. Further afield are woodland trails and walks, and finally an excellent restaurant and tea rooms to regale the wanderer on his return.

1½ m N of Haywards Heath on Balcombe road

TQ 3226 (OS 198)

Open Mar and Oct S and Su; Apr to Sept W, Th, S, Su and Bank Hol M 1000-1800 (dusk in Oct); reduced rates for parties of 20 or over

WC D D ⛱ ♨ ⚕
(by appt)

Denmans WEST SUSSEX

Mrs J. H. Robinson and John Brooks, Esq., Fontwell, nr Arundel.
tel. Eastergate (024 368) 2808

The gardens at Denmans have been created over the past 35 years by their energetic and single-minded owner, Mrs J. H. Robinson, who with the help of one gardener transformed a one-time market garden and smallholding into a home for many exciting plants. The setting is the old 19th-century bothy, stable block and service buildings of the adjacent Westergate House (since sold) and its walled garden. The exotic and secluded character of Denmans derives largely from the clever planting design using bold specimens and informal groupings, the emphasis being on the shape, colour and texture of the whole growing picture rather than the individual plants. The entrance drive is planted with mainly spring- and autumn-colouring trees and shrubs. A warm sunny terrace on the south of the cottage is luxuriant with massed cistus, brooms, grey-foliaged shrubs, dwarf conifers, groups of California tree poppies and many others. The main informal garden has winding paths through drifts and islands of specimen trees and shrubs, the surface material being mostly gravel. All manner of plants seed into this with most effective results. A more recent feature is a dry stream in pebbles and stones winding down through an arboretum, with willows, grasses and stony plantings. Ingenious plant associations are everywhere at Denmans, including a glasshouse full of luxuriant conservatory plants.

4 m E of Chichester on A27 turn S to Fontwell racecourse

SU 9407 (OS 197)

Open end Mar to end Oct daily 1300-1700 exc M and T; open Bank Hol M; other times by appt

🅿 ♿ (limited) 🚻 (by appt) 🍽 ♣

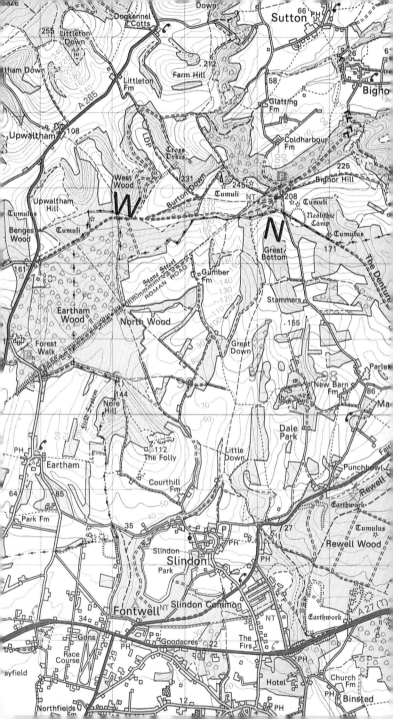

Leonardslee Gardens WEST SUSSEX

The Loder Family, Lower Beeding, Horsham.
tel. Lower Beeding (040 376) 212

Leonardslee is aptly described in its attractive guide book as one of the largest and most spectacular woodland gardens in England. And this is no exaggeration for there are over 80 acres (32ha) of gardens comprising one of the best collections of mature and unusual trees, shrubs, rhododendrons, azaleas and camellias in the British Isles. The sturdy Georgian-style house built in 1855 is superbly sited 300ft (91m) above a fine panoramic view of the wooded valleys and lakes with the South Downs on the horizon. Sir Edmund Loder was the first of this famous family to begin planting and developing the gardens in the 1890s, and it was he who raised many famous rhododendron cultivars, outstanding being the glorious Loderi crosses. These alone are worth seeing here in May and early June. The gardens have continued to flourish and develop under succeeding generations of the Loder family who still live here today. Plenty of time is needed to explore the gardens. Near the house are the massed shrubberies around the drives with spectacular specimen conifers, the rock garden ablaze with Kurume azaleas and dwarf rhododendrons in May, and then the long descending paths through groves of more rhododendrons, camellias, magnolias and many others, to the lakes (old hammer ponds) and dells in the valley. Wild flowers and birdlife also abound in this marvellous place.

4 m SE of Horsham on
A281

TQ 2225 (OS 198)

Open late Apr to mid
June daily 1000-1800;
Oct S and Su 1000-
1700; reduced rates for
parties by appt

Peak month mid May

P WC ⊖ (limited) ⊟ ☕
⊟ ⊛ ⚹ ★

Nymans WEST SUSSEX

The National Trust, Handcross.
tel. Handcross (0444) 400 321

Nymans is a large garden with associated woodland and parkland, noted for its many mature rare trees and shrubs and its association with the Messel family who have been largely responsible for its creation and development. Mr Ludwig Messel purchased a then-enlarged Regency house with fine lawns and cedar trees in 1890 and immediately began developing the gardens and grounds. He turned the old walled orchard into a delightful flower garden transected by the famous summer border inspired by Robinson and Jekyll, and planted out such rare trees as *Nothofagus* (southern beeches), magnolias and richly naturalized with bulbs. He made some of the first heather gardens in the country, a sunken garden with Japanese lanterns, and the great stone wisteria-clad pergola, a favourite feature of so many Italian gardens. After 80 years, a renovation programme is planned for this feature. His son, Colonel Messel, succeeded in 1916 and he became a tremendous gardener and plant enthusiast. He laid out more of the gardens, planting freely and developinG the area called Tasmania on the west side of the main road. He rebuilt the house in a Jacobean style but it was sadly destroyed by fire in 1947. His daughter, Anne, Countess of Rosse, still lives here and supervises the garden for the National Trust, to whom it was bequeathed in 1954. Allow plenty of time to explore the many contrasting features in this fine garden.

4 m S of Crawley on
A23 turn E after
Handcross onto B2114

TQ 2629 (OS 198)

Open Apr to end Oct
daily exc M and F 1100-
1900 (sunset if earlier)
also Bank Hol M;
parties of 15 or over by
appt at other times

P WC 🚻 🍽 🐕 🌿 ★

Parham House   WEST SUSSEX

The Hon. Clive and Mrs Gibson, Pulborough.
tel. Storrington (090 66) 2866

The venerable grey stone, gabled and mullioned house at Parham lies in its ancient oak-studded chase or deer park. Fallow deer have been here since monastic times. Sir Thomas Palmer built the house in the late 16th century but the stone office wings, stables and clock tower were added in the 18th century. Entrance is through the Fountain Court with its sparkling fountain and red water-lily-studded pond and then through a garden door for the many surprises that lie in store. A broad gravel path, a superb axial feature, invites one into the delightful recently planned and planted walled gardens. Peter Coats, the garden architect, has been responsible for their design and development, the aim being to achieve economy of labour while retaining the character of Tudor Parham. This begins near the gate with a very new knot garden of box, coloured gravels and yew sentinels. Mixed borders of silver, purple, grey and the long-flowering tree mallows lead to the central cross paths. Left is a striking blue border and right an effective gold border. Low-maintenance edging plants are a feature and there are many more carefully designed features in this still young, and yet surprisingly effective garden. The grounds at Parham also feature a lovely $2\frac{1}{2}$ acre (1ha) lake, a temple garden and the superb views across the deer park. A place to linger and refresh the senses.

3 m S of Pulborough on A283

TQ 0614 (OS 197)

Open Easter Su to end Sept W, Th and Bank Hol M also S in July and Aug 1300-1800

Peak months July and Aug

P WC ⌂ (reduced rates for parties by appt)D
🍴 ⛱ ⚘ ☎ (guided tours on certain days, otherwise unguided)

Standen WEST SUSSEX

The National Trust, East Grinstead.
tel. East Grinstead (0342) 23029

Apart from the delightful garden, the house at Standen is of especial interest, being one of the few Victorian houses owned by the National Trust. It was built for the Beale family in 1892 by the architect Philip Webb, a close friend of William Morris, the artist and reformer. A plan for the gardens by E. B. Simpson, a landscape gardener, was considered too formal and artificial and the Beale family seems to have developed its own more spontaneous and intimate style, in keeping with the house and the site, which in essence survives today. When the Trust took over in 1972 it found a much overgrown and neglected garden that is still being carefully and systematically restored and developed. The charm and surprise elements are a great feature of Standen because of the steeply sloping nature of the site with views towards the Medway Valley and the new reservoir. A winding path looks down into a cool, leafy dell made from an old quarry, now the home of the royal fern (*Osmunda*). From the informal woodlands and simply planted upper lawns, where wild flowers and native orchids grow, a long grass walk leads to a gazebo or summerhouse. The lower lawns are edged with massed effective ground cover and the house terraces are gay with summer flowers and scented subjects. One gardener looks after these delightful and tranquil gardens with great dedication and effect.

1 m SW of East
Grinstead on B2110
turn S to Saint Hill

TQ 3835 (OS 187)

Open Apr to end Oct W,
Th, S and Su 1400-1730

⬛ WC ♿ ♨ (by appt)
D (on woodland walk
only) 🐕 🌿 ★ 🍴

Wakehurst Place Garden WEST SUSSEX

The National Trust, Ardingly, nr Haywards Heath.
tel. Ardingly (0444) 892701

A very large and scenically magnificent garden covering a naturally dramatic site of woodlands, rocky valleys, streams and lakes where a vast collection of rare and unusual trees, conifers, shrubs and many other plants is grown. There is a spectacular display of rhododendrons and azaleas in May and early June. Gerald Loder, later to become Lord Wakehurst, purchased the Elizabethan house and 500-acre (202-ha) estate in 1903, and spent the next 30 years developing the gardens and landscaping and planting the estate on an ambitious scale. His successor, Sir Henry Price, continued the programme, and on his death in 1963 bequeathed Wakehurst to the National Trust, who then leased it to the Royal Botanic Gardens at Kew for scientific botanical and conservation research. Such is the scale, the diversity and the infinite variety of plants here that visitors are recommended to obtain a copy of the excellent guide to the gardens and the trail booklet. Notable features to summarise briefly here are the beautifully planted Sir Henry Price Memorial Gardens and the walled garden areas, the heather garden, the streamside walk called 'The Slips' and the rock garden where magnolias, acers and dogwoods flourish, and then for the adventurous the fascinating circulating ramble through Westwood Valley to the lake, along the rock walk and back by Bethlehem wood, marvellous with bulbs in the spring.

4 m N of Haywards
Heath on B2028

TQ 3331 (OS 187)

Open daily (exc 25 Dec
and 1 Jan); Jan, Nov
and Dec 1000-1600; Feb
and Oct 1000-1700;
March 1000-1800; Apr
to Sept 1000-1900;
reduced rates for
parties by appt

Peak months summer

P WC ⊕ (limited) ⊟
🍽 (Apr to Oct) ✁
★ (Apr to Oct)

DYFED

WEST
GLAMORG

Arlington Court
✿ Marwood Hill
Woodside
✿ Tapeley Park

✿ Rosemoor
Garden Trust

D

✿ Ca
D

✿ Tresco
Abbey

✿ Tremeer Gardens

CORNWALL

The Garden
House
Cotehele ✿
House   ✿ Buckland Abbey
Lanhydrock ✿
House   ✿ Moyclare   Bickham House
                Ince Castle   Plymouth
County   Antony House   ✿ Saltram   Dartin
Chyverton   Demonstration   House   Hal
                Garden   Mount Edgcumbe
                ✿
Trehane   ✿ Trewithen
Trelissick   ✿ Caerhays Castle
Garden ✿
                                          Overbecks ✿
Trengwainton   Fox-Rosehill ✿   Garden
   Penzance   Garden
               ✿ Glendurgan

The West Country

HEREFORD AND WORCESTER

POWYS

GWENT

MID GLAMORGAN

SOUTH GLAMORGAN

Cardiff

GLOUCESTERSHIRE

Gloucester

OXFORD-SHIRE

Swindon

AVON

Bristol

Clevedon Court

Dyrham Park

Corsham Court

Bowood House

Bath

Bath Botanical Gardens

The Courts

Wansdyke Nursery

WILTSHIRE

SOMERSET

Taunton

Stourton House

Stourhead

Heale House

Hadspen House

Salisbury

East Lambrook Manor

Barrington Court

Tintinhull

Knightshayes Court

Montacute House

Yeovil

Cranborne Manor Gardens

HAMPSHIRE

Brympton d'Evercy

Killerton House

Clapton Court

DORSET

Highbury

Forde Abbey

Parnham House

Minterne

University of Exeter Gardens

Ivy Cottage

Compton Acres

Exeter

Bicton Park

Abbotsbury Gardens

Bournemouth

Torbay

Bath Botanical Gardens AVON

City of Bath, Royal Victoria Park.

The Botanical Gardens of about 7 acres (3ha) in extent were formed within the Royal Victoria Park in 1887. Originally created to house the 2,000 specimens of trees, shrubs and herbaceous plants given by Mr C. E. Broome of Elmhurst Batheaston, bequests were later received from Mr T. W. Morris and Lady Lushington. On the lawn inside the lower entrance gates is a fine specimen of the silver lime, *Tilia petiolaris* and also the two largest examples in Britain of *Cornus controversa*, with variegated leaves and horizontal branches. Nearby stands *Cornus mas* 'Variegata', an equally outstanding small tree amongst the generally heavy foliage of August. Another splendid tree is the tall-growing, downy *Populus lasiocarpa*. The rock garden is at its best in spring; nearby is *Poncirus trifoliata*, the Japanese bitter orange, believed to be a cutting from Canon Ellacombe's famous garden at Bitton. The stream that runs through the garden and feeds the pools comes from the springs at Lansdown and was once the source of the city's water supply. Beside the pool grow maples, willows, bamboos and underplantings of *Gunnera manicata*, rodgersias and primulas. In spring the magnolias, particularly the lime-loving *M. kobus*, are outstanding. The variety of this small garden is amazing; so is the standard of upkeep, winning it many awards in the 'Britain in Bloom' competitions.

1 m from centre of Bath to N of A431 at juntion of Marlborough Rd and Upper Bristol Rd

ST 7365 (OS 172)

Open daily throughout the year 0900-dusk

P ⊖ 🄗 D 🄰

Clevedon Court AVON

The National Trust, Clevedon.

The south-facing terraces, which may follow the line of earlier defence fosses, are probably of 18th-century construction. The top, or Esmond Terrace, so named as Thackeray's 'Henry Esmond' was begun there, is delightfully informal, and upon it grows a strawberry tree, *Arbutus unedo*, which seeds itself, the dwarf palm, *Chamaerops humilis*, and a Judas tree, *Cercis siliquastrum*. From it there are views of the house, lower garden and the Octagon. The main or Pretty Terrace, castigated by Gertrude Jekyll for its over-formality, is now more as she would have liked it, and its sunny length houses a fine variety of tender plants, *Buddleia colvilei*, with crimson dropping trusses, the semi-double, yellow spring jasmine, *Jasminum primulinum*, and various ceanothuses. At one end stands an 18th-century octagonal garden house, overlooked by Chusan palms, and at the other a Gothic garden shelter. In the lower garden is a fine collection of magnolias, while posts support a huge specimen of the Himalayan musk rose, *Rosa brunonii*. The whole garden exhibits a long history of loving care which makes it a delight to visit.

1½ m E of Clevedon on B3130

ST 4271 (OS 172)

Open Apr to end Sept W, Th, Su and Bank Hol M 1430-1730

🅿 WC ⊖ 🚻 (by appt) 🍴 ✻ 🏠

Dyrham Park AVON

The National Trust, nr Chippenham.
tel. Abson (027 582) 2051

The curving drive, laid out in about 1780 by C. Harcourt-Masters, the Bath
surveyor, provides superb views of the house below. This part of the park was
originally an immense, formal, Baroque water garden with cascades,
fountains and pools of unrivalled quality, made by George London for
William Blathwayt in the latter half of the 17th century. By 1780 it was
neglected and was 'reconciled to the modern taste'; this landscape park,
containing a famous herd of fallow deer, has in turn required replanting. The
orangery on the east was built about 1701, and now, in addition to lemons and
oranges, is curtained with the pale blue of plumbago, and scented by *Jasminum
polyanthum*. The original stream still plunges underground to reappear on the
garden side of the house, to feed two pools connected by a cascade. This
garden is overlooked by a stone-paved terrace, level with the house and
church, and Humphry Repton is thought to have planted the leaning holm
oaks. The south-facing retaining walls provide warmth and shelter for
Magnolia delavayi, *Solanum crispum*, and the climbing roses 'Mermaid' and
'Gloire de Dijon'. In the southern end of the garden recent plantings have
reintroduced trees used in the time of William Blathwayt, including the
Virginia pine and the tulip tree. The dramatic position of this park and the
views over the Vale of Severn towards Bristol are unforgettable.

6 m N of Bath on A46,
and 1½ m S of M4
junction 18

ST 7475 (OS 172)

Open Apr, May, Oct
S-W; June to Sept daily
exc F 1400-1800; other
times with written
permission

🅿 (limited) WC
♿ (limited) 🚻 ♨ 🍴
🚗 ☎

Antony House CORNWALL

The National Trust, Torpoint, Plymouth.
tel. Plymouth (0752) 812191

From the avenues and tree-dotted park the south front of this early 18th-century house is viewed and entered through a central gate and square grass forecourt. The walls on either side of the gate are clothed with climbing roses and have a rose border in front and the brick arcades have some plants against them. A door on the west of the house leads to the now simplified grounds belonging to the National Trust. They include extensive lawns, some of which replace former Victorian flower beds, a great yew hedge and several free-standing *Magnolia grandiflora* and other individual trees. A clipped yew cone was designed as a garden pavilion and there are many ornaments associated with former generations of the Carew family. Borders in and outside the garden have been planted with many hemerocallis that once formed part of one of the largest collections of this genus in the country. This was the most easterly of the five estates in Cornwall visited by Humphry Repton but, like the other four, little from his 'Red Books' survives today. A bold group of flowering cherries was planted long after his visit and clumps of evergreen oak planted in 1760 were growing well before his time. A developing woodland garden around the perimeter of the estate with the usual camellias, magnolias and rhododendrons is open separately in the spring.

5 m W of Plymouth via
Torpoint car ferry; turn
N off A374 at Maryfield

SX 4156 (OS 201)

Open Apr to end Oct
T-Th and Bank Hol M
1400-1800

Peak months July to
Sept

P WC ⊖ (limited) 🚏 (by
appt) ⋇ ★ ☎

Caerhays Castle CORNWALL

F. J. Williams, Esq., Gorran, St Austell.
tel. Truro (0872) 501 310

This 150-year-old 'castle' stands about half a mile (0.8km) from Porthluney Cove and about 100ft (30m) above the sea. Well grown *Magnolia delavayi* and *M. grandiflora* at the foot of the south-west front indicate the scale of the house, and fuchsias and lapageria on the north-west tell of the mildness of the climate. From terraced lawns, paths and wider rides track steadily up across the steep slope of this wooded hillside behind the house, reaching some 250ft (76m) above sea level at the top. This hanging wood has massive native trees between which exotic conifers and the larger magnolias have emerged to the sky. The second layer consists of massed camellias and rhododendrons and other shrubs, some dating from seed sent home by Wilson and Forrest to J. C. Williams who helped finance their expeditions and who started this garden some 90 years ago. This is the home of *Camellia* x *williamsii* and many of its cultivars raised from crosses made by 'J. C.', who also raised new magnolias and rhododendrons. Some are now overgrown but the regular annual programme of slashing half-acre (0.2-ha) areas and replanting has produced many new groups and interesting glades. One group, planted in 1978 to celebrate the 21st birthday of the owner's son, bears witness to the interest of the next generation. Many plants are propagated here and sold at Burncoose, another Williams garden, on the A393 south of Redruth.

3 m SW of St Austell on A390 turn S onto B3287, after 2 m turn S to St Michael Caerhays

SX 9741 (OS 204)

Open Easter Su and few other Su for local charities; ring for details

Peak months Mar to May

P WC ⌂ (by appt only) D
🍴 (at beach café) ⛱ ✿
❀

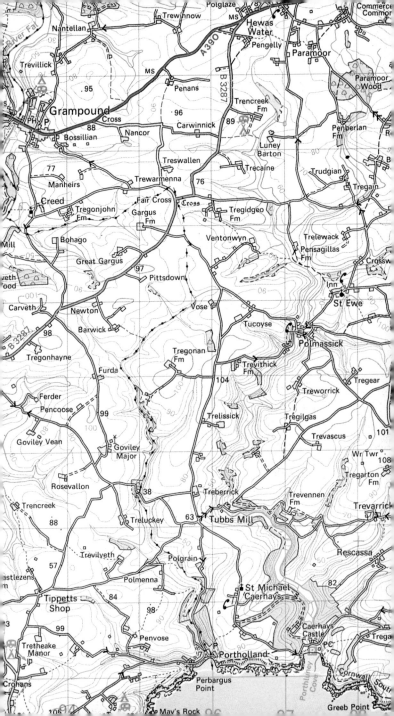

Cotehele House CORNWALL

The National Trust, St Dominick, nr Saltash.
tel. St Dominick (0579) 50434

This sloping garden may be entered from the car park at Cotehele Quay on the River Tamar or from one of the others near the 600-year-old house. Leaving the quay, a path above the riverside meadows, past the little 400-year-old chapel, leads to thick native woodland at the bottom of an east-facing valley. Paths on the north and south lead upwards through wicket gates, and occasional cultivated plants are seen on either side. Gradually among fewer trees the native flora grows less and more garden plants are to be found. Pondlets and damp areas beside the stream support moisture-loving plants. The small, 15 by 10yd (14 by 9m) ancient fish pond has water-lilies and other water plants. Still higher there are more shrubs and other plants until one passes through or under the medieval garden wall, to arrive at the foot of four-tier terraces below the east front of the house. Here are rose beds and, against the house, borders and wall shrubs as there are on other walls of the house and on the extensive garden boundaries. Paths lead round to the north, past shrubs in rough grass, to a formal pond with central island and surrounding lawns and flower borders. There is a garden for cut flowers and interesting old trees, all at about 250ft (76m) above the river. Beyond a back courtyard there is the south front and main entrance. The less energetic will enter here and enjoy the garden and the view from the terrace or below the roses.

5 m SW of Tavistock turn S off A390 at St Ann's Chapel onto road to Norris Green and Bohetherick

SX 4268 (OS 201)

Open Apr to end Oct daily 1100-1800; Nov to Mar dawn to dusk

P WC ⊔ (by appt only, not on Bank Hol)
🍴 (limited opening)
🌂 ★ (limited opening) 🕿 (Apr to Oct)
🕏

County Demonstration Garden and Rural Studies Centre CORNWALL

Cornwall County Council, Probus, Truro.
tel. Truro (0872) 74282

Lacking a horticultural college or department of an agricultural college, the Cornwall County Council established this 6½-acre (2.6ha) garden early in the 1970s. It serves as the education, demonstration and advisory centre for the Duchy and produces plants for schools and other county council plantings. On the typical shaly soil it stands between 250–300ft (76–91m) above sea level on former farmland on the Trewithen estate, in stark contrast to Trewithen's very well sheltered gardens. There are numerous demonstrations of small garden layouts for many situations and aspects, and methods of growing vegetables, pruning fruit, treating lawns, weed control and manuring are all on show. There are historical and economic gardens and those showing introductions and breeding by Cornish gardeners. Greenhouses for propagation and display, frames, cloches, labels and mulches in great variety are all to be seen here as well as lawn edgings, hanging baskets, patio bowls, ground cover and all the aspects of gardening that popular custom demands. There is a very good collection of the smaller trees, and conditions have been created to demonstrate the flora of the main types of the landscape of Cornwall: wetlands, towans, meadows and acid downs among others.

6 m E of Truro on A390

SW 9147 (OS 204)

Open Oct to Apr M-F
1000-1630; May to Sept
M-F 1000-1700 Su
1400-1800

Peak months June to
Aug

P WC ⊖ 🅗 ⚹

The Fox-Rosehill Garden CORNWALL

Carrick District Council, Melvill Road, Falmouth.

One of several gardens in the district made by the Fox family during the last
century, this one has been taken over by the local council and is preserved as a
rare and unusual public garden. Some 2 acres (0.8ha) in area it is near but not in
sight of the sea; it retains a number of massive trees and large shrubs including
vast griselinias, tree rhododendrons, an embothrium, pines and other forest
trees from early plantings. Lawns and some coarser grass planted with a range
of bulbs provide space for walking and sitting and set off the plants, while
broad smooth walks give access to all parts. Many tender shrubs found only in
the mildest gardens widen the interest and much recent planting will provide a
continuing display of camellias, magnolias and rhododendrons for many years
to come. Such rarities as cestrum, prostanthera, musa (banana), tibouchina and
many acacias are to be found against walls and in secluded corners. There are
large specimens of the palms, trachycarpus and cordyline, that are so common
in this part of Cornwall; the latter giving its alternative name to one of the
longer thoroughfares in the town – Dracaena Avenue. All is well kept, many
plants are well labelled, there is hardly a popular geranium or forget-me-not in
sight but *Geranium maderiense* and *Myosotidium hortensia* more than make up
for them in the eye of the plantsman. A modern touch is a group of variegated
and coloured phormiums from New Zealand.

On B3290, main road
through centre of
Falmouth

SW 8032 (OS 204)

Open daily

Peak months spring

Glendurgan CORNWALL

The National Trust, Helford, Mawnan Smith, nr Falmouth.

Two realistic, life-size stone foxes stand watch over the not easily seen entrance
to this valley garden. They remind us that this was one of several estates
developed locally by the Fox family of Falmouth in the 19th century and since.
Once inside, a drive curves through short grass under tall established and more
recently planted trees and shrubs, down to the house which stands some 200ft
(61m) above and 700yd (640m) from Durgan, a tiny former fishing village on
Helford river. Winding paths, some steeply sloping, take one to all parts of this
28-acre (11-ha) woodland garden and, finally, to the water's edge. Those that
would avoid the climb back may do so by turning off the main path, but still
enjoy lovely views and many plants. The plan shows sixteen viewpoints, most
of them in the upper half of the garden and giving a glimpse of the sea over and
through a canopy of exotic trees and shrubs. There is colour of flowers from
early spring through much of the summer but always variety of form
provided by many long-established conifers with deciduous and evergreen
trees. There has been steady recent planting giving greater interest and many
stretches of grass contain bulbs in their season as well as naturalised primulas
and columbines. Gunnera and bamboos add more variety to the pattern of leaf
and plants. A laurel maze is a great rarity in Cornwall and near the top a wall
garden has slightly more formality than the rest.

3 m SW of Penryn turn
S off B3291 to Mawnan
Smith

SW 7727 (OS 204)

Open Mar to end Oct M,
W and F (exc Good Fri)
1030-1430

Peak months Apr to
June

WC ⊖ (limited) 🚻 ⚹

Lanhydrock House CORNWALL

The National Trust, Bodmin.
tel. Bodmin (0208) 3320

The majority of visitors are attracted to the turreted gatehouse and impressive castellated house, with its long gallery and preserved living rooms. Outside there is much to see for those who would walk and sit. Three main gardens can be distinguished within the 28 acres (11ha) or so. First, the formal, levelled, well kept lawns with uniformly trimmed Irish yews among formal beds, some box-edged, filled with roses or bedding plants. Next, past croquet and tennis lawns among several huge trees and well-filled modern shrub borders, and then moving steadily upwards through the main part of the garden. There are several distinct sections here with herbaceous plants, a hosta collection, a small stream garden, trees and shrubs in variety from about 100 years old to recent plantings, including many magnolias and the rhododendrons that flourish in the more open conditions. The top of this semi-formality is well above the house and adjoining parish church and gives views of the buildings, the extensive wooded park and the distant car park. From this point at about 400ft (122m) above sea level a straight path leads steadily down to the third, more heavily wooded, completely informal section in which large-leaved rhododendrons have been more recently planted and are growing well above the bracken. This will no doubt fill to become a Cornish woodland garden of the future.

3 m SE of Bodmin off B3268

SX 0863 (OS 200)

Open daily Apr to Oct 1100-1800; Nov to Mar daylight

Peak months Apr to June

P WC ♿ (enter from B3268) D ♥ (Apr to Oct daily; Nov and Dec limited opening) ✿ ★ 🎁 (Apr to Oct) ♨

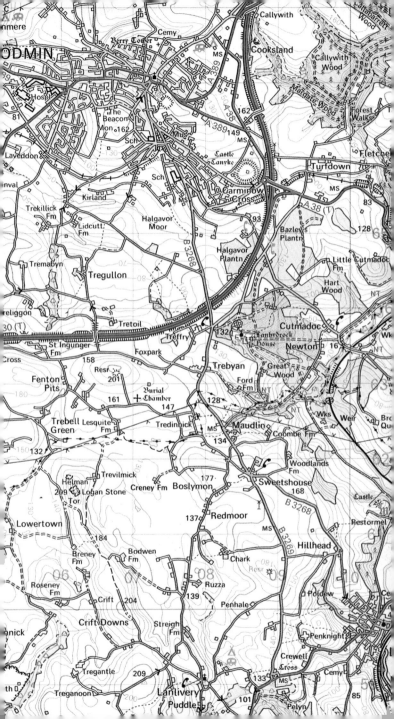

Mount Edgcumbe Gardens CORNWALL

Plymouth City Council, Cremyll.

In 1971 the Plymouth parks department, on behalf of the City and Cornwall
County Councils, took over this estate of a 1,000 or so acres (405ha) that the
war years, occupation by Normandy invasion forces and shortage of labour
had left overgrown but crossed by several solid concrete roads built for tanks
and troop-carrying vehicles. Previous generations of the Mount Edgcumbe
family had been keen landscapers and gardeners and, without directly
employing any of the well-known designers, had from the late 18th century
created the 9-acre (3.6ha) garden around the house, which is not open, and
some 27 acres (11ha) of striking formal gardens near the north-east entrance.
These comprise an Italianate garden near the large orangery, a French garden
with box edging to intricate beds and biannual bedding and English gardens,
each with unusual garden houses and mostly enclosed by tall hedges of
evergreen oak. Some old trees survive here and farther south facing Plymouth
Sound, and the whole is being restored to something of its former style. There
are follies and isolated trees; in denser woods around the amphitheatre the first
plantings of what is to be a comprehensive collection of camellias were made a
few years ago. Most of them are now thriving plants among the natural
vegetation and should add spring colour to this imposing background when
viewed from the edge of the sea. A popular place for summer outings from the
city and well worth exploring by the garden historians.

2 m SE of Torpoint at
end of B3247, or by
passenger ferry from
Plymouth

SX 4552 (OS 201)

Open daily

⓿ WC ⊖ 🚻 D (on lead)
🐾 🎪 ⛛ ☎

Trelissick Garden CORNWALL

The National Trust, Feock, nr Truro.
tel. Devoran (0872) 862090

With some 350 acres (142ha) of tree-dotted park and deciduous woodland this 20-acre (8-ha) garden has variety of form and magnificent views from many vantage points in lovely surroundings. The stately house with its small orangery stands 150ft (46m) above King Harry Ferry which crosses the River Fal nearby. It can only be seen from a distance as, with its terrace and immediate surroundings, it is not open to the public. There are several distinct and distinctive gardens within the whole. In the angle of two walls there is a collection of tender plants and, opposite, a fig garden with 10 cultivars of that luscious fruit, backed by a collection of ivies on other walls and brightened by many named fuchsias. The outer walls of the large kitchen garden, not open, provide many more lengths of backing for tender and half-hardy plants. A shaded dell has tree ferns and many other suitable plants. Crossing the public road by an old bridge one comes into a miniature parkland with many interesting trees, including conifers, and shrubs in lightly mown grass and a pleasant meander of closely cut grass paths. Back in the main garden more grass and gravel paths lead through camellias and rhododendrons to open lawns with trees and shrubs, including summer-flowering kinds of which hydrangeas are particularly plentiful. Everywhere are glimpses of the waters of the Fal and the surrounding park and wood which can be walked through.

4 m S of Truro on B3289 above King Harry Ferry

SW 8339 (OS 204)

Open Apr to end Oct
M-S 1100-1800 Su 1300-1800 (sunset if earlier)

Peak months Apr to Aug

🅿 WC 🚻 ⏺ 🌿 ★
🚶

Tremeer Gardens CORNWALL

Dr G. C. Haslam and Mrs C. Hopwood, St Tudy, Bodmin.
tel. Bodmin (0208) 850313

The drive is lined on the north by flowering cherries and then by the vegetable-garden wall. It ends at the east-facing front door of the 80-year-old house. To the north is a bank of heather and small-leaved rhododendrons. Above and beyond, narrow grass paths lead round beds and borders filled with others of the same genus. They feature all over this 7-acre (3-ha) garden for it once belonged to two dedicated rhododendron enthusiasts. Most are labelled and are probably between 10 and 30 years old. Returning to the start the obvious route takes one onto a terrace with borders under the south wall of the house and an extension to the west. The walls are mostly clothed with shrubs and climbers with low-growing plants at their feet. A few steps down there is another border of small rhododendrons and some other shrubs facing two level lawns. Across to the south one may plunge into more rhododendrons, opposite the foot of the steps or at either end, to find more narrow paths wandering so that almost every plant can be seen. They include some camellias and other shrubs and small trees. Situated 350ft (107m) above the sea and not many miles from the north Cornwall coast, at Tremeer the rainfall is high and the growth of lichen strong. Colour is provided well into the summer by other genera but also by many late-flowering hybrids mostly, say the labels, crosses involving the late-flowering *Rhododendron* 'Polar Bear'.

3 m NE of Wadebridge on A39 turn E to St Tudy

SX 0676 (OS 200)

Open Apr to end Sept daily

Peak months Apr to June

🅿 ⊖ 🍴 (by appt only)

Tresco Abbey ISLES OF SCILLY

R. A. Dorrien Smith, Esq., Tresco, Isles of Scilly.

Unique is an over-used word in descriptive writing but there is no garden quite like this sub-tropical outpost. Fourteen acres (6ha) of south-sloping gardens are protected by 50 acres (20ha) of sheltering trees. This shelter is essential for the plants that are grown on this low-lying island in the Atlantic. Augustus Smith from Hertfordshire started to make this garden nearly 150 years ago and several succeeding generations of his family have continued to collect and receive from collectors and to plant and maintain these truly magnificent gardens. Within the shelter of Monterey cypress and pine, plants from the Southern Hemisphere and the Mediterranean are grown as in a vast greenhouse. Large palms in greater variety look happier than on the mainland, acacias abound within the shelter plantations and pelargoniums act as ground cover. Cinerarias and other South African annuals seed themselves and the vivid red of the startling beschorneria contrasts with the flourishing arum lilies. Plants known as house plants elsewhere not only grow in the gardens but thrive among native plants outside it. Colour is everywhere so that the non-gardener must be impressed; the wide variety and rarity of trees, shrubs, climbers, bulbs, succulents, herbaceous and annual plants make a visit a necessity for anyone with any interest in plants or gardens, while the approach by sea or air is a spectacle in itself.

SW corner of island; heliport and landing stage nearby

SV 8914 (OS 203)

Open daily throughout year 1000-1600

Peak months May to Aug

WC ⊖ D ☕ ☺ ✿ ★

Trewithen CORNWALL

Mr and Mrs A. M. J. Galsworthy, Grampound Road, Probus, nr Truro. tel. St Austell (0726) 162087

Standing just above the 250-ft (76-m) contour this 28-acre (11ha), almost level, garden would often be swept by Cornish gales if it were not for the many mature native and exotic trees in and around it. They provide the framework in which George Johnstone, author of *The Asiatic Magnolias*, created the present garden in the 56 years before 1960. Many of his laurel windbreaks are no longer necessary and have been removed but there has been wise planting of new mixed shelter belts around the outside to maintain the serenity of this beautiful garden. The ha-ha beyond the east lawn and walk gives good views of massive trees in the well-farmed park. Among the numerous kinds of trees and shrubs the broad lawn, running some 200yd (183m) south from the 250-year-old house, is the hallmark of the place. Cross and recross this lawn to savour the views in both directions and the noble, 100-ft (30-m) tall trees. Many side paths reveal a wider range of woody and other plants, both mature and young. The newer plantings, often in gaps left by gale-felled old giants, include many modern camellias and rhododendrons which add to the numerous rarities and old favourites. Other plantings are in an area leading to the old cock pit and in a grass field within the new shelter belt. The formal walled garden, with its pool, roses and climbers, is worthy of attention; note the wisteria dominating the pergola and the old yew.

6 m E of Truro on A390 near Probus

SW 9147 (OS 204)

Open Apr to Oct M-S 0800-1300 and 1400-1700

Peak months spring

P WC ⊖ (by appt) D (occasional)

Bicton Park DEVON

Otter Leisure Enterprises Limited, East Budleigh.
tel. Budleigh Salterton (0395) 68475

Much of the gardener's craft of bygone days is preserved among the tourist
attractions in this extensive garden. Separate greenhouses contain cacti,
temperate and tropical plants, and birds. An important early greenhouse
(c.1820), built tall for palms, is now filled with many tender plants. Spring and
summer bedding provides splashes of colour when viewed from the curved
range of greenhouses over the Italian-style terraces. The view takes in a
rectangular pool, fountains and sculptures, to a distant obelisk through a
landscaped gap in hill and woodland. The many and varied old deciduous and
coniferous trees have received much skilled surgery and young replacements
are starting on their long life. The original mansion, now, with the
surrounding farmland, the Devon College of Agriculture, overlooks a large
lake and the trees. A comprehensive dwarf conifer collection is relieved by
drifts of heather and provides useful examples for those who would add a few
of these solid reliable plants to their own gardens. In the same way a new
pergola beside a canal will provide interest when covered by the newly
planted collection of climbing plants. There are rock gardens, wall and other
shrubs, herbaceous and water plants, all bearing witness of continuing skilled
attention – even if not within the gardeners' rules of 1842 still displayed on a
large board on one of the walls.

3 m N of Budleigh
Salterton on A376

SY 0786 (OS 192)

Open daily exc 23 Dec
to 1 Jan; Apr to Oct
1000-1800; Nov to Mar
1000-dusk

P WC ⊖ 🖶 D 🍽 ⛽ ⌘
🌿 ★

Castle Drogo DEVON

The National Trust, Drewsteignton.
tel. Chagford (064 73) 3306

A narrow Devon lane suddenly opens to a broad circle of tarmac and a mile-long (1.6-km) drive swings away through tall beeches and short grass to this dramatic Lutyens' castle that was started 70 years ago and completed in the early 1920s. The visitor must park his car in hiding behind the trees, and this helps the National Trust to prevent any intrusion on the architect's design. The forecourt is a bare gritted surface, yew hedges shut in the few staff cars that have to approach the castle and all around rough rabbit-cropped grass and natural vegetation surround the stark walls, with the exception of some solid planting in a small yard near the chapel. From below the forecourt the narrow end of the rhododendron garden runs some 400yd (366m) north with a good selection of the genus among other shrubs and tall trees. A path leads easterly and up and suddenly one is in a lovely English garden at about 750ft (229m) above the sea. In a rectangle of tall yew hedges well grown roses occupy the central lower part and colourful herbaceous borders fill the surrounds above partially clothed rock walls, all without the intrusion of the odd shrubs that seem to be found necessary in most modern borders. In the four corners parrotias are making good growth towards tall domes of shade. A herb garden is up more steps and another flight leads to a narrow path between many shrubs before entering a smooth lawn within a perfect circle of yew hedge.

4 m N of
Moretonhampstead on
A382 turn E to
Drewsteignton

SX 7290 (OS 191)

Open Apr to end Oct
daily 1100-1800;
reduced rates for
parties by appt

WC ⊖ (limited)
⊟ (by appt only) ☞
✳ ★ ⌂

Dartington Hall DEVON

Dartington Hall Trust, nr Totnes.
tel. Totnes (0803) 862367

Several youngish trees outside the imposing entrance prepare one for the extensive gardens within. Inside the gates a giant swamp cypress stands sufficiently aside to allow ample views of the ancient buildings, which are lightly clothed with restrained plantings of wall plants and flanked by a few trees and shrubs around the central lawn. Thence by way of the south-east, south and west, a series of gardens bear evidence of the work of the Elmhirsts, transformers from 1925 of this ancient and then derelict site, and of the succession of garden architects and advisers from both sides of the Atlantic who planned and suggested the planting and use of these varied and undulating grounds. Extensive lawns and rougher grass give space for long views and walks. Formal hedges shut off the private garden but well planned additional groups break the severe straight lines and add to the protection of the inner garden. Despite the decision to plant only to suit the design and situation and not merely to achieve a collection of plants there is a goodly range of interesting subjects among some stately trees of the past. Modern buildings blend with the old and their lines are broken or hidden by careful plantings. The main activities of the estate are in evidence much of the time and blend suitably with the artistic development of the gardens with Henry Moore's and Willi Soukop's figures standing among the shrubs.

2 m NW of Totnes on
A384 turn E

SX 7962 (OS 202)

Open daily dawn to
dusk

Peak months Apr to
May; Oct/Nov

P WC ⊕ ⊟ (by appt) D
🍽 🐕 ♨ ★ 🏃

University of Exeter Gardens DEVON

Northcote House, The Queen's Drive, Exeter.
tel. Exeter (0392) 77911

Reed Hall, the Victorian house formerly at the centre of the estate, still stands amid the many and varied university buildings on this modern campus and so do some of the trees that were planted in the old grounds about 120 years ago. Some larger shrubs also survive from the plantings made by and from the famous Veitch nurseries that flourished in the city. Since the development of the university a wide range of plants of all kinds has been planted. The sloping site, with mainly acid soil and running streams and a pond, has allowed the development of a number of variable habitats for garden plants from many sources, including some tender plants that thrive on the south sides of some of the larger buildings and, in contrast, some bright summer bedding. Some 500 acres (202ha) in all, including the roads, car parks, sports grounds and buildings, it has extensive lawns some of which are sites of future buildings already surrounded by recently planted trees. Among it all are many carefully designed groups of related and contrasting plants and, except for a few private enclosures adjacent to halls of residence, the whole is open to public view. The citizens of Exeter are fortunate in having such a well designed and still developing 'public park' in their midst. Visitors from farther afield must be impressed both by the imaginative arrangement of the interesting plants and the skilled maintenance of the whole.

On N outskirts of Exeter on A396 turn E onto B3183

SX 9193 (OS 192)

Open daily

Peak months Apr to June

🅿 ♿ 🚻 (by appt) D ✿
★

The Garden House DEVON

Fortescue Garden Trust, Buckland Monachorum, nr Yelverton.
tel. Yelverton (0822) 854769

A modern garden, created since 1945, in 2 acres (0.8ha) within the walls of part of a medieval monastery and now spread to some 7 acres (3ha) of mixed planting with closely trimmed lawns and flourishing trees. A small part of an ancient turret gives a bird's eye view of the enclosed garden. Known in the south-west for the very best forms of many of the numerous species and cultivars which, from the beginning, the first owner, Lionel Fortescue, collected from far and wide, the garden is not being allowed to ossify under the recently created Trust but is being cherished by the present gardener and opened to provide vistas to carefully selected trees and distant views, while former thoughtful groupings are being maintained and improved. Lines of Leyland's cypress, planted in the early days after the war, rather dominate some parts of the garden but provide essential shelter from cold winds from the moors above. The developing nursery is producing plants for sale from the rarer and better of the plants to be seen in flower or form by discerning visitors. The stony soil is naturally acid but the old walls have raised the pH in the enclosed part. There are borders of carefully blended rhododendrons near the entrance with other unusual shrubs extending down to where the less acid soil allows the cultivation of a wide range of herbaceous and alpine plants on the banks and flat ground among the ruins.

1 m W of A386 between Buckland Monachorum and Crapstone

SX 4968 (OS 201)

Open Apr to end Sept daily (exc Bank Hol) 1400-1700

Peak months May and July

P WC ⊖ ✿

Killerton House DEVON

The National Trust, Broadclyst, nr Exeter.
tel. Exeter (0392) 881345

The garden on this estate of more than 6,000 acres (2,428ha) is entered by a small door beside the house just beyond the front door. The first impression is of limited gardening on a flat site. There are several shrubs and climbers in narrow borders below the house and above the dwarf wall opposite that divides the garden from the lower farmland. Then, at the end of the short south front of the house, the 15 acres (6ha) of garden open up with extensive finely trimmed lawns rising to groups and banks of trees and shrubs. First there is a 'terrace' garden and borders beside the low wall with many herbaceous plants and a few shrubs. Beyond, the lawns and paths continue west and up past a rock garden in an old quarry. Alpine gardeners will find few of their plants among the shrubs and even trees that spring from the rocks. Up again beyond the long level beech walk the garden boundary is reached some 150ft (46m) above the bottom lawn and one can turn east through many trees and shrubs back to the house. John Veitch, the young Scot who founded the famous nursery, advised on planting here in the 1770s. Successive generations of that family have added many new trees and shrubs including, it is said, the first seedlings of the giant redwood that now stand tall among numerous neighbours. Under the National Trust the policy continues of felling old trees and replanting similar species to provide an interesting and well-kept garden.

6 m NE of Exeter on
B3185 between B3181
turn W onto B3183

SS 9700 (OS 192)

Open daily dawn to
dusk

🅿 WC ⊖ (limited)
🚌 (reduced rates for
parties by appt) 🐾
❀ ★ 🎁 (Apr to Oct)

Knightshayes Court DEVON

The National Trust, Bolham, Tiverton.
tel. Tiverton (0884) 254665

This Victorian house stands high above the site of once prim Victorian gardens now completely transformed by the former owners and, since 1973, by the National Trust. The top terrace now has rare and unusual permanent plants in the borders and on the walls above. South of the terrace semi-formal beds of roses and herbaceous plants thrive among fine lawns. Lower still the south garden has bulbs and rhododendrons. East from the house, up steps past modern junipers, there are separate and distinct small gardens: first a paved garden with statuary and mainly grey foliage and pink-flowered plants, fronted by a bank of alpines, then a former bowling green now with a pool in the middle and surrounded by statues and yew hedges. Opposite, mown grass emphasises the 60-year-old fox and hounds topiary. Still to the east the 'garden in the wood', the 'glade' and other areas provide contrasting settings for a wide range of plants. The beds and borders with shade-bearing plants are different from the wild and woodland shrub gardens elsewhere. Behind the house to the north-west a 20-year-old willow garden is growing rapidly around a pond and among earlier plantings of azaleas and rhododendrons. At 450ft (137m) above the sea there are extensive views of the park and woodland and the Devon countryside, but the gardens themselves, of more than 40 acres (16ha), hold the attention with their great variety of form, colour and species.

2 m N of Tiverton on minor road to Chettiscombe

SS 9615 (OS 181)

Open Apr to end Oct daily 1100-1800; reduced rates for parties by appt)

Peak months Apr to Oct

P WC ᕁ (by appt only) ᕁ ᕁ ᕁ ᕁ ★ ᕁ (open 1330-1800)

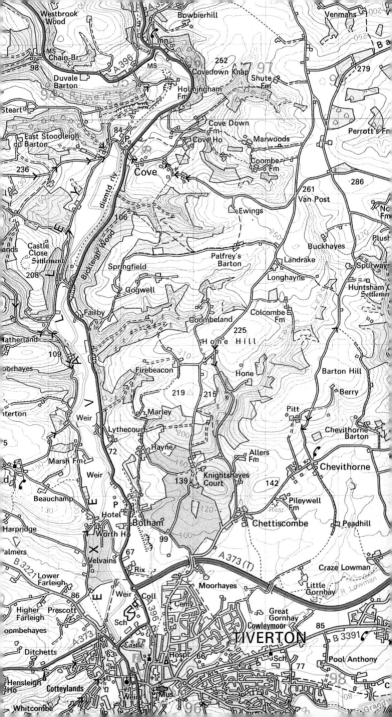

Marwood Hill DEVON

Dr J. A. Smart, Barnstaple.
tel. Barnstaple (0271) 42528

Only in 1962 did the owner burst forth from the confines of the walled garden, where he had gardened from 1949, to plant trees and shrubs on the sloping pastures to the south. Now 12 acres (5ha) of this and the opposite slope of mown grass are planted with species and cultivars of numerous garden plants, of many of which the owner can say 'from seed I collected in . . .'. An important interest is the camellia and a large greenhouse was built in 1969 to produce perfect blooms of many of the best of them. Neither they nor rhododendrons dominate the scene – a comprehensive collection of camellias is tucked away behind the church. In the same year the stream, which flows from east to west some 50ft (15m) below, was dammed, to be followed eight years later by a lower dam to give three broad ponds and a stretch of bog with a wide range of water-loving plants. Also in 1977 another greenhouse was erected for tender Australian plants. Earlier a rock garden was made in a hillside quarry. The walls of the first garden are very well clothed with climbing and scrambling plants; there is a well kept rose garden and many new plants are added to the whole each year. A recent feature is a Leyland's cypress/larch shelter belt to the west which is being steadily thinned to accommodate many potentially large and mostly uncommon trees that will grow rapidly upwards among the nurse crop of the belt.

4 m N of Barnstaple on B3230 turn W at Muddiford

SS 5437 (OS 180)

Open daily dawn to dusk

Peak months Apr to Aug

⊟ (any day Apr to Oct by appt) D ☕ (limited opening) ✿ (limited opening)

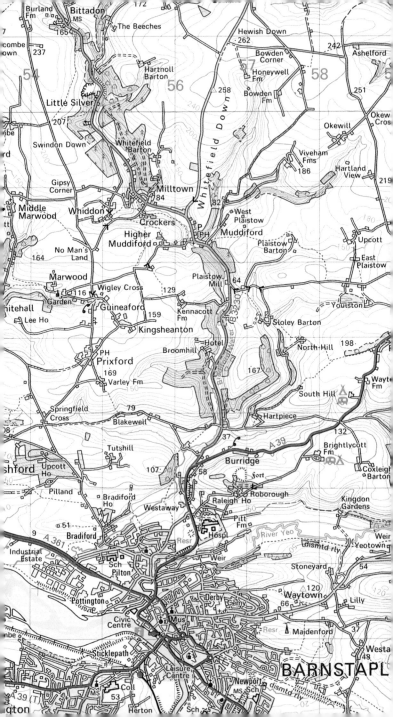

Overbecks Garden DEVON

The National Trust, Sharpitor, Salcombe.
tel. Salcombe (054 884) 2893

A first glance at the level rectangular lawn running to the west of this 70-year-old house might make one think that this is just another quite ordinary garden. Brief thought of the approach road and study of the interesting plants in the borders, a look up to the sheer cliff at the end of the lawn and another glance south to the sea and estuary gives a very different impression. In the 6 acres (2.4ha) of well-kept broken hillside there are many secluded corners in which to sit or stand and admire the views. Close at hand there are unexpected plants and groups of plants. There are recent plantings among 80-year-old trees and shrubs and several other areas of lawn or pathway, a rocky hollow with alpines and other suitable plants, narrow lawns with herbaceous plants and a wall from which to look down on to the propagating area (not open to the public). Other features include straight walks and walls shaded by magnificent magnolias and winding paths through large shrubs among which some clearing and replanting is going on. The Chusan palms are everywhere, grown from seed from the original specimens, and in every corner there are half-hardy and tender plants to interest the curious and test the knowledge of the plantsman. Below it all there is the sea and water with yachts in summer and wind and waves before and after. A small conservatory houses well-grown oranges and lemons.

From Salcombe take
road to SW for 1½ m to
South Sands

SX 7237 (OS 202)

Open daily 1100-1800

Peak months spring to
early summer

🅿 WC ⊖ (1½ m walk) ⌂
♨ ★ 🏛 (limited
opening)

Rosemoor Garden Trust DEVON

Lady Anne Palmer, Great Torrington.
tel. Torrington (080 52) 2256/3919

A steepish drive runs up through trees from a road beside the River Torridge
to the personal gardens which started out in 1959 from the small surroundings
of this pleasant country house. It now extends to 7 acres (3ha) and 'one more'
field is soon to be planted. Many rare plants surround and clothe the house and
there is always something new to be seen during each visit. Smooth lawns and
shrub borders extend eastwards to a pond with water-loving plants in and
around it. Peat banks support dwarf rhododendrons and other suitable plants.
Further on, at the end of the garden and exit drive, there is a collection of
smaller and truly ornamental trees and it is this type of planting that is to be
extended into the next paddock. A hard tennis court has been broken, covered
with soil and shredded bark and planted with shrub and trailing roses among
many other varied plants. Other larger roses fill spaces between and clamber
over pyrus, prunus and other trees to give generous colour for much of the
summer. In the conifer plantation, now being steadily thinned, on the steep
hillside above the main garden many species and cultivars of rhododendron
and related genera have been planted. Many of the rare plants in the garden are
propagated in the mist on benches under the tunnels and in frames. All is
carefully tended under the watchful eye of the owner and gives the impression
that every plant is separately cared for.

1 m SE of Great
Torrington on B3220

SS 5018 (OS 180)

Open Apr to end Oct
daily dawn to dusk;
reduced rates for
parties

P WC ⊖ (limited) ⊟ D
🍽 (on Bank Hols
also Su and W May to
Sept; otherwise by appt
only) 🎪 🐕 ✿

Saltram House DEVON

The National Trust, Plympton, Plymouth.
tel. Plymouth (0752) 336546

Emerging from the entrance through the old stable yard one finds large trees
and short grass leading up to the east front of the house. The south front looks
over a ha-ha to the extensive park while the 8-acre (3-ha) garden leads away
from the west front. Other detached buildings tend to attract visitors up to the
top of the long garden but the orange grove behind the chapel should not be
missed. There in summer are to be found orange and lemon trees in large tubs
brought from the adjoining orangery in spring and returned in the autumn, as
they were in the days when imports of such fruit were few. Other similar trees
are kept all the summer in this large glass-fronted building to provide, with
other tender plants, attractive surroundings and interest. Various paths lead
westwards through trees and shrubs to a small 'castle' or belvedere.
Continuing plantings of young trees, shrubs and bulbs can be seen on the way.
From there a long avenue of limes leads straight back to the house. Attractive
at any time it is particularly pleasant with old-fashioned daffodils in spring, the
scented lime flowers in high summer and cyclamen in autumn. Plantations of
young trees guard the walk from southerly winds and hedges enclose a small
vegetable and flower garden. This is a relaxing oasis high above the sprawling
city of Plymouth surrounded by its busy roads and motorways.

1½ m E of Plymouth on
A379 turn N to
Billacombe, after 1 m
left to Saltram

SX 5255 (OS 201)

Open daily dawn to
dusk; reduced rates for
parties at certain times
by appt

P WC ⊕ (¾ m walk) 🚻
D 🐾 (limited
opening) 🌿
★ (limited opening)
🍴 (limited opening)

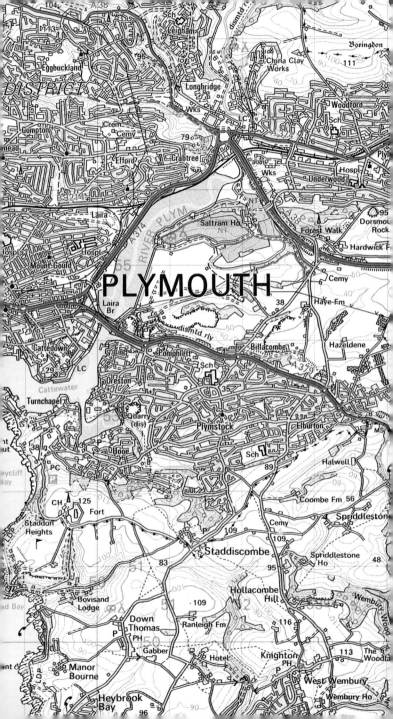

Abbotsbury Sub-Tropical Gardens DORSET

The Strangways Estates, Abbotsbury, Weymouth.
tel. Abbotsbury (0305) 871387

Set in a secluded position near Chesil Beach and protected from the cold
north-east winds by the lovely Dorset hills behind, the gardens were created
by the 1st Countess of Ilchester for her summer residence, Abbotsbury Castle.
They were enlarged by the 4th Earl of Ilchester, who planted many unusual
trees and tender shrubs in the damp shady woodlands surrounding the original
walled garden. The gardens, which were greatly changed under the guidance
of Lady Teresa Agnew, a descendant of the first owner, and John Hussey,
former head gardener, now cover nearly 17 acres (7ha) of largely informal
plantings where peacocks wander freely. Spring comes early to Abbotsbury
with its almost sub-tropical climate, beginning with a wonderful display of
camellias, azaleas, rhododendrons and magnolias, planted under such
magnificent trees as *Pterocarya fraxinifolia*, Caucasian wing nut. A small stream
feeds the ponds, where sloping banks provide ideal situations for moisture-
loving primulas, gunnera and lysichitum. In the walled garden, large Chusan
palms over 100 years old mix happily with *Cornus nuttallii* and *Robinia* 'Frisia'.
Lacecap hydrangeas and shrub roses provide summer colour with trees grown
for their coloured and textured bark, like the large collection of eucalyptus and
the spectacular cinnamon-bark myrtle.

9 m W of Weymouth on
B3157

SY 5685 (OS 194)

Open mid-Mar to mid-
Oct daily 1000-1800

Peak months Mar to
May, Aug and Sept

🅿 WC ♿ (limited) 🚻 D
🍽 🎪 ⚘ ✻

Compton Acres DORSET

J. and L. A. Brady, Canford Cliffs Road, Canford Cliffs, Poole.
tel. Canford Cliffs (0202) 708036

These famous gardens were first planned in 1914 by Thomas William
Simpson, whose idea was to design a series of completely different gardens
enclosed by hedges, walls and trees, thus making only one garden visible at a
time. Beginning at the tiny Roman garden, encircled by mellow brick walls, a
path leads through the herbaceous borders, seen at their best in summer, to the
Italian gardens where formal beds surround the lovely cross-shaped lake filled
with water-lilies. Behind these beds hundreds of roses grow in the long
borders together with clematis climbing gracefully round pillars of Bath
stone. A temple at one end of the lake and bronze statues of the 'Wrestlers of
Herculaneum' at the other add to the character of this garden. A sub-tropical
air is created by the eucalyptus, mimosa, palms and bamboos in the rock and
water garden. There is a superb Japanese garden, complete with a pagoda, an
Imperial tea-house over which wisteria elegantly climbs, and many oriental
statues that look down on a sunken lake which may be crossed by stepping-
stones. Every available space is massed with azaleas, flowering cherries and
lilies for blooming in early summer and mingling with maples which provide
a spectacular display of autumn colour.

2 m W of Bournemouth
on A35 turn S to
Canford Cliffs

SZ 0589 (OS 195)

Open Apr to end Oct
daily 1030-1830;
reduced rates for
parties of 35 and over

🅿 WC ⊖ 🍴 ☕ 🎁 ⛱ 🐕
🌿 ★

Cranborne Manor Gardens DORSET

The Marquess of Salisbury, Cranborne, Wimborne.
tel. Cranborne (072 54) 248

These very beautiful gardens were laid out in the early 17th century by Mounten Jennings and John Tradescant (who supplied some of the original plants) and contain many interesting features. Entering the gardens by the pergola walk, then wandering through church walk where trained fruit trees grow, one strolls down towards the river garden, a mass of daffodils under flowering cherries in spring. Many unusual kinds of bulbs are mixed with hellebores in borders either side of a little secluded path by the River Crane, sheltered from cold winds by a yew hedge. In June the air is filled with the scent of old shrub and species roses flowering in the north court where they mingle with herbaceous perennials. The Jacobean mount garden looks down on the west lawn and a small knot garden that is planted with 16th- and 17th-century flowers including crown imperials, *Fritillaria imperialis*. The chalk wall garden contains a mixed shrub and perennial border, underplanted with bulbs and spring- and autumn-flowering hardy cyclamen on one side, and a yew hedge, clipped in places to form windows, on the other. A herb garden crammed with many varieties of herbs set in small beds provides a final aromatic treat before leaving.

9 m N of Wimborne Minster on B3078

SU 0513 (OS 195)

Open Apr to Oct 1st S and Su of month 0900-1700 (S) 1400-1700 (Su and Bank Hol M)

Peak months May to July and Oct

🅿 WC ♿ 🚻 (preferably by appt) 🐕 ★

Highbury DORSET

Mr and Mrs Stanley Cherry, West Moors.
tel. Ferndown (0202) 874372

This fascinating half-acre (0.2ha) garden, filled with hundreds of unusual and rare plants in a setting of mature trees, was bought in 1966 by Mr and Mrs Stanley Cherry in a state of neglect. Since then it has been restored to the original design of 1909. There is much here to interest keen gardeners, plant collectors and botanists, and all the plants are clearly labelled. Variegated and silvery leaved shrubs and ground-cover plants grow in beds near the front of the house with a collection of slow-growing ones nearby. Overlooking these are two very beautiful *Amelanchier lamarckii* trees which provide blossom in spring and also good autumn colour. Crinodendron and embothrium mingling with other interesting shrubs help to enclose the small paved garden which is filled with a good collection of herbs. In a narrow bed between this and the north walk 16th- and 17th-century plants grow. The lower garden is full of exciting plants, *Cunninghamia lanceolata* and the variegated lily-of-the-valley, *Convallaria majalis* 'Variegata', blend with collections of dwarf conifers, grasses, herbaceous perennials and bulbs. Next to the orchard, which is underplanted with snowdrops, daffodils and bluebells and divided by a hedge, a mixed border runs down to the greenhouse and small weather station.

8 m N of Bournemouth
off B3072

SU 0802 (OS 195)

Open Easter Su or 1st
Su in Apr to 1st Su in
Sept; Su and Bank Hol
M 1400-1800; parties at
other times by appt

WC ⊖ 日 ● (limited) ⋤
❀ ⚹

Barrington Court SOMERSET

The National Trust, nr Ilminster.
tel. Ilminster (046 05) 2242

Though Barrington Court was built in 1514, the gardens were not designed until 1920 when Col A. A. Lyle leased the house and sent his plans for the garden to Gertrude Jekyll who made suggestions for the planting. Entering the gardens through the orchard, so beautiful in spring with many daffodils in bloom, a path leads towards the moat and the old 16th-century beef stalls where the old brick pillars and walls make an ideal background for climbing roses and honeysuckle. Nearby is the iris garden, looking at its best in early summer, with small beds filled with bearded irises. Large flowered (hybrid tea) and cluster flowered (floribunda) roses scent the summer air in the rose garden and next door is the lily garden where many water-lilies grace the pool and the mixed borders around contain crown imperials, crinums, azaleas and perennials. Very good use is made of every available area of wall space in these gardens, clematis and roses being the favourite climbing plants used. A well laid out kitchen garden is filled with many varieties of vegetables, the walls attractively covered with trained peach, apple and pear trees. The view from the lawn near the south border looks out to the tranquil park beyond the ha-ha, and an arboretum stands to the right of this lawn with a lime walk nearby.

3½ m NE of Ilminster on B3168 turn E

ST 3918 (OS 193)

Open early Apr to late Sept Su-W 1400-1730 also few days under NGS and Gardeners' Benevolent Society; reduced rates for parties

Peak months May to Sept

WC ⊖ ⊟ (by appt) ⬤ ⚹ ☎ (limited opening)

Clapton Court Gardens SOMERSET

Capt. S. J. Loder, Crewkerne.
tel. Crewkerne (0460) 73220/72200

One of the most beautiful and best kept gardens in the West Country, Clapton Court has only been open to the public since 1979. The fascinating 10-acre (4-ha) gardens are filled with many interesting plants and provide good all-the-year-round colour. The biggest ash tree in Britain is just one of the many fine specimen trees to be seen in the woodland gardens. Entering the garden through a gateway from the plant centre, the terraces come into view. Grey- and silver-leaved plants dominate the first terrace, while *Pyrus salicifolia* 'Pendula', the willow-leaved pear, is eye-catching planted as a central feature on the second terrace. A 'golden border' on the left of the highest terrace leads to the wild garden where old oaks and pine provide overhead protection for camellias, hydrangeas and the hundreds of small bulbs which carpet the ground in spring. The formal rose garden, enclosed by yew and hornbeam hedges, is fragrant on a hot summer's day with the blooming of many roses. Tiny streams meander through the delightful upper woodland which is filled with unusual and rare plants under a çanopy of mature beech and ash. Many varieties of rhododendron and azaleas fill the leafy glades with glorious displays of colour in spring, and ferns, hostas and primulas all act as ground-cover plants.

2½ m S of Crewkerne on B3165 turn E

ST 4106 (OS 193)

Open daily throughout year exc S but inc Easter S and all S in May 1000-1700; Su 1400-1700; reduced rates for parties by appt

WC (by appt only) (limited opening)

Montacute House SOMERSET

The National Trust, Montacute, nr Yeovil.
tel. Martock (0935) 823289

The very formal gardens were first planned when Montacute House was built in the late 16th century. They were later changed in 1845 by William Phelips and remain largely unaltered to this day. Entering the gardens through a yew hedge, clipped in such a way that it looks almost like a large moss-covered bank, the cedar lawn comes into view with two magnificent sweet chestnuts, *Castanea sativa*, standing in one corner. In the borders surrounding the east court, herbaceous perennials and roses give plenty of colour during the summer months. Tucked under the raised walk which separates the east court from the north garden, and edged with clipped yews and American thorns (*Crataegus lavallei*) is a border of shrub roses which includes *Rosa gallica officinalis*, *R. versicolor* and *R. alba* 'Maxima' with *Hosta fortunei* planted as ground cover. Passing the orangery that stands at the west end of the raised walk, the imposing west drive sweeps away from the house and is edged with yews, beeches, limes and cedars. Turning into the south drive where variegated hollies and golden yews grace the right-hand side, there stands one of the largest Monterey cypresses, *Cupressus macrocarpa*, in the country – its height is well over 100ft (30m). On the left California redwoods grow.

4 m W of Yeovil on
A3088

ST 4917 (OS 183)

Open daily throughout
year 1230-1800

🅿 WC 🚻 (by appt only)
🍽 (Apr to mid-Nov)
🎑 ♿ ★ 🏰 (limited
opening)

Tintinhull House SOMERSET

The National Trust, nr Yeovil.

After moving to Tintinhull at the beginning of this century, Dr S. J. M. Price laid out the very beautiful small formal gardens to the west of the house, starting with the walled Eagle Court. In 1933 Captain and Mrs F. E. Reiss came to live at Tintinhull and they were responsible for planning the lovely gardens to the north of the house and for introducing many of the unusual plants. The running of the gardens is now in the capable hands of Penelope Hobhouse. A path from the west front of the house leads through the Eagle Court with bergenias and hellebores blooming in spring in the left border under splendid flowering cherries, while tulips and bearded iris mingle with perennials on the right. Charming dog-tooth violets, anemones and hardy cyclamen contrast well with cone-shaped clipped box along the stone path. Before walking through the tranquil fountain garden, look back at the superb view of the west front of the house. Kniphofias (the red hot pokers), peonies and sweet peas trained up tripods blend well with the vegetables and a good collection of herbs in the kitchen garden, where the summer air is filled with the scent of the roses and honeysuckle climbing the pillars by the central path. A tranquil scene is viewed from the loggia in the pool garden where water-lilies bloom in early summer.

9 m NE of Ilminster on A303 turn E

ST 5019 (OS 183)

Open Apr to end Sept
W, Th, S and Bank Hol
M 1400-1800

P WC ⊖ ⊟ (by appt)
⚹ ☎

Bowood House WILTSHIRE

The Earl of Shelburne, Calne.
tel. Calne (0249) 812102

The summer spectacle of hundreds of roses blooming in neat beds on the formal terraces in front of the magnificent orangery, contrasts well with broad columnar clipped yews standing in areas of lawn and divided by gravel paths, stone steps, walls and balustrades. *Magnolia grandiflora* and climbing roses are trained against the walls with lavender used as an edging plant in some places, stone urns placed at intervals along the walls are filled in summer with pelargoniums. From the East Terrace a breathtaking view of the pleasure grounds and long 40-acre (16-ha) lake can be seen, the latter designed by Capability Brown. A broad path leads towards the cascade and Doric temple at the north end of the lake, passing hollies, acers and hydrangeas planted in the shelter of the kitchen garden wall. Under the many superb trees, narcissi grow in great drifts, mingling with the carpets of bluebells. The pinetum that lies to the left of the path was designed in 1848 and contains many notable conifers including redwoods, Sitka spruce, Monterey pine and monkey puzzle trees. During May and June, the rhododendron walks in the separate woodland gardens are open; beech and oak shelter the numerous varieties of rhododendron that create such a blaze of colour.

1 m W of Calne on A4
turn S to Buck Hill

ST 9769 (OS 173)

Open Good Fri to end
Sept daily 1100-1800;
reduced rates for
parties by appt

Peak months Apr to
Sept

P WC 🚻 🍽 ⛱ 🐕 ♿ ★ 🎁

115

The Courts WILTSHIRE

The National Trust, Holt, nr Trowbridge.
tel. Trowbridge (0225) 782340

Once an old wool mill, but now forming one wing of the house, 'The Courts'
was made larger by 17th-century additions, when the building was converted
for use as a court. By incorporating the old ponds and ditches once used for
washing the wool, Lady Goff designed a series of very intriguing gardens
sheltered by clipped yew hedges and joined by mossy stone paths. In 1950
many unusual trees were planted by Miss Goff in a meadow beyond the
boundary of yews, including the elegant fern-leaved beech, *Fagus sylvatica
heterophylla*. Many interesting features fill this 7-acre (3-ha) garden. In the cool
fern garden rodgersia grows with many varieties of ferns round a tiny pool.
The long rectangular lily pond is filled with pink water-lilies, blooming from
May onwards, and bordered by a long bed of phlox on one side and roses on
the other, the whole area being enclosed by mixed shrub and perennial
borders. From the old wool washing pond where gunnera is planted, the path
winds between little channels of water, before entering a garden filled with
roses and old-fashioned plants such as honesty, cowslips, bluebells and
bergenias naturalising even between the slabs of stone on the paths and steps.

2 m NE of Bradford-on-
Avon on B3107 turn S at
Holt

ST 8661 (OS 173)

Open Apr to end Oct
M-F 1400-1800; other
times by written
application

🅿 🚻 (by appt only) ✧

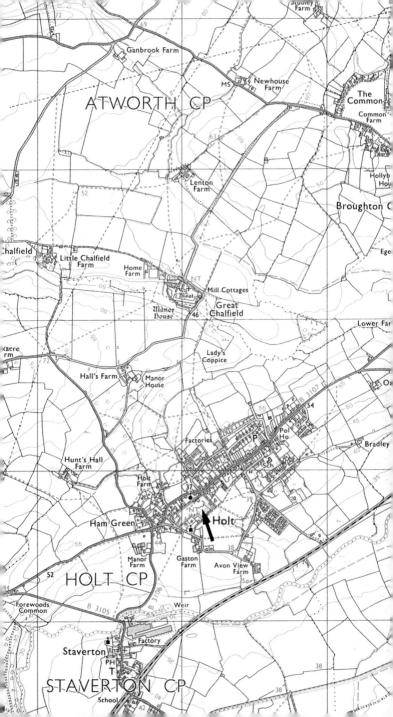

Stourhead WILTSHIRE

The National Trust, Stourton, Warminster.
tel. Bourton (0747) 840348

The breathtaking landscape gardens of Stourhead were designed in 1741 by Henry Hoare the Second when he created a series of lakes in a sloping woodland setting with vantage points to view the monuments and temples across the sparkling waters of the lake. Looking from the Temple of Flora the view is of the Pantheon standing serenely on a grass mound, more often than not reflected in the still water. Walking northwards along the path that encircles the lake one passes rhododendrons, magnolias, acers and magnificent specimens of sequoiadendron, metasequoia (the dawn redwood) and London plane. Many varieties of pine and abies are planted on the hillside above the path as it turns westwards, winding its way to the damp and rather eerie grotto from which a marvellous view of the stone bridge, the Bristol cross, brought from Bristol in the 18th century, and church is seen. The Temple of Apollo towers above an enormous tulip tree, *Liriodendron tulipifera*, planted at the water's edge and when the leaves turn a brilliant yellow in the autumn, the bright red foliage of adjacent acers provides a striking contrast of colour. In the same area, a very good specimen of *Davidia involucrata*, the handkerchief tree, can be seen at its best in early summer.

1 m W of Mere on A303 turn N onto B3092 to Stourton

ST 7734 (OS 183)

Open daily 0800-1900 (or sunset if earlier)

🅿 WC 🚻 D (Oct to Feb only) 🕭 ⚘ ★ (Mar to mid-Dec) 🚌 (limited opening; parties by appt only)

Stourton House WILTSHIRE

Col. and Mrs A. S. Bullivant, Stourton, nr Warminster.

This lovely 4-acre (1.5-ha) garden is filled with very interesting plants, including flowers that are grown specially for drying such as achillea, delphiniums and *Physalis franchettii*, the Chinese lantern. Elegant tree peonies, so beautiful in June, and herbaceous perennials grow in fan-shaped beds enclosed by high hedges in the small sheltered formal garden. In spring hundreds of unusual narcissi with split coronas bloom in an area next to the tiny water garden and rock garden. Not far from the front of the house, dwarf conifers and heathers fill the newly made peat beds, together with dog-tooth violets and the splendid deep purple-flowered *Fritillaria persica*. The high leafy canopy provided by mature trees in the woodland garden helps to protect the many rarities growing below: spectacular magnolias, rhododendrons, camellias and the marvellous pink-tinged green and white leaved *Pieris japonica* 'Variegata', mingle with primulas, meconopsis and the fern-leafed *Corydalis cheilanthifolia*, a mass of dainty yellow flowers in April. Nearby, in the shade of an enormous holly tree, many different kinds of hydrangea grow, giving good colour in late summer and featuring the most attractive white and green foliage of the variegated hydrangea.

1 m W of Mere on A303
turn N onto B3092

ST 7734 (OS 183)

Open Apr to Nov S,
Th and Bank Hol M
1100-1800; other days
by appt

⚑ WC ♿ (by appt) ⛱
❀ (also dried flowers)

Bangor

Plas Newydd

Penrhyn
Castle

Bodnant
Garden

GWYNEDD

C

Aberystwyth

POW

Llandrinc
Wells

DYFED

Carmarthen

WEST
GLAMORGAN

MID
GLAMORG

Swansea

S
GLAM

Dyffryn Gard

Wales and Western Counties

MERSEY-SIDE

Liverpool

Manchester
Dunham Massey

Sheffield

Arley Hall ✿

Tatton Park ✿

Lyme Park ✿

University of Liverpool
Botanic Gardens ✿

✿ Chester Zoo Gardens

Capesthorne Hall

Chester

C H E S H I R E

DERBYSHIRE

Y D

Wrexham

Little Moreton Hall ✿

Stoke-on-Trent

Nottingham

✿ Cholmondeley Castle

✿ Erddig

Derby

k Castle ✿

STAFFORDSHIRE

Hodnet Hall ✿

Shrewsbury

Telford

Leicester

vis Castle ✿

SHROPSHIRE

Weston Park ✿

LEICESTERSHIRE

Benthall Hall ✿

WEST MIDLANDS

Dudmaston ✿

Birmingham

Coventry

Berrington Hall ✿

✿ Burford House

Worcester

WARWICKSHIRE

✿ Hergest Croft Gardens

HEREFORD

✿ Spetchley Park

WORCESTER

Kiftsgate Court ✿

Moccas Court ✿

Hereford

The Priory ✿

Hidcote Manor ✿

The Weir ✿

✿ Batsford Park

✿ Abbey Dore Court

Snowshill Manor ✿

Sezincote ✿

Sudeley Castle ✿

Westbury Court Garden ✿

Llanfihangel Court ✿

Gloucester

GLOUCESTERSHIRE

OXFORDSHIRE

Oxford

G W E N T

✿ Barnsley House

Berkeley Castle ✿

Westonbirt Arboretum ✿

Swindon

Cardiff

A V O N

Bristol

WILTSHIRE

BERKSHIRE

Chester Zoo Gardens CHESHIRE

North of England Zoological Society, Chester.
tel. Chester (0244) 380280

To see Victorian bedding-out at its most highly colourful go to Chester Zoo Gardens, where the mosaic carpets of flowers, changed three times a year and using 80,000 plants, are a floral experience. The colours are quite staggering and the beds set amidst extensive lawns centred by fountains of bronze statuary make for a delightful picture. To add to the colour are 15,000 roses in beds throughout the garden. In this 110 acres (44.5ha) of zoo and gardens, developed by Mrs Mottershead, wife of the zoo founder, even the animal enclosures are planted with trees, climbers and shrubs to make as natural a habitat as possible. Such is the high, arching tropical house where exotic birds fly free and animals peer through naturally growing philodendrons, datura, bougainvillea, anthurium and orchids and a cascade 20ft (6m) high among towering shrubs gives a jungle effect. A rock garden with running water created in 1968 in memory of Mrs Mottershead is clothed in interesting rock plants and bounded by spiring conifers including the fossil tree (*Metasequoia glyptostroboides*) now 30ft (9m) high. On this side of the garden is a new South American garden where tender subjects from that tree and shrub treasure land are being tried out, and the Jubilee garden which, until 1977, was a hole in tHe ground, but is now a green amphitheatre centred by a most distinctive fountain of bronze, Noah and the Four Winds.

N outskirts of Chester
off A41 outer ring road

SJ 4170 (OS 117)

Open daily exc 25 Dec
1000-1800 (summer);
1000-1 hour before dusk
(winter)

P WC D (guide dogs
only) 🍴 ⚲
★ facilities for disabled

Cholmondeley Castle CHESHIRE

The Marchioness of Cholmondeley, Malpas.
tel. Cholmondeley (082 922) 202/3

Gardening here dates from the castle building between 1801–4 when cedars, taxodiums, wellingtonias and oaks were planted as were the massed, massive 'haystacks' of ponticum rhododendrons, bamboos and laurel. Since 1950, when Lord and Lady Cholmondeley came here, large-scale planting and redesigning has taken place in which both Mr McKenna and Mr James Russell lent their practised hands, the former for the rock garden and waterfall and the latter, over nine years, planted hundreds of rhododendrons, azaleas, flowering shrubs and redesigned the herbaceous borders. A lake was dug in the temple garden and a circular, open, domed pavilion placed on an island and water-lilies planted. Today the planting is most diverse, colourful and full of year-round interest. A cherry walk, the high castle terrace and its walls, are stages for choice climbers as well as camellias, clematis, herbaceous and unusual roses and hydrangeas. Steps from the terrace enter a grey and silver Jubilee garden. The high-hedged rose garden featuring raised beds and arches over the paths is aglow with a grand collection. In the glade rhododendrons, viburnums, hydrangeas, acers, cornus, roses, other flowering shrubs and early bulbs for spring make a delightful feature. There are wide views over garden and surrounding countryside from various vantage points and infinite care has been taken with planting to give such pictures of colours, foliage and form.

8 m N of Whitchurch
on A49

SJ 5351 (OS 117)

Open Easter to end
Sept S and Bank Hol
M 1200-1800

🅿 WC ⊖ 🖽 D 🍽 ⛱ ⚙
🌿 ★

University of Liverpool Botanic Gardens (Ness) CHESHIRE

Mr J. K. Hulme (Director), Ness, Neston, South Wirral.
tel. (051) 336 2135

Now the botanical gardens of the University of Liverpool, this 50 acres (20ha) of land on the Wirral started as the private garden of A. K. Bulley, who first sent George Forrest, Kingdon Ward and R. E. Cooper plant hunting. Many of the plants introduced by the collectors were first grown at Ness and the original *Pieris formosa forrestii* and many of Forrest's Asiatic primulas are still grown there. Ness has the finest heather garden in the country, a rose garden set out to demonstrate the evolution of the family, a woodland garden sheltering rhododendrons and many of the tender South American trees and shrubs. A large rhododendron and azalea collection dazzles the eye while collections of sorbus and magnolias add interest. A long double herbaceous border contrasts with the smaller scale, but delightful, terrace garden with delicate climbers on its walls. Two small, compartmented gardens are paved and parterred to make colourful resting places. The Ledsham Herb Garden laid out in 1974 displays all the culinary herbs in separate beds and nearby is a rose pergola and laburnum arch. A lower area called the 'Pingle' is a stream- and pool-fed garden and there is a bulb meadow too. A water garden houses endangered native plants and there are greenhouses for a tropical touch.

9 m NW of Chester on
A540 turn S to Burton

SJ 3075 (OS 117)

Open daily exc 25 Dec
0900-dusk

Peak months May, early
June, July to Oct

Lyme Park CHESHIRE

The National Trust, Disley, Stockport.
tel. Disley (066 32) 2023

Originally a hunting park, the Palladian mansion terraces still look over more than 1,000 acres (405ha) of parkland and moorland on the edge of the Peak District. It was in the late 19th century that Lord Newton laid out the surrounding sunken gardens, steps, terraces, the graceful glass-roofed orangery and the Italian garden and fountain still to be seen from above in all its formal parterred glory, planted up twice a year to give a blaze of floral colouring. Other flower beds and two long herbaceous borders continue the floral interest across the lawns to a hedged rose garden and even the borders which are hedged by hollies and yews are full of roses and other climbing plants lacing the hedging. There is a pond, a setting for a statue of Neptune fishing, and a water feature bridged by a stone construction of 1756. In the distance is an eyecatcher, a lanthorn tower, and by the streamside a ravine is now a garden glade side-planted for a long season of flowering with primulas, hostas, rhododendrons, azaleas, hydrangeas, astilbes and a mixture of philadelphus for fragrance. Looking over the Italian, or Dutch garden as it is sometimes called, on the west front is the Vicary Gibbs' garden, to commemorate the gift of this once celebrated gardener from Aldenham, of choice trees and shrubs, the Algerian oak, *Aesculus* hybrids, *Cornus kousa*, *Malus* 'Gibbs' Golden Gage', and *M.* 'Aldenhamensis'.

8 m SE of Stockport on A6 turn S at Disley

SJ 9682 (OS 109)

Open daily 0800-sunset

WC ⊖ (1½ m walk) 🚌 (by appt) D 🍽 (limited opening) 🎋 ★ 🎁 (limited opening) 🚲 cycle hire; pitch and putt; fishing; various events throughout year

Tatton Park CHESHIRE

The National Trust, Knutsford.
tel. Knutsford (0565) 3155

The gardens of 60 acres (24ha) and its 1,000 acres (405ha) of parkland show the changes of over 200 years. The garden at Tatton is divided into two, east and west, by the long walk terminating in a Grecian temple of 1820. Repton drew up a 'Red Book' for landscaping the parkland for the Egertons, and the Italianate terraces, fountain and formal pool were laid down by Paxton in 1847, the vista over them being to deer grazing in parkland, tree studded and marked by a long mere or lake. Tatton has the best representation of a Japanese garden, dated 1910, in this country, with its Shinto temple brought from Japan, tea-house, miniature pagoda and Fuji Yama. The 'Golden Brook' and lake mirror exotic trees and a host of azaleas and rhododendrons, many planted since 1940, a last count giving over 600 different species and varieties. A Victorian fernery houses Antipodean tree ferns; there is an orangery of 1818 by Wyatt still housing oranges, a maze of box, an African hut and a glade of *Metasequoia glyptostroboides*, a leach pool with fountain and clipped topiary work. A paved rose garden with fountain is enclosed by a yew hedge and nearby the tower garden is the home of flowers and rare shrubs. The long L-shaped border is divided into sections by buttressed yew. Roses and clematis clamber through clipped holly, there is both an arboretum and a pinetum, a magnolia collection, a tiered fountain and an arbour.

4 m S of Altrincham
on A5034

SJ 7481 (OS 109)

Open Easter to mid-May and Sept to early Oct daily exc M 1200-1630 (S and Bank Hol M 1100-1700); mid-May to Aug daily exc M 1100-1750 (S and Bank Hol M 1100-1800); early Oct to Easter daily exc M 1300-1600 (S and Bank Hol M 1200-1600); closed 25 Dec; parties at other times by appt

WC (reduced rates for parties by appt) D ⚭ ✻ ★ 🐕 (limited opening)

Erddig CLWYD

The National Trust, nr Wrexham.
tel. Wrexham (0978) 355314

The remains of formal gardening in Britain are few. Capability Brown saw to that. Badeslade's engraving of 1738 shows a layout of a central gravel walk leading to a long, straight canal and through the White Gates there is a view of the country beyond. This is the arrangement of the original garden made by John Meller in 1718. The intention has been to return the garden as far as possible to the condition of the Badeslade engraving. The orchards have been replanted, and fruit trees, of ancient varieties especially propagated, have been placed against the walls. The middle section of the broad walk has been planted with double rows of limes, *Tilia euchlora*, which are pleached to make a low formal connection between the lawns and the canal. The gates at the end of the canal made by Robert Davies, the Wrexham smith, replaced the earlier White Gates in 1905. The south-facing side of the garden terminates in a fishpond, but the remainder was devoted to fruit, and has been replanted with ranks of apples, trained into pyramids. There will also be pears, peaches, apricots and plums from the walls. South of the canal walk the central section is devoted to a Victorian flower garden, which includes the rambler rose 'Dorothy Perkins' and *Clematis jackmanii*. This garden lies between yew hedges and a moss walk.

1 m SW of Wrexham on A483 turn E to Hafod-y-bwch

SJ 3248 (OS 117)

Open Apr to end Sept daily exc F but inc Good Fri 1200-1730; Oct W, S and Su 1200-1530 (last admission 1 hour before closing); reduced rates for parties of 20 or over by appt

P WC ♿ (by appt only) ⬤ ⚘ ★ 🏠

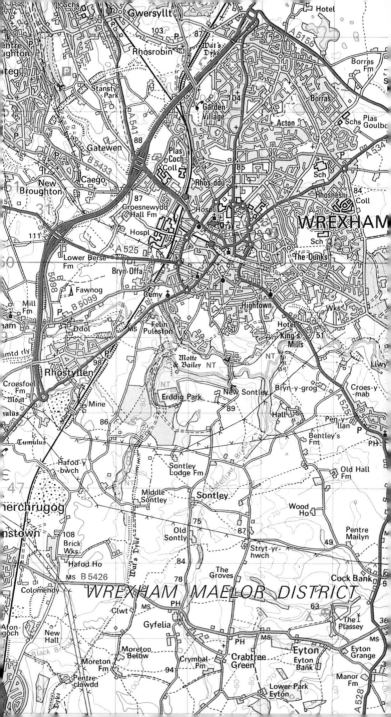

Dyffryn Botanic Garden

SOUTH GLAMORGAN

Mr D. V. Goddard (Director), St Nicholas, Cardiff.

Situated in the Vale of Glamorgan, this 50-acre (20-ha) garden was landscaped in the 20th century by Thomas Manson for the owner John Cory, who was a prominent figure in the commercial, religious and philanthropic life of South Wales. The garden was further developed by his son, Reginald Cory, an eminent horticulturist, who increased the plant collections and established Dyffryn as one of the finest botanic centres in Wales. As a botanic garden, priority is given to the collection of plants, but the garden is also open to the public to encourage ideas in planting and design and as a venue for leisure events. Its chief features are individually designed gardens (e.g. paved, sunken, pool, heart, and Roman gardens each enclosed by magnificent yew hedges), an extensive arboretum, herbaceous borders, a newly established heather and rock garden, a rose garden, lawns and attractive water features. Of the plant houses, the 50-ft (15-m) high palm house is the most dramatic architecturally and contains many exotic plants and a large collection of citrus fruits. Other houses contain interesting collections of orchids, cacti and succulents. Among the trees are large specimens of paper bark maple, Brewer's weeping spruce, wing nut and roble beech. The Japanese maples and magnolia species are particularly outstanding.

4 m W of Cardiff on A4232 turn S onto A4050 and then W to Dyffryn

ST 0972 (OS 171)

Open Apr to Sept daily 0900-dusk

Peak months May, July to Sept

WC & D 🍴 A ⊗ ✻ ★

Barnsley House GLOUCESTERSHIRE

Mrs Rosemary Verey, nr Cirencester.
tel. Bibury (028 574) 281

Although not large this garden is worth a lengthy visit, for it contains as many ideas and plants as any comparable space in England. It is tempting to compare David and Rosemary Verey with Harold Nicolson and Vita Sackville-West, the husbands contributing a strong sense of architectural design and the wives the controlled but profuse planting. Mrs Verey's second great contribution is her knowledge of garden history, which is shown not only in the arrangement of plants, but in such features as the tunnel of *Laburnum* 'Vossii', the knot garden and her intricate 'potager' with pyramids of roses and clematis, and cunningly contrived arbours. In the borders round the house, particularly those facing south, is a fascinating collection of plants chosen for shape, colour, scent and year-round interest. The pattern of the garden is set by a wide path of Cotswold stone pointed by pairs of Irish yews, which leads to the garden gate and crosses at right-angles the laburnum tunnel and its parallel box-lined path, terminating in the rain fountain. To the left of the path lies a Doric temple, its columns and the echoing junipers reflected in a lily and goldfish pool. The main lawn to the west of the house has as its chief ornament an 18th-century summerhouse and terminates in a collection of sorbus and other interesting trees, including a paulownia. In a garden of this kind the house is of great importance, and Barnsley House is worthy of its gardens.

4 m NE of Cirencester
on A433

SP 0805 (OS 163)

Open W 1000-1800
(dusk if earlier) also 1st
Su in May, June and
July; parties at other
times by appt

Peak months Apr to Oct

P WC ☐ ☐ ⌂ ✿

Batsford Park Arboretum GLOUCESTERSHIRE

Batsford Estates Company, Moreton-in-Marsh.
tel. Moreton-in-Marsh (0608) 50722 or Blockley (0386) 700409

The foundations of this garden arboretum were laid by Lord Redesdale, who created a garden in the oriental style with carefully considered groupings of water and rocks, garden buildings and ornaments, set among a collection of trees and shrubs. During the war, and until the present Lord Dulverton succeeded in 1966, little change was made to the garden. He then decided to reclaim it and to expand its contents into an arboretum. The collection is now outstanding. A guidebook describes the arboretum in detail; among the evergreens there are fine groups of cedars, Californian redwoods, Western hemlocks, and of that often bare-legged tree *Chamaecyparis lawsoniana* 'Erecta Viridis'. Batsford is naturally at its best either in spring, when the magnolias and cherries are in flower, or in autumn when the reds, yellows and golds from Japanese maples, red oaks, beeches, chestnuts, and cherries flame against the background of evergreens. There is an enormous variety of trees at Batsford, a mecca for students, but its well contrived effects make it a place that everyone will enjoy.

5 m N of Stow-on-the-Wold on A429 turn W at Moreton-in-Marsh

SP 1833 (OS 151)

Open Apr to Oct daily 1000-1700

Peak months May, June and Oct

🅿 WC 🚻 (by appt only) D
🍽 ⛱ ♿ ⚘ ★

Berkeley Castle GLOUCESTERSHIRE

R. J. E. Berkeley, Esq., Berkeley.
tel. Dursley (0453) 810332

The sheltered terraces that form the garden are in sharp contrast to the overpowering gloom of the castle walls. Facing south, and with the shelter that these walls provide, it has been possible to grow a wide selection of sun-loving and semi-tender plants. The planting was originated by the present owner's father, Major Robert Berkeley, who had as his mentor his aunt, Ellen Willmott of Warley Place. The wall plants include the evergreen magnolias, *M. grandiflora* and *delavayi*, Banksian roses, and species of ceanothus, eucalyptus, clematis, cestrum and *Cytisus battandieri*. A wisteria rises the whole height of the castle walls as did *Magnolia delavayi* until cut by a savage winter. Interesting herbaceous plants and shrubs include acanthus, aloes, cistus, *Clerodendrum bungei*, red hot pokers, tree peonies and yuccas. What was once the swimming pool, denuded of its topiary elephants, is now a formal lily pool. From here or from the flat meadows, which formerly could be flooded at will, the best views of this formidable castle are to be obtained.

At Berkeley on B4066

ST 6898 (OS 162)

Open Apr and Sept daily exc M 1400-1700; May to Aug T-S 1100-1700 Su 1400-1700; Oct 1400-1630; Bank Hol M 1100-1700; reduced rates for parties of 25 or over by appt

Peak months May to Sept

🅿 WC ♿ (limited) 🚻 (by appt only) ♥ 🍴 ★ 🏠

Hidcote Manor Garden GLOUCESTERSHIRE

The National Trust, Hidcote Bartrim, Chipping Campden.
tel. Mickleton (038 677) 333

Hidcote, created by the American, Major Lawrence Johnson, is one of the seminal gardens of the 20th century. The Hidcote style has been, and largely still is the accepted manner in which to lay out gardens today. Johnston started work before the First World War and continued until his death in 1958. He was working at a time when the plants of the world were available to him, and when the history of gardening had become a subject of interest. Hidcote is thus a synthesis of much that has gone before. Its emphasis on structure, the avenues, the cross vistas, the thrust of the central spine starting in the old garden, through the circle, up the red borders, mounting the steps by the garden pavilions, along the stilt garden to a magnificent view of the open country, is derived essentially from the classical period of French gardening, but its planting is English, the planting of cottage gardens, but with an immeasurably enriched palette. Colour control is Miss Jekyll's principal contribution to gardening, and Lawrence Johnston learned her art; his red borders, the greens and yellows of the garden he named after his mother, Mrs Winthrop, the whites, silvers, pinks and mauves of the old garden testify to this. After a period of decline, in Johnston's later years, the garden is now meticulously and sympathetically maintained by the National Trust.

3½ m N of Chipping
Camden on B4081 turn
E at junction with A46
to Hidcote Bartrim

SP 1742 (OS 151)

Open Apr to end Oct
daily exc T and F 1100-
2000; parties of 15 or
over by appt only

P WC D (guide dogs
only) ☂ (limited
opening) ♨ ★

Kiftsgate Court GLOUCESTERSHIRE

Mr and Mrs J. G. Chambers, Chipping Campden.
tel. Mickleton (038 677) 777

It is amazing to have two gardens as great as Kiftsgate and Hidcote within a stone's throw of each other. Kiftsgate wins on drama, for it is planted above and on the Cotswold scarp with long, pastoral views over the Vale of Evesham; it leads also on individuality. Despite its structure, there is a sense that, as it developed, Hidcote outgrew its strength; Kiftsgate is tighter, the sense of personal creation stronger. Its intimacy makes it less suited to absorb crowds; come therefore at off-peak times the better to appreciate the sitting-out gardens that surround the house, to give time for an unhurried examination of the skilfully planted borders, using the excellent garden guide and plant list, to descend winding walks to the swimming pool lawn with its magnolias, and to marvel at the hedges of the striped Gallica, 'Rosa Mundi', and to admire the outrageous vigour of the Himalyan musk rose, *Rosa filipes* 'Kiftsgate', that now covers several trees, and flowers in July. Remember also that the sales barrows are happy hunting-grounds for interesting new plants.

3½ m N of Chipping Camden on B4081 turn E at junction with A46 to Hidcote Bartrim

SP 1743 (OS 151)

Open Apr to end Sept W, Th, Su and Bank Hol M 1400-1800

P WC ♿ (by appt only)
🍴 (limited opening)
✿ ⚘

Sezincote GLOUCESTERSHIRE

Mr and Mrs D. Peake, Moreton-in-Marsh.

This is Xanadu come to England. The house, an amazing Hindu-Mogul fantasy in the manner of Akbar, was completed in 1805 by Samuel Pepys Cockerell for his brother Charles, who had served in the East India Company. The finest view of it can be had from the bridge over the lowest pond, where its amber walls, copper dome and the pinnacles of the pavilions, temples and stables stand out among the trees. Reverse the position and from the front of the house or from the curving orangery, surely the most enticing greenhouse corridor in England, look at the park. The great Lebanon cedars to the left were planted by Humphry Repton, their under-canopy, misty pink cherries, by Lady Kleinwort and Graham Thomas; the lake is Repton's, while the view across the Evenlode valley is English countryside at its most magical. Three parts of the garden in particular retain an exotic atmosphere. The south garden, between the house and the orangery, is laid out in Mogul fashion with canals and paths crossing at right-angles, representing the rivers of life. At the temple pool there is a temple, designed by Thomas Daniell, to Surya, Hindu god of the sun. The Indian influence culminates at Daniell's bridge decorated with Brahmin bulls, and below which, coiled round a tree trunk, is a metal three-headed serpent. The planting of the stream expands and contracts, until it reaches the island pool, spanned by a bridge, where cedars are reflected in the clear water, and in spring the turf is bright with anemones and bluebells.

2 m W of Moreton-in-Marsh on A44 turn S

SP 1730 (OS 151)

Open Jan to end Nov Th, F and Bank Hol M 1400-1800

P WC ⚘ 🏠 (limited opening; parties by appt only)

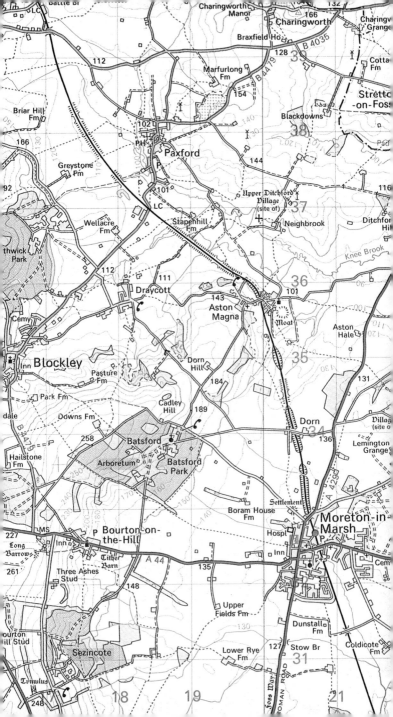

Snowshill Manor GLOUCESTERSHIRE

The National Trust, nr Broadway.
tel. Broadway (0386) 852410

By 1919 Snowshill had become a semi-derelict farm when it was bought and restored by the architect Charles Wade. By 1923 Mr Wade, using Mr H. Baillie Scott as designer, had laid out the garden, incorporating the old farm buildings including the dovecot, and using the spring that rises under the house to feed a series of pools and troughs. 'One of his maxims was that the plan of the garden is more important than the flowers', writes Graham Thomas. Wade favoured gardens that do not disclose all their delights at a single glance, so his garden is organised in a series of terraces and outdoor rooms. He also had a predeliction for mauve and blue flowers which he considered to contrast ideally with surroundings of Cotswold stone. Visitors will notice that the doors, windows and gates of the house and farm buildings are painted in a deep turquoise blue that has become known as Wade Blue. It is no mean achievement to have made a garden of great variety in a small space which is in complete empathy with the house it surrounds. This garden is in the Hidcote and Sissinghurst tradition, full of charm, and only lesser in renown as it is smaller in scale.

3 m S of Broadway on road to Snowshill
SP 0934 (OS 150)

Open Apr and Oct S, Su and Easter M 1100-1300 and 1400-1700; May to Sept W-Su and Bank Hol M 1100-1300 and 1400-1800

P WC ♿ (by appt only) ✿ ★ 🏠

Sudeley Castle GLOUCESTERSHIRE

The Lady Ashcombe, Winchcombe.
tel. Winchcombe (0242) 602308

This is a large and popular place, so try to choose a time when crowds will not spoil the Tennysonian atmosphere of the garden. Maude might easily have wandered among the lavender and rosemary of the Queen's Garden, laid out in imitation of a medieval original by Emma Dent in the mid-19th century. Victorian too are the domed, clipped yews by the park balustrade, and the bastion-like yew hedges with openings and tunnel walks that flank this charming knot garden. The pleasure grounds are well planted with cedars and limes, and many younger specimens of planes and sweet chestnuts. The canal is now devoted to a collection of waterfowl. Another romantic incident is provided by the ruin of the magnificent tithe barn; in front there is a rectangular lily pool, and at either side it is buttressed by hedges of yew and groups of the white Japanese cherry 'Shirotae'. Strong climbers, such as wisteria and *Clematis montana*, clothe it appropriately. The castle is in itself highly romantic, so the whole – park, wide views, and garden – combine together to create a place in which Scott and Tennyson would have delighted.

6 m NE of Cheltenham on A46 turn E at Winchcombe

SP 0327 (OS 163)

Open Mar to end Oct daily 1100-1750; parties in winter months by appt

WC ⊖ 🚻 🅿 🍴 🎠 ★ 🐕 Falconry on W, Th and Su pm, May to end Aug

Westonbirt Arboretum GLOUCESTERSHIRE

Forestry Commission, Tetbury.
tel. Westonbirt (066 688) 220

The idea of an arboretum can be daunting, but this is not true of Westonbirt, for Robert Holford, who began the plantings in 1829, had a genius for grouping and was as much concerned to satisfy the eye as to form a scientifically arranged collection. This was the time when David Douglas was exploring North America and it is inevitable that Holford's arboretum should concentrate on the flood of new conifers that he introduced. Their arrangement, however, into glades and avenues and the subsequent underplanting with flowering trees and shrubs avoids boredom while allowing us to view from sufficient distance the grandeur of Douglas fir, noble pine, coast redwood and sequoia. The Forestry Commission, which now owns and runs the arboretum, is carrying on the planting tradition and developing new collections notable among which is the Hillier Glade of ornamental cherries. Visitors should not confine their visits to the original arboretum but cross the valley into Silk Wood, where in the shelter of old oak woods and hazel coppice are collections of native and American species, and where a major delight is in walking among magnificent trees on a spring carpet of primroses, wood anemones and bluebells. Come without fail both in spring and autumn, when the colours of leaves are at their best, and choose, if you can, a sunny day.

3½ m SW of Tetbury
on A433

ST 8590 (OS 162)

Open daily 1000-dusk

P WC 🚻 (by appt only) D
🍽 ㄷ ⚘ ★ 🐕

Bodnant Garden GWYNEDD

The National Trust, Tal-y-cafn, Colwyn Bay.

Bodnant must be rated as one of the great gardens of the world. Developed since 1874 by three generations of Aberconways with three generations of Puddles as the head gardeners, it is distinguished firstly for its amazing range of plants, next for its superb views to the mountains of Snowdonia, and then for the variety and scope of its design. The garden falls into three main sections, the Italianate terraces descending in front of the house constructed by the late Lord Aberconway between 1905 and 1915, the shrub borders above the River Hiraethlyn and flanked by the park, and the Dell, deep below full of great conifers, rhododendrons, and primulas. The soil is a stiff boulder clay, overlying a friable shaly rock. Pride of place goes to the rhododendrons, magnolias and camellias, all spring flowering. The summer display is concentrated on the terraces, roses, water-lilies and clematis, but throughout the garden there is leaf colour in the autumn. The basic structure of the garden is achieved by backgrounds of large native trees, mostly planted about 1792, by abundant running water, and by the dramatic fall of the land. Horticulturists will be overwhelmed by the endless variety of the species grown, and every visitor will be impressed by the views, the dramatic changes from sunny terrace to shady depths, and by the knowledge and devoted skill that has made Bodnant into one of the wonder gardens.

8 m S of Colwyn Bay on A470, entrance on road to Eglwysbach

SH 8073 (OS 116)

Open mid Mar to end Oct daily 1000-1700; reduced rates for parties of 20 or over by appt

Peak months mid Apr to end Sept

P WC ⊖ 🚻 ➤ (exc Oct) ✾

Berrington Hall HEREFORD AND WORCESTER

The National Trust, nr Leominster.
tel. Leominster (0568) 5721

The house was begun in 1776 for the Hon. Thomas Harley, the MP for Herefordshire, by Capability Brown and his son-in-law, Henry Holland. Today the park remains much as Brown left it, including the 14-acre (5.7-ha) lake in the south-east corner. The present Lord Cawley has been responsible for planting the collection of interesting, and sometimes rare, shrubs and plants. The drive leading to the south front is flanked by the Chinese wintersweet (*Chimonanthus fragrans*), magnolias, mountain ashes, and the Syrian hibiscus. A woodland garden runs along much of the west boundary and is planted with many agreeable shrubs including the May bush (*Kolkwitzia amabilis*), mock orange, and deutzias. The lawns in front are, in early autumn, bright with the spires of ladies' tresses orchids, and followed by a carpet of *Cyclamen neapolitanum* in pink and white. The rare shrubs are planted on the sunny walls of the walled garden. The rarest is that perennial relation of the vegetable marrow *Thalidiantha oliveri*, a climber with rich yellow flowers. A striking combination is the large-flowered *Clematis* 'William Kennett', lavender blue, and the orange flowers of *Eccremocarpus scaber* from Chile. The mild climate also allows *Buddleia colvilei*, varieties of crinodendron, and *Carpenteria californica* to flourish. As a combination of Brown park and unusual plants Berrington has much to offer.

4 m N of Leominster on A49

SO 5063 (OS 149)

Open Apr and Oct S, Su and Bank Hol M 1400-1700; May to Sept W-Su and Bank Hol M 1400-1800

🅿 WC ♿ 🚻 (by appt) 🍴 ✿ ★ 🎁

Burford House Gardens HEREFORD AND WORCESTER

John Treasure, Esq., Tenbury Wells.
tel. Tenbury Wells (0584) 810777

Control is the essence of this garden; nothing has been done without consideration. The self-discipline of its maker is matched by his creative flair, and informed by an architectural training. John Treasure and his brother bought this fine 18th-century house with a derelict garden in 1954, their ambition being to create a modern garden, in keeping with the formality of the building, and to found a nursery to sell the plants grown. The starting point was 4 acres (1.6ha) of ground, bounded on one side by the River Teme, containing a London plane, a copper beech, a Scots pine, and a few boundary trees. It is not easy to invent a style that is suitable for the growing of a wide variety of plants, which creates points of view, vistas, open areas of parade and sequestered, secret gardens harmoniously blended, still providing the essential element of surprise, but this John Treasure has achieved. For those less interested in design, the wealth of plants is its own reward. Clematis were Mr Treasure's first love and some 130 examples are to be found, not all pinned against walls, but mounting trees, tangling with shrubs, or pegged along the ground. There are alpine gems below the heather slope, old-fashioned roses back several of the borders, and the stream gardens are rich with moisture-loving plants – all are healthy, and have been placed with artistry and care.

7 m SE of Ludlow on A456; ½ m W of Tenbury Wells

SO 5868 (OS 137)

Open Good Fri to early Oct daily 1100-1700 Su 1400-1700; reduced rates for parties of 25 or over by appt

WC (by appt only)

Hergest Croft Gardens

HEREFORD AND WORCESTER

W. L. and R. A. Banks, Kington.
tel. Kington (0544) 230218

There are herbaceous borders as good, rock and water gardens of equal interest, but nowhere that rhododendrons can be seen in a more spectacular manner than in Park Wood at Hergest Croft. In 1910 W. H. Banks purchased Park Wood and planted it with masses of rhododendrons, mostly the standard garden hybrids of the time. A pool has been created in the cleft of Park Wood by damming a stream, and from the bridge the full effect of 'Flower Fall', a cascade of rhododendrons, can best be seen. The Loderi hybrids are particularly splendid. The edges of the pool at Park Wood are planted with bamboos and with such bog plants as lysichitums, osmundas and rodgersias. The garden proper begins with small rock and water gardens. In spring this part is brilliant with snowdrops, and daffodils. *Scilla bifolia* has naturalised, as has *Crocus vernus* and *Anemone apennina*. The walled garden is an interesting mixture of vegetables and herbaceous borders; iris and anemones stand out. The other great feature of Hergest Croft is its range of trees, planted over most of the 50 acres (20ha). Acers are particularly well represented. There are large specimens of *A. griseum* and *A. palmatum* 'Senkaki'. There is also an extensive collection of deciduous azaleas.

20 m NW of Hereford, ½ m S of A44 on W outskirts of Kington

SO 2755 (OS 148)

Open May to mid Sept daily; Oct Su 1330-1830; reduced rates for parties of 20 and over by appt

Peak months May, June and Oct

P WC ⊖ ⊟ D 🍵 (limited opening) 🎪 🐕 ✿ ★

The Priory   HEREFORD AND WORCESTER

Mr and The Hon. Mrs Peter Healing, Kemerton, nr Tewkesbury.

Mr Healing is a lover and grower of plants, interested in the unusual but not in thrall to novelty; he has had the vision to combine rare treasures with the less rare in colour groupings deriving from William Robinson and from Gertrude Jekyll. The soil is limy, ph7.5, so it is encouraging to find *Meconopsis regia* at home and cardiocrinum, grown from seed, about to flower. *Hebe hulkeana* is happy under a wall, and the fern, 'Mrs Goffey's Very Fine Variety', is a feathery wonder. The new garden, used for vegetables until 1974, has been designed to be at its best in June and July, and here the tones are soft, silver, pink and lavender. *Polemonium* 'Pink Beauty', is a key plant in May. The central path is of round stepping stones, dug up by the Healings while making the garden, over which the plants spill. Behind them rise old-fashioned and species roses, and then the dark wall of a yew hedge, a fine example of controlled profusion. Knowledge, the eye for a good plant, and the capacity to plan (the original layout was done on paper during Mr Healing's wartime service with the RAF, and he has found little need for change) have combined to produce a garden of unusual distinction, the whole animated and infused by the owner's evident love of the place and of its plants.

5 m NE of Tewkesbury off B4079

SO 9436 (OS 150)

Open May to Sept Th also several Su under NGS and for other charities 1400-1900

Peak months June to Sept

P WC 🅗 D 🍵 (Su in July and Aug only) 🕭 ⌗

Spetchley Park HEREFORD AND WORCESTER

R. J. Berkeley, Esq., Spetchley, nr Worcester.
tel. Spetchley (090 565) 213/224

In the time of Rose Berkeley, sister of the great gardener Ellen Willmott, Spetchley Park was one of the wonders of England, and although it is no longer possible to maintain it to the highest standards, it remains a place to be admired and loved. The entrance is now through the melon yard, where a foretaste of the quality of the planting is obtained, for on the walls are *Bignonia capreolata*, *Campsis* 'Madame Galen', *Fremontodendron californicum*, and *Trachelospermum jasminoides*. Here also are to be found specimens of the olive, the double pomegranate and of lemon-scented verbena. Magnificent borders full of rare shrubs surround the old kitchen gardens. The alcove of Bath stone faces the fountain gardens, inspired by Ellen Willmott herself, in which the 36 beds within yew hedges and flanked by stone paths, were filled with botanically arranged families of plants. The rose lawn, with the conservatory to the north, a fine cut-leaved beech, *Fagus sylvatica heterophylla*, beside it and frame of tall pines and cedars is the focus of the garden; and from here the pattern of the lake, moat, woods and garden becomes clear. A walk past the cork lawn, dominated by the Luccombe oak, an evergreen cross between the turkey oak and the cork oak, leads to the new lawn with its collection of sorbus, and other trees for autumn colour. Return through the copse with its magnolias, azaleas, low-growing trilliums and huge cardiocrinums.

3 m E of Worcester on A422

SO 8953 (OS 150)

Open Apr to Sept M-F 1100-1700 Su 1400-1730 Bank Hol M 1100-1730

Peak months Apr to June

P WC ⊖ 🅗 🍴 (Su only) 🎋 ⛲ ✂

Powis Castle POWYS

The National Trust, Welshpool.
tel. Welshpool (0938) 4336

It is difficult to overpraise Powis, for it has everything: a marvellous site, a park whose natural contours out-landscape Brown, formal terraces, flowing woods, lime and lime-free soil, a head gardener of exceptional ability, the whole dominated by its rose-red castle. Designs for the terraces were probably commissioned by the first Marquess between 1680 and his exile in 1688. They are a unique example of the formal Italianate style in Britain, and command views as extensive and superb as any villa in Tuscany. The planting is carefully documented in the excellent guide to the gardens by Graham Stuart Thomas and John Sales, and the list of plants excites envy. The key to the romantic appearance of the terraces lies principally, however, in the huge clipped yews, which date from the original planting, and in lead figures, probably by Van Nost, that adorn the balustrade above the orangery. The area below the castle hill to the north was converted to a pleasure garden some 70 years ago. The woods surrounding the main lawn below the terraces have been developed horticulturally during the present century. The acid soil is favourable to conifers and rhododendrons, which mingle happily with the original oaks. From the main vista there are magnificent views of the castle and terraces in one direction and of the Long Mountain and the Clee Hills in the other. The planting is remarkable at all seasons of the year for variety and artistry.

1 m S of Welshpool
on A483

SJ 2106 (OS 126)

Open Apr, May, June
and Sept W-Su 1300-
1800 (exc Good Fri);
July and Aug T-Su
1300-1800; Bank Hol
M 1130-1800; reduced
rates for parties of 12
or over by appt

P WC 🚻 ♿ ✳ ★ ☎

Hodnet Hall Gardens SHROPSHIRE

Mr and the Hon. Mrs A. Heber Percy, Hodnet, Market Drayton.
tel. Market Drayton (0630) 84202

The gardens of Hodnet Hall have enormous natural advantages. The house stands high and below it a series of terraces descends to the main pool, the last of a string of lakes. At the level of the house, beyond the private garden, stretches a wide grassy meadow overlooked by hanging bluebell woods, while to the south is the run of fascinatingly shaped lakes. A walk along the mown paths beneath the yellows and greens of the springtime oaks, looking across grass thick with bluebells and ragged robin to their reflections in the water, is pure pleasure. It is only as we approach the more heavily planted areas that questions arise. It is unfortunate that some of the most frequently planted azaleas and rhododendrons come in violently clashing colours, chrome yellow, cerise, magenta and scarlet. They flower together and the result is visual cacophony. The magnolia walk, alongside a path leading from an entrance gate to the tea room is excellent. The white theme continues with a snowdrop tree, *Halesia monticola vestita*, and on the lower level a bed of white camassias, with white Persian lilac nearby. Spring and autumn are the peak periods for this large, handsome garden. The smell of the azaleas is overwhelmingly seductive, and the space is large enough to take their blaze.

12 m NE of Shrewsbury at junction of A53 and A442

SJ 6128 (OS 127)

Open Apr 1 or Easter to late Sept M-S 1400-1700; Su and Bank Hol M 1200-1800; reduced rates for parties of 25 or over

Peak months May and June

P WC 🚻 D 🍴 (limited opening; parties by appt) 🚻 ⚘ ⚘ ★

Central England

GREATER MANCHESTER
Manchester

W YORKS

SOUTH YORKSHIRE
Sheffield

CHESHIRE

LINCOLN-SHIRE

Chatsworth ✿
Haddon Hall
Hardwick Hall ✿
✿ Thoresby Hall

DERBYSHIRE

NOTTINGHAMSHIRE
✿ Newstead Abbey
Flintham Hall ✿

Stoke-on-Trent
Alton Towers ✿
Kedleston Hall
Clive Memorial Garden ✿
✿ Trentham Gardens
Derby
Nottingham

STAFFORDSHIRE

Stafford
✿ Shugborough
Melbourne Hall ✿

✿ Whatton
LEICESTERSHIRE

Chillington Hall ✿
✿ Moseley Old Hall
✿ Wightwick Manor
WEST MIDLANDS
Birmingham
Leicester
✿ Leicester University Botanic Garden

ROP-IRE

✿ Deene Park
Rockingham Castle ✿
Boughton House ✿
✿ Dower House, Boughton

Coventry
NORTHAMPTONSHIRE
CAMBS

✿ Lamport Hall
✿ Coton Manor
✿ Holdenby House

HEREFORD AND WORCESTER

✿ Packwood House
WARWICKSHIRE

✿ Charlecote Park
Farnborough Hall ✿
Stratford-upon-Avon
Upton House ✿
Brook Cottage ✿
✿ Wroxton Abbey
Banbury
Northampton

Chicheley Hall ✿
BEDFORD-SHIRE

Broughton Castle ✿

✿ Stowe School
Milton Keynes

✿ Rousham Park
BUCKINGHAM-SHIRE

GLOUCESTERSHIRE

Blenheim Palace ✿
OXFORDSHIRE
Oxford College Gardens ✿
Oxford
Oxford University Botanic Gardens ✿
Waddesdon Manor ✿
Ascott ✿
✿ Nether Winchendon House
Waterperry Horticultural Centre ✿

HERTS

Buscot Park ✿
Pusey ✿
✿ Kingston Bagpuize House

Milton Cottage ✿

AVON

Swindon
Kingstone Lisle Park ✿
West Wycombe Park ✿
Cliveden ✿
London

WILTSHIRE

Reading

BERKSHIRE

Ascott BUCKINGHAMSHIRE

The National Trust, Wing, nr Leighton Buzzard.
tel. Aylesbury (0296 668) 242

Ascott was just a 17th-century farmhouse until purchased in 1873 by Baron Mayer de Rothschild, whose seat was the neighbouring mansion of Mentmore, for use as a hunting box. It was then purchased by Leopold de Rothschild who used the architect George Devey to build a rambling Tudor-style gabled house in which he housed his famous collection of fabulous works of art. He was also a talented gardener, and with the help of Sir Harry Veitch of Chelsea nurseries' fame, he laid out a remarkable garden of some 30 acres (12ha) whose essential features still survive today. They were completed by 1900. On a pronounced south-facing slope, the gardens offer remarkable contrasts of formality and informality, remarkable and unusual in that the more formal gardens tend to be on the perimeters with essentially spacious lawns and parkland and orchards nearer the house. There is a splendid long terrace walk backed by a wall superbly planted in themes of blue, purple and white. A circular pool with Venus in a shell chariot provides an exotic incident along this terrace, which then ends in a loggia. An evergreen sundial is another unique feature. Further west is another surprise formal flower garden at right-angles to the long terrace, superbly bedded out in the summer around a marble tiered fountain. A rock garden (rather wild), a fernery, and informal shrub areas are to be found and fine specimen trees nearer the house.

2 m SW of Leighton
Buzzard on A418

SP 8922 (OS 165)

Open Apr to June Th
1400-1800; July to end
Sept daily exc M (but
inc Bank Hol M) 1400-
1800

⓹ WC ⊖ 무 (by appt)
❀ ☎ (limited opening)

Cliveden BUCKINGHAMSHIRE

The National Trust, Taplow, Maidenhead.
tel. Burnham (062 86) 5069

On a magnificent site high above the River Thames, these landscape gardens and grounds of over 180 acres (73ha) have an intriguing history of development covering more than three centuries. The Duke of Buckingham was the first to build here in 1666, followed by Lord Orkney who altered and enlarged the house to Italian design. He also laid out the formal gardens, especially the great parterre (1723–4). Bridgeman helped at this stage with the amphitheatre (compare the Claremont feature here) and yew walks above the river. Two successive disastrous fires destroyed corresponding houses, the present mansion being built by Sir Charles Barry in 1850–51. Lord Astor bought Cliveden in 1893 and added the great Fountain of Love, and the very elaborate and natural style water gardens with a graceful pagoda from the Paris Exhibition. The carp in the pools are enormous and the maples, azaleas and waterside planting most effective. The 2nd Lord Astor gave Cliveden to the National Trust in 1942. Plenty of time is needed to explore these grounds where endless surprises await the energetic. The views are breathtaking, and there are leisurely walks through sylvan glades and everywhere garden buildings, Italian classical statuary, and hidden gardens. The plan and guidebook are essential if the visitor is to discover all the pleasures of Cliveden.

4 m N of Maidenhead
on A4094 turn E at
Bourne End on road to
Hawks Hill

SU 9185 (OS 175)

Open Mar to end Dec
daily 1100-1830

⚑ WC ⊖ ⊟ (by appt)
🐾 (limited opening)
🌾 ★ (limited
opening) 🎪 (limited
opening)

Waddesdon Manor BUCKINGHAMSHIRE

The National Trust, Waddesdon, nr Aylesbury.
tel. Aylesbury (0296) 651211/651282

The resplendent mansion built for Baron Ferdinand de Rothschild from 1877 to 1889 was designed in the French château style by Gabriel Hippolyte Destailleur and it dominates the now richly wooded hill on which it stands. A massive operation transformed the cone-shaped hill. Bath stone for the mansion was transported by steam and cable railway, rock gardens were built, drives to a suitable gradient traversed the estate and many semi-mature trees were brought on specially constructed carts. The great terraces were adorned with fountains and statuary in the formal French style, and the house was filled with a priceless collection of books, paintings, china and furniture. In 1957 James de Rothschild bequeathed the house, contents and grounds to the National Trust. A long winding drive from the village leads to the Triton fountain, a terminal axial feature from which great avenues lead to the mansion. A very French-style parterre to the south with central fountain is bedded out with over 7,000 display plants, tulips and wallflowers for the spring, followed by pelargoniums and ageratums for summer effects. The rest of the gardens and grounds are informal and Edwardian in character, irregular paths among specimen trees, shrubs and sculptures. A magnificent aviary set in a formal garden is like a grotto with its central fantasy of rock ferns and free-flying macaws and the song of many exotic birds.

6 m NW of Aylesbury on A41

SP 7316 (OS 165)

Open late Mar to end Oct W-S exc W after Bank Hol 1300-1800; Su 1130-1800; Good Fri and Bank Hol M 1100-1800

P WC ⊖ ⊟ (by appt) D 💌 ♨ (braille leaflet available) ★ ☎ (limited opening)

West Wycombe Park BUCKINGHAMSHIRE

The National Trust, West Wycombe.
tel. High Wycombe (0494) 24411

This beautiful landscaped park is now considered to be 'one of the most perfect expressions in England of the Natural School of Gardening'. The Dashwood family acquired the manor of West Wycombe in 1698. The 2nd Baronet, Sir Francis Dashwood, enlarged the house to its present-day appearance and created the park. He began work on the park in 1735, and continued it until 1785. A pupil of Capability Brown was involved with damming a stream to make the great lake. Humphry Repton 'tidied up the park' in about 1794, removing odd buildings and thinning trees. The 10th baronet gave the house and grounds to the National Trust in 1943. The present Sir Francis Dashwood runs the estate of 4,000 acres (1619ha) and the house. A plan available to visitors shows the main features to see: the fine views from the house, the lake, its islands, cascades, and temples. New planting and renovation is in progress to restore the park to its 18th-century grandeur. Nearby are the famous Hell Fire Club caves, another of the 2nd baronet's diversions, and the church he rebuilt on the hill. Close by is the dominating mausoleum with its niches to take the urns in which were to be preserved the hearts of the members of the club. The beautifully preserved village is also owned by the National Trust.

3 m W of High
Wycombe on A40
SU 8294 (OS 175)

Open Easter and Spring
Bank Hol Su and M;
M-F in June; daily exc
S in July and Aug 1415-
1800

P WC ⊖ ⊟ (by appt)
⚹ ☎ (limited opening)

Chatsworth DERBYSHIRE

Chatsworth House Trust Limited, Bakewell.
tel. Baslow (024 688) 2204

Successive generations have left their mark on Chatsworth gardens but what one sees now is mainly the work of the 6th Duke of Devonshire and Joseph Paxton. Of 17th-century provenance are the brick-built orangery, Flora's Temple, the Seahorse Fountain and the Great Cascade of 1694 with its water-spouting temple by Archer of 1703. In 1761 Brown altered the line of the river and planted up the park as it is today. Paxton's work is most evident in his clothing of what were bare hillsides in woodland and pinetum, in his canal and Emperor Fountain – where lime trees date back to 1784 – his water works, the Wellington Rock, the Robber Stone Cascade, the ruined aqueduct, the Willow Tree Fountain and the site of his Great Stove, now a maze. His conservative wall greenhouse still houses camellias. A new greenhouse, however, houses the Amazonian lily which Paxton was the first in this country to bring to bloom. There is a grotto of the late 18th century, an azalea dell and a water and bog garden following the streams down the steep hillsides. A rose garden enhances the orangery lawns and a long, double herbaceous border leads from the house orangery. The round pond, with its Kentian Chiswick statuary, is surrounded by thick beech hedges and a serpentining beech walk of 1953 planting leads away from it. There can be few gardens which offer so much both historically and in beauty.

2 m S of Baslow on B6012

SK 2670 (OS 119)

Open late Mar to end Oct daily 1130-1630

Peak month May

🅿 WC ♿ (limited) 🍴 D
🍽 ⛱ ♨ ✂ ★
📷 (special events th'out year)

Hardwick Hall DERBYSHIRE

The National Trust, Doe Lea, nr Chesterfield.
tel. Chesterfield (0246) 850430

Bess of Hardwick's house of 1597 still retains its original surrounding garden
walls, heavily crenellated, the gatehouse and the 18th-century parkland in
which is ancient timber, one of them, the Hardwick Oak, of 15ft 5in (4.7m)
girth and probably growing in Bess's time. One of the original walled
enclosures, the one on the south, is the garden proper. A long border is a
feature in the entrance courtyard and from here the visitor reaches the south
garden laid out by Lady Egerton from about 1870. It is divided into four by
yew and hornbeam hedges and walks, and in arbours cut in the hedge are 18th-
century lead statues. The north side is marked by a mixed border of
herbaceous plants and shrubs with a silvery sheen, while on the east is a wild
border in which plants such as the 10-ft high (3m) giant hogweed are to be
seen. A lawn here with magnolias contrasts with the two eastern sections
planted as an ornamental orchard. Borders here are of shrub roses and
lavender, while on the south side is a row of mulberry trees. During recent
years part of the old vegetable garden has been turned over to an Elizabethan
herb garden and here can be seen the white-margined foliage of the Hardwick
lily-of-the-valley. An 18th-century gate leads to the east garden with pond,
yew hedges, lots more shrub roses and a double row of limes planted in the
shape of an inverted wine glass in the 1930s to be seen over the park.

4 m NW of Mansfield on
A617 turn S at Glapwell

SK 4663 (OS 120)

Open Apr to end Oct
daily exc Good Fri 1200-
1730 (or dusk if earlier)

Peak months June and
July

🅿 WC ♿ (by appt only) 🅳
🍽 (limited opening)
🍴 ⧉ ★ (limited
opening) 📷 (limited
opening) ♿

Melbourne Hall Gardens DERBYSHIRE

The Marquess of Lothian, Melbourne, nr Derby.
tel. Melbourne (033 16) 2502

Probably the only existing formal garden of the early 18th century left in England is at Melbourne Hall, where London and Wise from 1701 onwards created this Le Nôtre French-style layout for Thomas Coke. There are some 16 acres (6.5ha) from the house terrace to the far side of the Great Basin framed by tall, mature taxodiums and on which is situated one of the most elegant of British garden ornaments, the open, wrought-iron 'Birdcage', or arbour, of 1706 by Robert Bakewell. By the side of the main lawns, bisected by a path edged with tonsured yews and leading the eye to the lake and the Birdcage, is the 200yd (183m) yew tunnel, older by many years than the garden layout. To the south between hedges there is a vista stopped by Van Nost's great Urn of the Four Seasons, a gift from Queen Anne to Coke. From this focal point and from fountain basins radiate a series of allées between woodland discovering many more Van Nost lead statuettes of cherubs, Mercury, Perseus, and Andromeda in yew niches. There is a Victorian grotto enclosing a mineral water spring with a verse inscribed by Caroline Lamb, wife of the 2nd Lord Melbourne, Queen Victoria's first Prime Minister. There is a 17th-century dovecot with an ogee roof, now a muniment room.

6 m S of Derby on A514
turn SE onto B587

SK 3924 (OS 128)

Open Apr-Sept W, S, Su
and Bank Hol M 1400-
1800

Peak months June, July
and autumn

▨ (limited) WC ⊖ ⊟ (by
appt) D ▶ (limited
opening) ▩ (occasional)
※ ★ (limited
opening) ▣ (limited
opening)

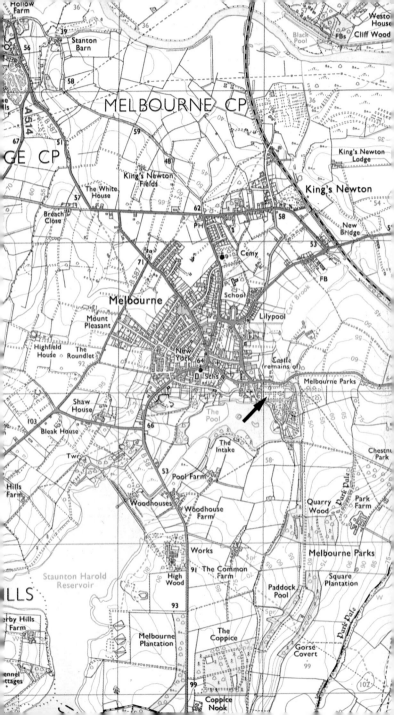

University of Leicester Botanic Garden
LEICESTERSHIRE

Council of the University of Leicester, Beaumont Hall,
Stoughton Drive South, Oadby, Leicester.
tel. Leicester (0533) 717725

The University of Leicester has in the years since 1947 achieved successfully the
very difficult feat of creating a botanic garden from a number of separate
private gardens – four in this case, with the houses of the original properties
being converted into student residences. All the houses were built early this
century and their presence adds much to the interest of the 16-acre (6.5-ha)
garden, especially as the character of the plantings around them have, to a
considerable extent, been preserved, and mature trees, many fine specimens of
their kind, abound. Special features include an arboretum, a collection of
hollies and others of roses and skimmias. The rose beds depict the evolution of
this most popular flower from ancient times to the present, while the skimmias
are the national collection of this valuable genus of evergreen shrubs. Other
features include limestone, sandstone, water and herb gardens, and a
conservation garden, which will house national collections of garden cultivars
of *Viola* and *Hesperis*. Heathers, woodland and herbaceous perennial plants are
all well displayed. There are no less than nine glasshouses housing diverse
collections of plants, from alpines to succulents and mixed ornamentals.

3 m SE of city centre off
A6 opposite racecourse

SK 6200 (OS 140)

Open M-F 1000-1700

Peak months May to
Oct

WC ⊖ 🅿 ♿ ✿

Boughton House NORTHAMPTONSHIRE

His Grace the Duke of Buccleuch and Queensberry K.T., Geddington, Kettering.

tel. Kettering (0536) 82248

Originally the property of the Abbey of Bury St Edmunds, Boughton House passed into the ownership of the Montagu family in the early 16th century to be metamorphosised into the impressive mansion it remains to this day. The 1st and 2nd Dukes of Montagu created, in the late 17th and early 18th centuries, major parterres and water features. Avenues, almost all of elm, were also planted at this time on a monumental scale. Because of Dutch elm disease none of these avenues remains, except some of small lime trees by the house, a magnificent lime tree avenue to the south of the house and an avenue to the west of the house, originally of elm but replanted with poplar. Virtually all the other garden features referred to were to fade away in the following two centuries. Some, however, have been re-created by the present owner, whose ancestors acquired the property in the mid-18th century. So, today, it is possible to enjoy once more at Boughton the view of the Broad Water over sweeping lawns; the well-stocked lily pond and the star pond fed by the cascade. Also, a delightful, circular rose garden, a long south-facing herbaceous border, a symphony of soft colours in summer, and an abundance of magnificent trees in equally magnificent surroundings. Superb vistas abound.

3 m N of Kettering off A43

SP 9081 (OS 141)

Open frequently between spring and autumn, phone for details

Peak months Apr and July

⓿ WC ♿ 🚻 D 🍽 (when house open; parties by appt) 🎪 🐕 ✂ ★ 🏛 🚶

Coton Manor Gardens NORTHAMPTONSHIRE

Commander and Mrs H. Pasley-Tyler, Coton.
tel. Northampton (0604) 740219

Rarely can the past and the present have been so successfully related as at Coton Manor, where some 10 acres (4ha) of modern gardens have as their focal point a house with a long and eventful history. The original manor house, mentioned in the Domesday Book, was destroyed in the Civil War to be replaced by a small farmhouse in 1662, and much added to to become the present manor house in 1926, when the gardens had their origins. These gardens might have been created specifically for gardening enthusiasts to visit, such is their interest in terms of fine plants – trees, shrubs, herbaceous perennials, roses and so on – most beautifully displayed in what is, in effect, a series of interrelated gardens on different levels. Water features figure prominently, including a stream trilling through a natural garden with moisture-loving plants on its margins which flows into a large pool in the lowermost part of the property. These gardens, created by the parents of Mrs Pasley-Tyler, are a splendid achievement, restored (after unavoidable one-time neglect) and developed with the utmost dedication since 1950 by Commander and Mrs Pasley-Tyler. One unusual feature of the gardens is the extensive collection of water-fowl and other birds which have a home there.

8½ m N of Northampton on A50 turn NW to Hollowell and Coton

SP 6771 (OS 141)

Open Apr to end Oct T, Th, Su and Bank Hol M, also W in July and Aug; Oct Su 1400-1800; parties at other times by appt

P WC D 🚻 ⛲ 🏛 ⚘ ★

Dower House Garden NORTHAMPTONSHIRE

Sir David and Lady Scott, Boughton House, Geddington, Kettering.

The Dower House, the home of Sir David and Lady Scott (Valerie Finnis), needs no introduction to plantsmen for its garden, alas only opened to the public a few times a year, is a Mecca for those who appreciate fine plants. It comprises an intimate, enclosed garden adjoining the house which includes a superb collection of choice plants, from climbers and wall shrubs to roses, hardy plants in beds, and other dwarf plants in 23 stone sinks and a large stone trough. On a higher level, across a driveway, is a fruit and vegetable garden and some 200yd (183m) of raised beds which provide an ideal environment for another collection of outstanding small plants. Beyond that is some 2 acres (0.8ha) of garden devoted to trees, shrubs, bulbous plants and woodland plants grown for the most part in island beds set in mown grass. This is an exceptional garden of especial interest to the horticulturally well-informed, for the care that has been taken to include only the best plants is matched by the skill exercised in finding them the most congenial locations from a cultural point of view. This is, therefore, a garden in which to observe and learn as well as to enjoy its purely visual attractions. Unusual plants propagated at the garden are on sale on open days. Situated as it is within the grounds of Boughton House, the garden also offers the visitor the advantage of comparing the intimacy of the one with the spaciousness and grandeur of the other – a memorable experience for any gardening enthusiast.

3 m N of Kettering off A43

SP 9081 (OS 141)

Open few times each year under NGS and occasionally by appt

Rockingham Castle NORTHAMPTONSHIRE

Commander L. M. M. Saunders-Watson, Corby.
tel. Rockingham (0536) 770240

Few gardens have such a spectacular or historical setting as that at Rockingham Castle with its views over no fewer than five counties and, as a backdrop, the magnificent edifice which was built by William the Conqueror. It was a royal residence until the 16th century when it became the property of the Watson family and is still in their possession today. The gardens date from that time. The most striking feature in these gardens, which cover 12 acres (5ha), is the magnificent double row of yews – or yew alley – which bisects the west garden with its sweeping lawns and vistas. These specimen yews, fashioned into elephantine shapes in a multiplicity of sizes, are reputed to be more than 400 years old. Another notable feature, to the south of the castle, is the yew-enclosed, circular rose garden, occupying the site of the old keep, and, in the valley to the west of that, the mature wild garden where many notable trees and shrubs are grown. A stroll through these tranquil gardens before visiting the castle itself is calculated to make anyone receptive to the nine centuries of history and cultural change represented, in one form or another, within its walls.

2 m N of Corby on A6003

SP 8691 (OS 141)

Open Easter Su to end Sept Su, Th, Bank Hol M and T, also T in Aug 1400-1800; other times by appt; reduced rates for parties of 20 or over

Peak months Apr, late June and July

P WC ㅂ D ● 무 ⚘ ★ ⌂ ⚲

Newstead Abbey NOTTINGHAMSHIRE

Nottingham City Council, Linby.
tel. Mansfield (0623) 792822

Founded as a priory between 1163 and 1173, Newstead Abbey gardens and grounds have evolved over the centuries. The poet Byron lived here and there is a statue and verses to his favourite dog. The millpool of the priory was enlarged to make the upper lake. Water from this lake runs into the garden lake by an ornamental cascade behind which the visitor can view the Abbey and pleasure grounds through the 'window' of water. From the lake, by two streams, the way is to a Japanese garden of the early 20th century with stepping stones, humpbacked bridges and appropriate plantings. The old walled kitchen garden is now the rose garden with a fountain and many old-fashioned, shrub and climbing varieties. The rock garden nearby is an early elaborate example with a heather garden of recent planting. Old yews here form a tunnel. Through the rose garden is the iris garden, formerly the fruit garden, where pears, quite old, are festooned over and around the paths. Sheltered by massive yews is what was once a tropical garden and nearby is a stew pond. There is Eagle Pond in Devil's Wood surrounded by walnuts. Adjacent to the Abbey is the so-called Spanish garden centred by an Iberian wellhead, but really a knot garden where the compartments, box-edged, are filled with flowers in season. The monks' garden is a dense planting of trees and many paths. There are trees planted by Dr Livingstone and Stanley.

4 m S of Mansfield
on A60 turn W at
Ravenshead

SK 5453 (OS 120)

Open daily exc 25 Dec
1000-dusk

P WC ⊖ 🖥 🍵 (limited
opening) ✼ ★ 🏛

Thoresby Hall NOTTINGHAMSHIRE

Mr R. P. H. McFerran (Agent), nr Newark-on-Trent.
tel. Mansfield (0623) 822301

An estate map of 1680 shows extensive parkland and a pleasure garden at Thoresby, which by 1725 was altered to show a lake, radiating avenues and the river's course canalised. The present garden came after Repton had supplied a 'Red Book' in 1791 and worked on a cascade feature on the river which has been restored. When Salvin designed the present elaborate Elizabethan-style house Nesfield was called in, but it would seem that Salvin was responsible for the terraced parterre of Victorian bedding out. The south terrace, which overlooks the lake, is of large, geometrically patterned parterre beds holding brightly coloured flowers punctuated by large clipped shrubs including golden yews. A lower terrace sets off a fountain and pool, on either side of which are gazebos for long vistas over the parkland or the gardens. On the west side of the house is another formal layout with a semi-circular sunken lawn, and to the north parkland trees have been underplanted with azaleas, rhododendrons and cedars in variety. The vista from the east front is particularly fine, with treed avenues stretching into the distance. The mile-long (1.6-km) lake in the park, on land enclosed from Sherwood Forest in 1683, is reached by a footpath from the formal gardens where a Gothic eyecatcher, Budby Castle, can be seen at the western end.

7 m SE of Worksop on B6005 turn E at junction with A616 on road to Thoresby

SK 6371 (OS 120)

Open June to Aug Su also Bank Hol M 1100-1800

Peak months July to Aug

P WC ⊖ ⊟ ● ⼊ ★ ⊞

Blenheim Palace OXFORDSHIRE

His Grace the Duke of Marlborough, Woodstock.
tel. Woodstock (0993) 811325

Blenheim can justly claim to be one of the grandest and most spectacular gardens in Britain. The 1st Duke of Marlborough employed Sir John Vanbrugh as the architect and Queen Anne's gardener, Henry Wise, to build the magnificent palace and formal gardens. A great 77-acre (31-ha) formal parterre was laid out to the south of the palace and half a mile (0.8km) away a huge high-walled kitchen garden was made in the wooded park. Vanbrugh constructed the monumental grand bridge over what was then the very meagre River Glyme. In 1764 Capability Brown arrived to transform the garden and parkland, sweeping away the great parterre (his 'grass to the very door' approach), planting many belts and clumps of trees in the 2,000-acre (809-ha) park and, most brilliant of all, damming the River Glyme at its south end to create two great winding lakes, flowing through Vanbrugh's bridge, ending with a dramatic cascade in a rocky, picturesque landscape. A double avenue of elms was planted to the north representing the battle formation at Blenheim. Some restoration of the formal style came in the 1920s when the 9th Duke engaged the French designer Achille Duchene to make an Italian garden and new terraces with fountains and hedged scroll pattern. All these features can be enjoyed today with many added family attractions to bring the vital revenue needed to maintain such a vast enterprise.

9 m NW of Oxford on A34

SP 4416 (OS 164)

Open mid Mar to end Oct daily 1100-1800; reduced rates for parties

Peak months summer

P WC ⊖ 日 D ● 🚻 ⌂ ❀
🌣 🏛 🕏 Butterfly house; special events

Brook Cottage OXFORDSHIRE

Mr and Mrs David Hodges, Alkerton, nr Banbury.
tel. Edge Hill (029 587) 303

A lovely garden, outstanding in its clever and attractive designs, and modern in that it was begun less than 20 years ago and has been developing ever since. The original cottage, now sensitively enlarged, stands on quite a steep north-west facing slope. When Mr and Mrs David Hodges came here in 1964 they quickly realised the potentialities of the site, and in designing the garden they concentrated on four features in particular – terracing and levels, enclosure, the clever and varied use of water, and above all, a wonderful variety of plant associations carefully selected for colour and contrast of effects. The main terrace beyond the house leads from a tiny paved courtyard contained by the L-shaped house with cool green hostas and climbers. A new stone wall and yew hedges partially enclose the terrace, and a border along one side is of mainly a blue, pink and grey theme. Columnar cypresses in sunken 'pedestals' of old millstones give a sense of formality here. Water suddenly appears as tiny rills running down each side of broad steps leading to the next level, the main lawn. Other features of Brook Cottage also offer mystery and surprise: copper beech hedges around a secret garden, a beautifully planted pool, a broad expanse of the valley lawn with its new lake and tree planting, a wilder tree and shrub area with spring bulbs and, high above the garden, a prospect from the terrace, where a stone wall shows off marvellous plant associations.

6 m W of Banbury on
A422 turn W towards
Alkerton and turn
opposite war memorial

SP 3743 (OS 151)

Open Apr to end Oct
daily by appt and
several weekends
under NGS

■ WC ⊖ (limited) ⊟ D
🐦 (limited opening
and for parties by appt)
🎋 ⊛ (occasional)
★ (limited opening)

Oxford University Botanic Gardens

OXFORDSHIRE

University of Oxford, Rose Lane, Oxford.
tel. Oxford (0865) 242737

These, in fact, comprise three separate botanical gardens. The first is the main garden described here. The second is the one-acre (0.4-ha) Genetic Garden located at the edge of the University Parks. Finally there is the 50-acre (20-ha) Nuneham Arboretum founded in 1830 and situated at Nuneham Courtenay, south of Oxford. The main botanic gardens are the oldest in Britain and the second oldest in Europe, being founded in 1621 as Physic Gardens with the main purpose of cultivating plants for use by herbalists and apothecaries. In 1840 they became known as the Botanic Gardens and Professor Daubeny, an assistant curator, proposed many new and wider fields of study involving co-operation with botanists and zoologists. There are many fine trees and groups of plants and different areas to be discovered here: collections of shrubs, of herbaceous, rock and water plants in beautifully constructed habitats; a fine and comprehensive range of 300 species and varieties of wall plants, many rather rare or half-hardy but enjoying the protection of the warm walls; a valuable demonstration of historical roses illustrating the origin of garden roses; and the glasshouses rebuilt in 1970 and housing a wide range of tropical, economic and ornamental plants.

In town centre off High Street, entrance opposite Magdalen College and in Rose Lane

SP 5205 (OS 164)

Open Mar to Oct M-S 0830-1700 Su 1000-1200 and 1400-1800; closed Good Fri; Oct to Mar M-S 0900-1630 Su 1000-1200 and 1400-1630; closed Dec 25; glasshouses open weekdays and Su 1400-1600

Oxford College Gardens OXFORDSHIRE

University of Oxford

Only a limited selection of College gardens is mentioned here of the many that
exist. The selection concentrates on those that are usually open more regularly
during the vacations. In most colleges the gardens are in the form of
quadrangles of great diversity of size, character and planting, but surrounded
invariably by wonderful architecture. Founded in the 13th century, the
gardens of Balliol have a quiet and austere stateliness with many unusual
climbers, attractive borders and fine trees. More than five centuries old, the
main gardens of New College have the romantic background of the old city
walls against which a great mixed border is a splendid sight from May to the
autumn. The famous mound or 'mount', a popular feature of Tudor gardens,
was built about 1530. Lofty mature trees are also a feature of this garden. The
unique tiny quad of St Edmunds Hall is worth a visit alone for its atmosphere
of a remote past wholly undisturbed. The old cloisters of Magdalen lead into
the great second quad with its mixed borders, while away to the north-east
side but with groves of trees are the famous Magdalen walks. Other
remarkable gardens include those of St John's and Trinity, Worcester with its
extensive lake, terraces and superb standard of maintenance, and Christ
Church Meadow, an ancient river water pasture, where in May thousands of
fritillaries are in flower.

In town centre

SP 5106 (OS 164)

Open daily pm but
times vary

⊖

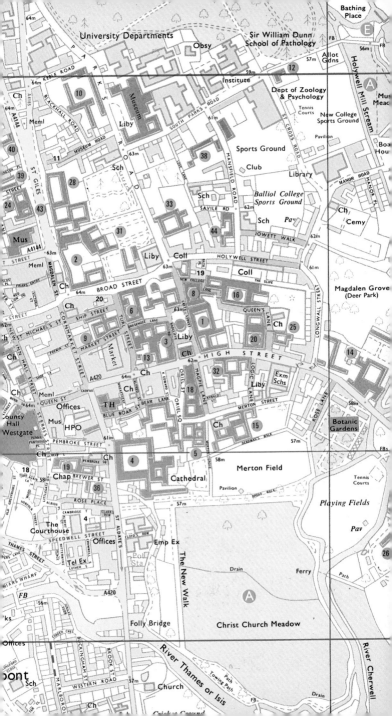

University Departments

Obsy

Sir William Dunn
School of Pathology

Bathing
Place

E

FB

56m

FB

Allot
Gdns

57m

Holywell Mill Stream

Institute

59m

12

A

Dept of Zoology
& Psychology

New College
Sports Ground

Meml

64m

KEBLE ROAD

10

Museum

Liby

South PARKS ROAD

61m

Tennis
Courts

ST CROSS ROAD

Pavilion

Manor Meac

Ch

Meml

64m

BLACKHALL ROAD

MUSEUM ROAD

63m

11

Sch

28

31

Sports Ground

Club

38

Library

MANOR PLACE

MANOR ROAD

Boat
Hou

40

ST GILES

39

24

43

Mus

A4144

Meml

2

Ch

Liby

Sch

33

44

SAVILE RD

Balliol College
Sports Ground

Sch

Pav

62m

JOWETT WALK

62m

Cemy

Ch

Coll

63m

Coll

19

62m

HOLYWELL STREET

61m

Magdalen Grove
(Deer Park)

MAGDALEN STREET

Ch

64m

BROAD STREET

20

6

8

NEW COLLEGE LANE

16

THE SLYPE

QUEEN'S LANE

LONGWALL STREET

ST MICHAEL'S STREET

Ch

CORNMARKET STREET

TURL STREET

BRASENOSE LANE

63m

Ch

25

14

9

Market

MARKET STREET

3

Liby

Ch

20

ROSE LANE

13

62m

HIGH STREET

A420

Ch

64m

Ch

KING EDWARD

MAGPIE LANE

ORIEL STREET

32

LOGIC LANE

Exm
Schs

Liby

58m

Ch

Meml

QUEEN ST

CARFAX

BEAR LANE

18

MERTON STREET

Botanic
Gardens

Ch

ST EBBES

Offices

TH

BLUE BEAR ST

15

FBs

County
Hall
Westgate

Mus

HPO

61m

Ch

PEMBROKE STREET

5

57m

Ch

18

19

PEMBROKE SQ

Chap

BREWER ST

4

Cathedral

Merton Field

Pavilion

BROAD WALK

58m

Playing Fields

Tennis
Courts

36

ROSE PLACE

CAMBRIDGE

CLARK'S

Pav

The
Courthouse

SPEEDWELL STREET

4

Offices

ST ALDATE'S

57m

26

THAMES STREET

Tel Ex

LUTHER

Emp Ex

Drain

Ferry

Path

A

A420

Pol
Sta

The New Walk

FB

56m

Folly Bridge

Christ Church Meadow

River Cherwell

Offices

Sch

BUCKINGHAM ST

MARLBORO

BROOK ST

WESTERN ROAD

57m

RIVER THAMES OR ISIS

Church

Towing Path

Path

Drain

FB

Pusey OXFORDSHIRE

Pusey Garden Trust, nr Faringdon.

When Mr and Mrs Michael Hornby bought Pusey in 1935 they found the house neglected, the lake silted up and the parkland and trees engulfed in Victorian shrubberies. Their first decision was to ask Geoffrey Jellicoe in 1937 to create a spacious paved terrace from which to view the lake and distant vistas beyond. From 1947 they began creating the ornamental garden. Borders were carefully planned and planted, the water garden developed across the lake and the many walks furnished with suitable plants. Visitors can follow a circular tour of the gardens. After the entrance gate comes a fine double border with reds shading to blues and yellows and silver and white as the distant lake comes into view. A great mixed border sweeps in a curve to the right, against the walls of the kitchen garden, also richly stocked with roses, clematis and many other plants. The paved terrace in front of the house is studded with pads of carpeting rock plants and bright with urns of flowers. To the left is an area of shrub roses and ground-cover plants, then the orange bed and thence across the lake by the Chinese bridge to a series of luxuriant water gardens, and through glades to pleasure gardens and shrubberies until one completes the circuit at Lady Emily's garden – walled and bright with flowers from spring to November. There are also many fine trees at Pusey, from the huge old planes, cedars and beeches to many new and vigorous magnolias, sorbus and maples.

10 m SW of Oxford on A420 turn S onto B4508

SU 3596 (OS 164)

Open Apr to late Oct daily exc M and F; Bank Hol weekends S-M 1400-1800; reduced rates for parties by appt

Peak months June, July and Oct

WC ⊖ ⊟ D ⬤ ⏗ ⚫ ⤳

Rousham Park OXFORDSHIRE

C. Cottrell-Dormer, Esq., nr Steeple Aston.
tel. Steeple Aston (0869) 47110

Rousham is an almost perfect example of the first English landscape park of the early 18th century. It was largely the work of William Kent, who also remodelled the 17th-century house. In the gardens he softened an earlier formal design by Bridgeman and fully exploited the charming setting of the River Cherwell and its valley. From the house he created vistas, the main one to the north looking towards a fine statue of a lion and horse, and in the far distance a triple arched 'ruin' or eye-catcher. Kent's main gardens lie in pleasant woodland glades on the north slope of the Cherwell, where by means of serpentine paths its classic features are cleverly sited, the Cold Bath with its elaborate waterways, the seven-arched arcades or portico (Praeneste) and the ponds and gentle cascades in Venus Vale, a green, quiet place where great carp swim lazily in the pools. A Temple of the Mill in rustic Gothic is also here and everywhere fine trees. In complete contrast is the series of charming walled gardens. The main former kitchen garden, with dipping pond and old espalier apples, is now combined with a mixture of luxuriant climbers on pergolas with herbs and flowers beneath. A charming pigeon house (its revolving ladder still operates) stands in a miniature parterre or knot garden of box hedges and roses. There are mulberries, magnolias and restful grass and seats here, a perfect place for meditation.

14 m N of Oxford on
A423 turn E

SP 4724 (OS 164)

Open daily 1000-1630

P WC ⊖ (exc Su) 🚻 🎪
🕿 (limited opening; no
children under 15
admitted, even if
accompanied; school
parties, however, may
be arranged)

Moseley Old Hall STAFFORDSHIRE

The National Trust, Fordhouses, Wolverhampton.
tel. Wolverhampton (0902) 782808

This is the house where Charles II fled, and was hidden, two days after the Royalists' defeat at Worcester. When the National Trust was given the property in 1962 by Mrs W. Wiggin, the garden had disappeared and the half-timbered house was hidden in a skin of blue-grey bricks. A complete replanting was necessary, so Graham Thomas, with the advice of Miles Hadfield and money raised by the National Trust's Wolverhampton Centre, set about the re-creation of a garden of the mid-17th century. Do not expect a gaudy misrepresentation of a knot garden of the kind that became fashionable under the Victorians. Remember that garden plants were still cultivated for practical purposes, for food, medicine, or to scent the house; remember also that the vast riches of China and Japan were still untapped. The Moseley knot garden is a copy of one designed in 1640, and portrayed in a manuscript in the library of Magdalen College, Oxford. A box hedge surrounds beds edged with dwarf box, and filled with gravel of differing colours. On the wooden arbour are trained *Clematis viticella*, and the deliciously scented virgin's bower, *Clematis flammula* from southern Europe. A nut walk and roundel leads to the King's Gate. A small herb garden and an orchard planted with fruit trees current in the 17th century completes this small but interesting garden.

4 m N of
Wolverhampton on
A449 turn E

SJ 9304 (OS 127)

Open Mar and Nov Su;
Apr to end Oct W, Th, S,
Su also Bank Hol M and
following T 1400-1800
(sunset if earlier);
parties at other times
by appt

Peak months summer

P WC ⊖ 🚻 (by appt) D
🍽 ⚘ ★ 🏛

Upper Laches Farm

Slade Heath

Far Laches Farm

Oaklands Farm

422

353

CANAL

PH

Cross Green

Manor House

Featherstone Farm

Whiteh Farr

Cross Green Farm

Three Hammers Farm

Featherstone Hall Farm

Brinsford

Depot (dis)

363

Hostel

Sch

Brinsford Farm

Brook House

Coven Heath

FEATHERSTONE

395

Pol Sta

Moseley Old Hall (NT)

Lesscroft Farm

365

Boro Const

443

B4l

Works

378

Moseley Hall

400

d. Houses

Moseley

375

Works

Moseley Court

Northycote Farm

School

Westcroft Farm

BUSHBURY

Sch

Moat

Cemy

Bushbury Hill

Schs

Beeches Farm

Underh

602

Schs

Bushbury Hall

Sch

Shugborough STAFFORDSHIRE

The National Trust, nr Stafford.
tel. Little Hayward (0889) 881388

Shugborough is the result of Admiral Lord Anson's voyage round the world, from which he returned in 1744 bringing with him a prize ship that made the family fortune. He also brought *Lathyrus nervosus*, a blue, scented pea, eaten by his sailors in Patagonia, and always known as Anson's Blue Pea. What makes Shugborough unique is its array of garden monuments, of which a painting by Nicholas Dahl (when all were complete and as yet unravished) can be seen in the house. They are based on Revett's drawings and include the Tower of the Winds, a Triumphal Arch and the Lanthorn of Demosthenes. A Chinese pagoda was swept away in a disastrous flood in 1795. To the south of the house by the River Sow is the wild garden. The dark purple rhododendrons and pale yellow azaleas create a pleasing contrast, without the usual incursions of cerise and scarlet. Walk as far as the Chinese House, erected in 1747 by the Admiral from a sketch made by one of his officers in 'Centurion'. The present cast-iron bridge, erected in 1813, is painted in the colour of Chinese lacquer. The clipped yews round the house are remnants of a Victorian layout, revitalised in 1966 by Graham Thomas, who designed a rose garden with arched entrances, pillars, and standards reminiscent of Bagatelle, near Paris, in which grow favourite roses of that period.

5½ m E of Stafford on A513

SJ 9922 (OS 127)

Open mid Mar to late Oct T-F and Bank Hol M (closed Good Fri) 1030-1730; S and Su 1400-1730

🅿 WC ♿ (1 m walk) 🚻 D
🍽 (limited opening)
★ (limited opening) 🎏

Trentham Gardens STAFFORDSHIRE

J. L. Broome, Esq., Stone Road, Trentham, Stoke-on-Trent.
tel. Stoke-on-Trent (0782) 657341

The great terrace, designed by Nesfield and Sir Charles Barry, is a marvel. In the dour Potteries landscape it is impossible to conceive of anything more lavish. In 1847 67 men were employed in the garden. Now the consumption of gardeners and bedding plants has been much reduced but the effect remains sumptuous and in excellent taste, probably better than when the garden was at its height in the 1840s under the 2nd Duke of Sutherland. The drama of the contrast between the elaborate Italian garden and the smooth immensity of Brown's lake beyond is breathtaking. The central walk thrusts straight down and from the steps in front of the now demolished house to the copy of Cellini's statue of Perseus with the head of Medusa, reinstated in its old position after a stay at Sutton Place. The attraction is so strong that the eye is held firmly to the central vista, the statue, the lake, and the eyecatcher on the hill beyond; but this is not all the garden has to give. The rose garden, the clematis walk, the rock garden and the peat garden are all of horticultural interest, as is the garden for flower arrangers. But these can be found elsewhere; the point of Trentham is prodigious display on a scale unequalled since the days of absolute monarchs, and of which Le Nôtre, master of a million flower pots, would not have felt ashamed.

3 m S of Stoke-on-Trent on A34

SJ 8640 (OS 118)

Open daily exc 25 Dec and 1 Jan 0900-dusk

Peak months July and Aug

P WC ⊖ ⊟ D ● ⅋

Charlecote Park WARWICKSHIRE

The National Trust, Wellesbourne.
tel. Stratford-upon-Avon (0789) 840277

Would that Charlecote still had the beguiling water garden to be seen in the painting of 1696 now hung in the drawing room. Alas this delight was swept away when Capability Brown was commissioned 'to alter the slopes and give the whole a natural easy corresponding level with the house on every side'. Gone are the fishing canal, the long sanded walks, the enclosed formal gardens, though the lime avenue he was forbidden to touch. Much of the house and of the garden that we see today is Victorian, the result of alterations instituted by that lively and effective lady, Mary Elizabeth Lucy. In her day 20,000 bedding plants were produced annually, mostly for beds in the forecourt. Now there are good shrubs in the borders, and after the removal of brambles and overrun plants a border in the north garden contains a selection of flowers mentioned in Shakespeare's plays, primroses and heartsease, violets, columbine and cuckoo flowers. From the rose-planted terrace above the banks of the River Hele, the sound of the cascade is clearly audible and the herds of fallow deer, presumably descendents of those in Shakespeare's time, flicker up to its walls. For tranquillity Charlecote ranks high in the list of magic places.

4 m E of Stratford-upon-Avon on B4086

SP 2556 (OS 151)

Open Apr and Oct S, Su, Bank Hol M and T 1100-1700 (sunset if earlier); May to Sept daily exc M and Th but inc Bank Hol M 1100-1800

P WC ⊖ ⊟ (by appt) ♥ (exc Oct) ⌂ ⌇ ★ ⌂

Packwood House WARWICKSHIRE

The National Trust, Lapworth, Solihull.
tel. Lapworth (056 43) 2024

Traditionally the clipped yews were said to have been planted during the Commonwealth, and to represent Christ preaching to the multitude. In fact modern research reveals that the greater part of them were planted as small topiary specimens in the middle of the last century. The attractions of this garden are, however, by no means limited to the austere beauty of these clipped trees. The south, or Carolean, garden has a gazebo at each of its four corners, from which it was possible to look over the surrounding countryside. The raised terrace walk was originally built to provide views of the elaborate parterres below. It is now planted with flowers whose colours blend with those in the lower garden. The colour scheme changes annually but is always striking. On the south face of the terrace wall are 30 round-headed niches in pairs, built to house a colony of bee-skeps. In the area to the west, originally known as the fountain court, is a cold plunge called the Roman bath, but few Romans would have been tempted by this dark water. Anyone interested in historic parterres or in Jekyll-style planting will delight in this unusual place.

11 m SE of central Birmingham on A34 turn E onto B4439 at Hockley Heath

SP 1772 (OS 139)

Open Apr to end Sept W-Su exc Good Fri but inc Bank Hol M 1400-1800; S and Su 1400-1700

P WC 🚐 (by appt only) 🌿 🐕

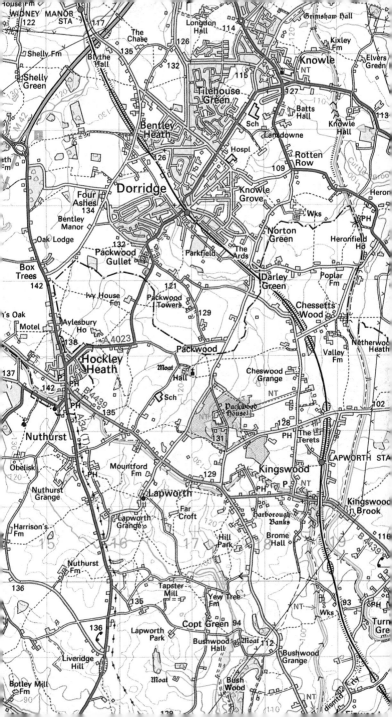

Upton House WARWICKSHIRE

The National Trust, Edge Hill.
tel. Edge Hill (029 587) 266

Upton House stands less than a mile (1.6km) to the south of the battlefield of Edgehill, and the ground behind it slopes into a deep coombe. In 1927 Lord Bearsted's architect, Morley Horder, developed wide terraces behind the house and planted them with lavender, catmint and the old Scots rose 'Williams Double Yellow'. A good time to visit is June when this rose is in flower. The garden was originally laid out to provide food for the household – fruit and vegetables on the warm south slope, and fishponds in the valley below. On the slope between further, descending terraces, shrubs and low-growing perennials are planted which flourish in conditions of shallow soil and sharp drainage: valerian, tree lupins, lavender, sages, laburnums, brooms, irises, lithospermums and aubrieta, well worth study by those faced with similar conditions. Good borders of sun-loving perennials are set beneath the terrace walls. A neat vegetable garden, laid out in the style of a French potager, is the last trace of the once extensive vegetable and fruit growing. In a combe below, round the corner, were three ponds, now reduced to one. The sites of the other two are occupied respectively by a bog garden and a planting of flowering cherries.

7 m NW of Banbury on A422

SP 3645 (OS 151)

Open Apr to end Sept M-Th 1400-1800, also several summer weekends (see National Trust Handbook); reduced rates for parties by appt)

Peak months June to Sept

WC ⊖ (limited) ⊟ (by appt only) D 🌣 ⚘ 🎫

Eastern Counties

Kingston-upon-Hull

MBERSIDE

Grimsby

Lincoln

❀ Doddington
Hall

Harrington ❀
Hall

Gunby ❀
Hall

LINCOLNSHIRE

❀ Marston
Hall

Springfields ❀
Gardens

Sandringham ❀
House

Sheringham ❀
Hall

Mannington ❀
Hall Gardens

Stody ❀
Lodge

Blickling ❀
Hall

Kings
Lynn

NORFOLK

Norwich

Great
Yarmouth

CESTER-

SHIRE

Peckover ❀
House

Peterborough

Talbot Manor ❀

Oxburgh Hall ❀

Somerleyton ❀
Hall

RTHAMPTON-
SHIRE

CAMBRIDGESHIRE

Bressingham ❀
Hall

Heveningham ❀
Hall

Bury St
Edmunds

Haughley ❀
Park

Beares ❀

Helmingham Hall ❀

Magnolia ❀
House

Anglesey ❀
Abbey

Ickworth ❀

Cambridge College ❀
Gardens

❀ Cambridge Univ.
Botanic Garden

Cambridge

Duxford ❀
Mill

Great Thurlow ❀
Hall

SUFFOLK

Lime Kiln ❀
Rosarium

Akenfield ❀

Ipswich

The Crossing ❀
House

BEDS

Wrest ❀
Park

Audley End ❀

Luton

Luton Hoo

HERTFORD-

Benington ❀
Lordship

SHIRE

Saling ❀
Hall

Colchester

Glazenwood ❀

The Beth Chatto ❀
Gardens

ESSEX

❀ Ashridge

Hatfield ❀
House

The Gardens ❀
of the Rose

Harlow

Chelmsford

Watford

Capel ❀
Manor

The ❀
Magnolias

Hyde Hall ❀

CKS

GREATER

LONDON

Southend-on-Sea

ERKS

Gillingham

SURREY

KENT

Canterbury

Guildford

Wrest Park BEDFORDSHIRE

Dept. of the Environment, Silsoe.
tel. Cambridge (0223) 358911 ext. 2285

Both the 19th-century mansion and gardens are French Renaissance in style -
elegant, and almost uncannily well suited to the flatness of the Bedfordshire
terrain. To stand by the rose garden and look over the parterre is to have the
eye drawn with magnetic compulsion to the great garden below the terrace. A
magnificent marble fountain, lead statues from Holland dating back to the
17th century and others brought to the gardens after the Great Exhibition of
1852, link with the formal Long Water canal which provides the axis for the
whole design. Beyond the canal is the domed pavilion, the work of Thomas
Archer in 1709–11 and a focal point of commanding presence. This scene of
grandeur, with acres of mown grass and magnificent trees framing the formal
features, was created by the 1st Duke of Kent in the early 18th century.
Capability Brown was engaged between 1758 and 1760 to carry out
alterations, these consisting of rides and vistas through the woods and the
creation of a river. On the west side of the gardens is the 18th century Bowling
Green House, in the Palladian style; an orangery dating from 1836, a bath-
house and a cascade. With their long vistas and matchless symmetry, these
gardens are a tribute to the artistry of man and nature.

9 m N of Luton on A6

TL 0935 (OS 153)

Open Apr to end Sept S
and Su 0930-1830

WC 🅿 D 🚻 ★ ⛩

Anglesey Abbey CAMBRIDGESHIRE

The National Trust, Lode, Cambridge.
tel. Cambridge (0223) 811200

Anglesey Abbey was purchased by the first Lord Fairhaven in 1926 and during the next forty years, on flat, windswept farmland, he created a major work of art. The chosen style was a combination of 17th-century formal and 18th-century landscaping, thus the garden is divided by magnificent avenues of chestnut, lime and hornbeam whilst the land between is planted informally with a mixture of interesting trees. For a garden made in this century the scale is immense. The Great Avenue is over half a mile (0.8km) long and has four rows of trees on each side, whilst a broad grass walk between Norway spruce and a beech hedge, and decorated with busts of Roman emperors, stretches for a quarter of a mile (0.4km). The main components of the design are trees, grass, sculpture and water. Flowers there are, but in the 18th-century manner they are hidden from the main views. There are hedged enclosures for hyacinths, dahlias and classic herbaceous borders designed by Vernon Daniel. These are at their best in mid-summer. The wealth of antique garden ornaments and statuary is unrivalled and it has been placed with the same care and grasp of scale that characterises the whole of this magnificent garden.

6 m NE of Cambridge on B1102

TL 5362 (OS 154)

Open early Apr to mid Apr S and Su; late Apr to mid Oct daily 1400-1800; reduced rates for parties of 15 or over by appt

⬛ WC ⊖ ⊟ (by appt) 🍽 (limited opening) ⏸ ⚹ ★ (limited opening) ☎ (limited opening)

Cambridge University Botanic Garden

CAMBRIDGESHIRE

Cambridge

Cambridge University moved its Botanic Garden to the present 40-acre (16ha) site in 1831. From the first it was developed not only to provide facilities for botanical and horticultural education but also as a delightful park. It goes without saying that anyone with a knowledge of botany or ecology will find much of interest, but so can the ordinary flower lover and garden maker. There is an excellent range of glasshouses, and a winter garden devoted to plants which provide interest from flowers, bark, berries or evergreen leaves in the darkest months, and which will be a revelation to those who think that a garden must of necessity lack colour between November and March. An outstanding feature is the rock garden. This rises dramatically from the edge of a small lake and has one section built of limestone and a second of sandstone. This allows a wide range of plants to flourish. Garden historians will enjoy the chronological bed, in which familiar plants are placed in their order of introduction to this country, and in the arrangement of roses to illustrate the descent of present-day hybrids from their wild ancestors, whilst conservationists will wish to see the collection of wild flowers of eastern England.

Near station; entrances on A10, A604, Bateman St and Brooklands Ave

TL 4557 (OS 154)

Open throughout year M-S (exc 25 and 26 Dec) 0800-1830 (or dusk if earlier), also Su (May to Sept) 1430-1830

WC ⊖ 🚻 🍴 ♿ ★ 🐕

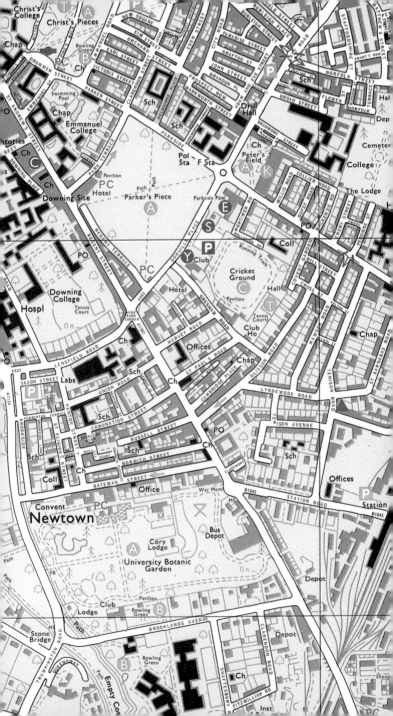

Cambridge College Gardens
CAMBRIDGESHIRE

Because there is such a wealth of fine architecture and historical assocations, few writers about Cambridge pay sufficient attention to the college gardens, which is unfortunate for without exception they are well planted, expertly maintained and contribute enormously to the beauty and atmosphere of the place, whilst several are major creations in their own right. The two features which do receive recognition are the velvety lawns and the 'Backs' which have been called the most perfect man-made view in England and which are at their loveliest when the meadows by the River Cam are filled with crocus and daffodils and the weeping willows are bursting into leaf. Amongst the best college gardens are those of Emmanuel, which has attractive ponds, superb copper beeches and a dramatic herb garden; Christ's, with an ancient mulberry and modern roof garden; Pembroke, in which one court is treated quite informally; and John's, which has a Georgian 'wilderness'. Best of all is the Fellows' Garden of Clare. This covers 2 acres (0.8ha) and has been skilfully subdivided into a number of smaller enclosures and planted with artistry. Created in 1947 by Walter Barlow, then head gardener, it incorporates a sunken and a scented garden, and separate borders of blue, yellow and red flowers.

In town centre

TL 4458 (OS 154)

Opening times vary, apply to Tourist Information Centre, Wheeler Street; parties of 10 or more should register at the Information Centre

The Crossing House CAMBRIDGESHIRE

Mr and Mrs D. Fuller, Meldreth Road, Shepreth.

Although only a quarter of an acre (0.1ha) in extent, and sandwiched between a main railway and a road, this garden is outstanding in three respects. Firstly it contains an amazing number of choice plants, many rare, others old favourites, but all selected by the eye of a connoisseur; secondly it shows how a strong, simple plan can transform an unpropitious site; and lastly it is that most exceptional thing, a successfully scaled down garden – a real 'tour de force'. This small masterpiece has been created over fourteen years by Margaret Fuller aided by her husband, who controlled the level crossing until automatic gates were installed. The design, which is full of original touches, incorporates a tiny lawn, pools with a cascade, banks for alpines and two hexagonal greenhouses. The spread of perennials and alpines and the size and shape of trees and shrubs are skilfully controlled to keep them in scale and prevent overcrowding. If a plant does get too big it is given away and some new discovery takes its place. Bare patches are not allowed and there are annuals and half-hardy plants in pots ready to fill any gaps. Every inch is used and the garden has even spread to the far side of the tracks!

5 m NE of Royston on
A10 turn NW to
Shepreth then SW to
Meldreth

TL 3847 (OS 154)

Open throughout year
daily 1000-dusk

Peak months Apr to
Sept

⊖ 🚻 D

Peckover House CAMBRIDGESHIRE

The National Trust, North Brink, Wisbech.
tel. Wisbech (0945) 583463

Peckover is a handsome Georgian house but the garden is essentially early
Victorian, laid out at a time when many strange new plants were arriving
from foreign lands, and designed to show off these acquisitions. It affords a rare
opportunity to see a garden of this period. In recent years, while care has been
taken to respect the original style – for instance a newly planted border
reinterprets carpet bedding using hardy instead of tender plants – more flowers
have been added, particularly roses, honeysuckles and clematis. The sensitively
maintained garden covers 2½ acres (1ha), most of it surrounded and subdivided
by high walls, creating that sense of mystery which old town gardens often
possess. The section immediately behind the house is most strongly Victorian,
with trim lawns, gravel paths and shady walks through shrubberies of laurel,
spotted aucuba and variegated holly, underplanted with ferns, hostas and
asarum. There are two summerhouses, one rustic with columns of pine logs,
the other white-painted with green lattice decoration which faces a circular
lily pool and topiary peacocks with herbaceous borders beyond. A greenhouse
contains ancient orange trees which fruit regularly, and colourful
conservatory plants including plumbago and begonias. Near by is a shady fern
house.

In centre of Wisbech on
N bank of R Nene on
B1441

TF 4509 (OS 143)

Open Easter to mid Oct
S-W 1400-1730

⓿ WC ♿ 🚻 (by appt)
🅿 ♨ 🏠

The Beth Chatto Gardens ESSEX

Mrs Beth Chatto, Elmstead Market, Colchester.
tel. Wivenhoe (020 622) 2007

This is amongst the few influential gardens to have been created since the last war, and it is full of lessons for the modern gardener on cultivation and maintenance, and above all on plant selection and grouping. The style is naturalistic and achieves its effects by the artistry with which the plants have been combined with each other and used in conjunction with water, grass and paving. On a 4-acre (1.6ha) site differing habitats have been created so that a wide range of plants can be cultivated. For plants adapted to grow in boggy conditions there are the banks of five large spring-fed ponds, whilst for those which must survive the long hot summers of countries drier than our own, there is a sharply draining gravel slope. Between these extremes are lightly shaded moist areas for woodland plants like hellebores and hostas. The emphasis throughout is on foliage, and in particular that provided by perennial plants, many of them uncommon, and on species rather than cultivars. At the same time there is no shortage of flowers, and in this bulbs play a major part, from the crocus and snowdrops of late winter through to sternbergias and nerines, which are still in flower in November.

5 m E of Colchester just beyond Elmstead Market on A133

TM 0624 (OS 168)

Open few times each year under NGS; parties at other times by appt

Peak months Apr to Aug

P WC ⊟ D ● (open days and by prior arrangement) ⋔ ⽕ (open days only) ⋇
★ (open days only)

Hyde Hall ESSEX

Hyde Hall Garden Trust, Rettendon, Chelmsford.
tel. Chelmsford (0245) 400256

This major garden has been created around an old Essex farmhouse during the past 25 years, but the owners had no intention of doing this when they purchased it. Had they done so they might not have chosen a wind-swept hilltop, heavy clay overlying in places impermeable gravel, and the lowest rainfall in England! There were, however, compensations; plenty of sunshine, little frost, neutral soil and several old ponds. There is no hint now of early struggles – even apparent drawbacks have been used to advantage. Trees and hedges planted for shelter have provided shade for rhododendrons and camellias whilst the dry, sunny climate has encouraged ceanothus, watsonias, hebes and other tender plants to thrive. The garden covers 8 acres (3.2ha), with a further 12 acres (5ha) devoted to specimen trees. The range and quality of the plants is impressive, as is the meticulous maintenance. Roses form a major element, from climbers to miniatures which are grown in raised beds. There is a mainly herbaceous border with a graduated colour scheme, an iris border and a corner devoted to golden foliage. The garden possesses the national collections of viburnums and malus. A high greenhouse accommodates treasures such as mimosa, daturas and lapageria.

7 m SE of Chelmsford on A130 turn E at Rettenden to East Hanningfield

TQ 7899 (OS 167)

Open Mar to end Oct M-S; Nov to end Feb M-F 0900-dusk

Peak months Apr to Oct

P WC ⊖ ⊟ (by appt) ⊼ ⊛ (also mail order catalogue) ✧

Saling Hall ESSEX

Mr and Mrs Hugh Johnson, Great Saling, Braintree.

The present owners began to develop this garden about 10 years ago, but the previous occupant, Lady Carlyle, had laid excellent foundations, notably around the house. The land extends to 12 acres (5ha) and the opportunity has been taken to create areas of distinctive character, in both style and atmosphere. Each section skilfully leads to the next via a suitable area of transition. The old Dutch-gabled house is approached past natural ponds, fine chestnuts and a group of Japanese cherries. Formality then takes over, with rows of Lombardy poplars and pleached limes flanking the forecourt. The house overlooks, on the south side, a symmetrically planned walled garden. Around the sides and flanking the middle path are borders of shrubs, roses, plants and bulbs, producing mostly blue, pink and pale yellow flowers. Rows of slim conifers stand like sentinels, with *Chamaecyparis lawsoniana* 'Pottenii' against the walls and shorter *Juniperus hibernica* along the path. A paved walk leads through a semi-woodland area with good ground cover to a shady water and bog garden. An alternative route leads into a park-like arboretum containing many interesting young trees. Against a steep shrub-covered bank has been built a curving pool, the design of which shows oriental influence.

3 m W of Braintree on A120 turn N to Great Saling

TL 7025 (OS 167)

Open early May to mid Oct exc Aug W-F 1400-1700; parties at other times by appt

Peak months May, June and Oct

P WC ♨

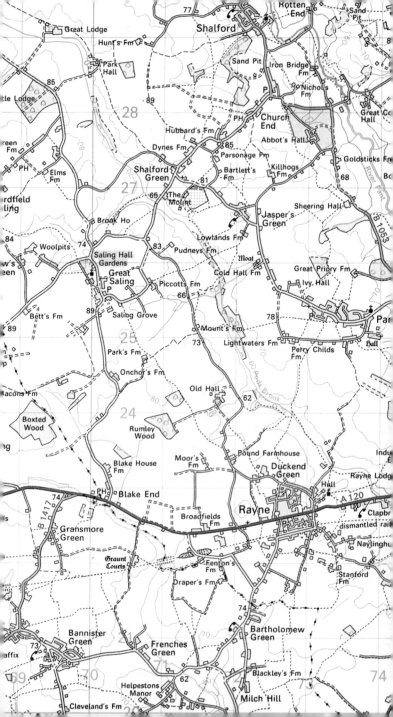

Ashridge HERTFORDSHIRE

Governors of Ashridge Management College, Berkhamsted.
tel. Little Gaddesden (044 284) 3491

The garden at Ashridge, covering some 90 acres (36ha), can fairly be described as one in which every prospect pleases, from the long vistas over coiffured lawns to the fine specimen trees on every hand and the grandeur of the mansion, which is the personification of early 19th-century elegance in the Gothic style. Running the length of the mansion on the south elevation is a terrace bordered throughout its length by plant beds enclosed by cube-shaped, clipped yews. It is from this terrace vantage point that the most impressive vista unfolds: a magnificent avenue of wellingtonias (*Sequoiadendron giganteum*), some 120 years old, which are seen in the middle to far distance across sweeping tree- and shrub-framed lawns. One of the features of Ashridge is its series of individual gardens such as a circular, yew-enclosed rose garden ('The Rosarie') and another sunken rose garden; the Monk's Garden with its Holy Well and parterres of clipped box; and a heather and conifer garden in a Westmorland limestone rock setting. There is a conservatory; great banks of rhododendrons and a fine arboretum featuring a ring of incense cedars (*Calocedrus decurrens*). For its first 250 years Ashridge was a monastery and then a Royal residence before passing into private ownership in the year 1605. The grandeur of the gardens owes much to Humphry Repton, who in the early 19th century laid out the gardens for the then new mansion.

4 m N of Berkhamsted on B4506

SP 9912 (OS 165)

Open Apr to Oct S and Su 1400-1800

Peak months May and June

🅿 WC ♿ (by appt only) 🚻 (limited opening)

Capel Manor HERTFORDSHIRE

London Borough of Enfield Education Committe, Bullsmoor Lane, Waltham Cross.
tel. Lea Valley (0992) 763849

For anybody living in north London or its adjoining counties (and especially those with easy access to the M25 and A10, which are adjacent to this establishment) regular visits to Capel Manor would be deeply rewarding. Administered by the London Borough of Enfield Education Committee, it comprises a series of delightful formal gardens grouped around a late 18th-century house. These gardens with their botanical-type plant collections provide interest at all seasons. There is a 17th-century knot garden, a herb garden, a collection of old roses, and also ornamental display glasshouses and a demonstration garden where fruit, vegetables, ornamental plants, formal bedding and so on can be seen at their best. The grounds also include a copper beech, reported to be the largest and oldest in the country, and a superb *Zelkova carpinifolia* and *Liriodendron tulipifera* (tulip tree). Courses for amateur gardeners leading to a City and Guilds of London Institute Certificate cover a wide range of subjects. There are also special-interest courses on many aspects of gardening, as well as flower painting and botanical illustration. Details of courses are available from the address above. Overall, the Institute occupies 100 acres (40ha) of land on the Capel and Theobald's Park Estates.

3 m N of Enfield on A10
at junction with M25

TQ 3499 (OS 166)

Open Apr to end Oct
M-F 1000-1630 also
Bank Hols and special
open weekends 1000-
1730

WC ⊖ 🚻 (limited
opening) D
♿ (limited opening)
🍴 🦮 ⚕
🕴 (occasional)

The Gardens of the Rose HERTFORDSHIRE

The Royal National Rose Society, Chiswell Green Lane, St Albans.
tel. St Albans (0727) 50461

This 12-acre (5-ha) garden contains one of the finest – some would say the finest – collection of roses in the world, with around 30,000 bushes representing every category of rose, modern, species and old-fashioned. Situated at Chiswell Green, some two miles from the centre of St Albans, it has been the home of the Royal National Rose Society since 1960. The display gardens surround a substantial house which is the Society's headquarters, with the main axis of the garden being the broad, rose-flanked pathway leading from the house to a circular pool bisected by an extensive curved pergola, a feature of great beauty when the climbing roses with which it is adorned are in bloom. This is but one of many major features and, in addition to the main displays, there is also a series of small, intimate gardens where roses are grown in association with other plants in conditions approximating to those obtaining in countless home gardens. These include a garden of miniature roses. Of great importance, too, is the trial ground, where new roses are subjected to three years of rigorous judging, with those which are deemed worthy of it receiving the Society's coveted awards.

2 m SW of St Albans, W of A405 off B4630

TL 1204 (OS 166)

Open early June to end Sept M-S 0900-1700, Su 1000-1800

Peak months late June to early July; Rose Festival early July

 P WC ⊖ ⊟ D ⬤ ⚹
★

Hatfield House HERTFORDSHIRE

The Marquess of Salisbury, Hatfield.
tel. Hatfield (30) 62823

Hatfield House is a place of pilgrimage. Architecturally distinguished and full of treasures, it has a fitting counterpart in the beautiful gardens which surround it – gardens which have changed greatly since the house was built by Robert Cecil, 1st Earl of Salisbury, in the early 17th century. This was due to changing fashions and the vicissitudes of the Cecil family. Indeed, the original gardens disappeared in the 18th century to allow landscaped parkland to sweep right up to the walls of the mansion. In the mid-19th century, however, both house and gardens were restored to the original Jacobean style. To the west of the mansion is an extremely attractive parterre garden enclosed by yew hedges in which patterned beds planted with roses, shrubs and herbaceous perennial plants have as their centrepiece a formal pool and fountain. Beyond this, on a lower level, is the scented garden, opened in 1979, a place of enchantment with its wealth of aromatic herbs, its scented trees, shrubs and other flowering plants in beautiful associations. Another addition is the knot garden, completed in 1981, in the courtyard of the remaining wing of the 15th-century Palace of Hatfield. Here plants grown in the 15th, 16th and 17th centuries are displayed. Another parterre garden of great charm and the famous maze lie to the east of the mansion, while to the south is the wilderness garden.

Opposite Hatfield
station on A1000

TL 2308 (OS 166)

Open late Mar to early
Oct M 1400-1700, T-S
1200-1800, Su 1400-
1730; reduced rates for
parties by appt

WC ⊖ ⊟ D ⬤ ⛱ ⛄
⚘ ★ ☎ (exc M)

Doddington Hall LINCOLNSHIRE

Antony Jarvis, Esq., Lincoln.
tel. Doddington (0522) 694 308

Approached through a Tudor gateway, the historic Doddington Hall with its turreted, brick- and stone-faced façade has not altered since the day it was completed between 1593 and 1600. The walled courtyard lorded over by two cedars of 1829 (there were four) and the garden layout show a remarkable likeness to the Kip view of 1705. On the west side of the house the original walls to the garden are more or less as built, but the layout accords with a Kew Gardens design of 1900 taking the form of a Jacobean knot garden with box- and grass-edged parterres. Nearer the house this garden is a home for iris and old-fashioned roses. In the centre of the west wall, through an 18th-century Italian gate of wrought iron, can be seen the replanting of an avenue shown by Kip; the nearer section is of Irish yew and the further of Lombardy poplar. Four acres (1.6ha) of wild garden have been planted with a wealth of spring bulbs, flowering shrubs, rhododendrons and a rich treasury of old-fashioned and climbing roses. The large walled kitchen garden still resembles Kip's drawing in its layout with its three massive sweet chestnuts most probably planted at the time. Near the house is also an ancient holly with a girth of 9ft 10in (3m). During the last 30 years there has been extensive planting of trees, some fine musk roses and many new rhododendrons. Among the plantings are those collected by Kingdon Ward on his last expedition.

5 m W of Lincoln on
B1190

SK 8970 (OS 121)

Open May to end Sept
Su, W, Bank Hol M also
Easter Su 1400-1800;
parties of 20 or over at
other times by appt

Peak months May to
July

WC ⊖ 🚽 D 🍽 🚻 ⚘ ★
🏠 🕭

Gunby Hall LINCOLNSHIRE

The National Trust, Gunby, nr Spilsby
tel. Scremby (075 485) 212

Known for their veteran roses, Gunby Hall gardens were first laid out when
the house was built for Sir William Massingberd in 1700. The existing garden
on the main front is of 1900 vintage, a yew-bounded enclosure with a central
sundial and formal flower beds, a paved central path and clipped golden
privet. Enclosures beyond, formed by yew hedges, make bowling alleys. On
the east are mellowed brick-walled gardens originally containing vegetables
and orchards. There are still apples, along with clematis and trained fruit on
the walls, and in beds are roses, many of which are rarely seen today such as
'Reine Marie Henriette', raised 100 years ago and exclusive to Gunby until
propagated by the National Trust, 'Mrs Oakley Fisher' (1921), which has
come to be known as the Gunby Rose, 'Mrs Wemyss Quin' (1914), 'Cardinal
de Richelieu' (1840), and 'Easlea's Golden Rambler' (1932). Among them are
modern shrub roses, and many climbing Bourbons and the old walls make a
fitting backcloth for herbaceous borders and a herb garden. Within these
walled gardens several old buildings survive, a pigeon house or dovecot
possibly older than the house itself and a stone summerhouse. Along the
southern wall of the gardens is a long pool. A cedar of 1812 planting on the east
has other young ones round to follow on, a characteristic of the house that
contains the Gunby Tree Book – a record of planting from about 1670.

7 m W of Skegness on
A158

TF 4666 (OS 122)

Open Apr to end Sept
Th 1400-1800; T, W and
F by written appt only

Peak months June and
July

P WC ⊖ 日 ⚹ 🕿

Harrington Hall LINCOLNSHIRE

Lady Maitland, nr Spilsby.

All the evidence seems to point to the Harrington Hall Garden as being the one Tennyson invited Maud to enter. It is still unspoiled by the passage of time, and matches in planting and design the 17th century with an early Elizabethan origin. Old brick walls surround one garden where gate piers, dated 1722, stand by steps leading to a raised terrace from which it would have been possible to see the once elaborate Jacobean parterres laid out in knots. Today its supporting walls are clothed in roses and its herringbone brick pathways are spilled over by herbs and herbaceous planting while a large holly, *Ilex aquifolium* 'Ferox Argentea', stands sentinel. *Rosa banksiae* 'Lutea' climbs the house walls while the entrance drive is through rhododendrons and azaleas to a large lawn bounded by a mellow brick wall on which sprawl honeysuckle and climbing roses. Under it luxuriates a herbaceous border of reds, mauves, pinks and white. The kitchen garden, approached by way of a high hedge of yew, has a flower border and a mulberry of 17th-century planting. A summerhouse built into the wall of the second terrace lawn leads to a south-facing walk where the wall supports shrub roses, *Pittosporum tenuifolium*, magnolias and viburnums. Some very old roses are planted in a box-edged square to be viewed from the drawing room window – 'Charles de Mills' (1836), 'Mme Pierre Oger' (1878), 'Alister Stella Gray' (1894), and, 'La Reine Victoria' (1872).

4 m SW of Alford on A1104 turn W

TF 3671 (OS 122)

Open Apr to end Oct W and Th 1200-2000 (or dusk if earlier) also several Su for charity inc NGS 1400-1800; other times by appt

🅿 🍴 ♿ ⚘ ★ 🚂 (limited opening)

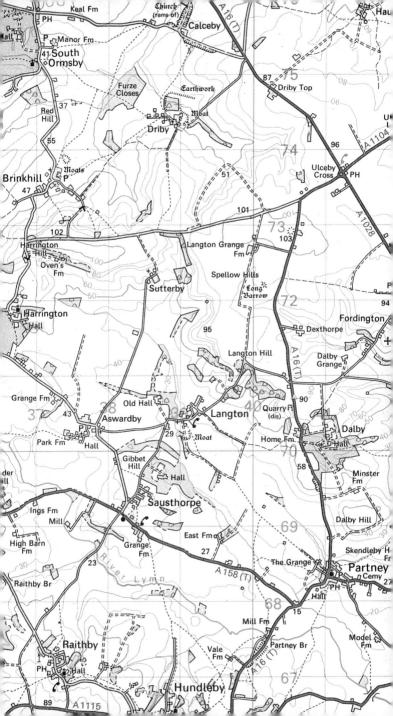

Springfields Gardens LINCOLNSHIRE

Springfields Horticultural Society Limited, Camelgate, Spalding.
tel. Spalding (0775) 4843

A show garden for British bulbs and corms was opened here in Spalding in 1966 after over two years of work. The 25 acres (10ha) of lake, woodland, sunken garden, paved walks, lawns and glasshouses in spring display over 1,000,000 bulbs and corms of more than 3,000 varieties. Some 300 tulip varieties are to be seen in two large greenhouses. Narcissi from the country's experimental horticultural stations and the Daffodil Society are grown in trial beds along with tulips from the Agricultural Development Advisory Service. This congress of beauty can be seen from early April to late May. In 1976 Springfield's opening season was extended to September, with the highlight the blooming of over 12,000 roses, both old and new, selected by the British Association of Rose Breeders. There are water-lilies in the lake, bedding-out and dahlias on the terraces, an eclectic collection of summer-flowering plants, trees and shrubs, all providing interest and brilliant colour in late summer. There is a maze of *Cupressocyparis leylandii* planted in 1977 to commemorate the Queen's Silver Jubilee. The gardens were designed by Carl Van Empelen, known for his Sterling Forest Gardens in New York and work on the Continent. In February every year the largest forced flower show in Britain is held in the gardens.

1 m NE of Spalding on A151 turn N

TF 2624 (OS 131)

Open Apr to end Sept daily 1000-1800; reduced rates for parties of 30 or over by appt

Blickling Hall NORFOLK

The National Trust, Blickling.
tel. Aylsham (0263) 733084

The enormous 400-year-old yew hedges flanking the forecourt give an
indication of the delights to be enjoyed in the superbly maintained gardens of
this romantic Jacobean house. They include a large parterre with clipped
topiary and a central fountain, designed in the 19th century by Nesfield and
Digby Wyatt, but simplified in the 1930s by Nancy Lindsey who reduced the
number of beds and planted them with perennials and polyantha roses. It is
unusual to employ herbaceous plants in such a setting but they are entirely
successful, due to the subtle colour schemes and carefully graduated heights.
Beyond the parterre a wide path bisects a 17th-century formal woodland
garden and leads through azaleas and rhododendrons to a Doric temple. The
woodland is intersected by radiating rides and surrounded by a raised terrace
walk from which can be reached an orangery, probably designed by Repton
or his son. The remainder of the garden consists of an early landscaped park,
later improved by Repton, with a beautiful man-made lake over a mile
(1.6km) in length. There is much of horticultural interest, including tender
climbers, unusual shrubs, naturalised cyclamen, and a famous oriental plane
which, by means of layering, has grown to a tremendous size.

10 m S of Cromer on
B1354

TG 1728 (OS 133)

Phone for information;
reduced rates for
parties of 15 or over
by appt

Peak months May to
Aug

P WC 🚻 D 🍽 🎪 ♿
★ 🐕 (limited opening)

Bressingham Hall NORFOLK

Alan Bloom, Esq., Diss.
tel. Diss (0379) 88243

Bressingham Gardens are a place of pilgrimage for all who enjoy beautiful and original gardens, but especially for those who love hardy herbaceous plants, for here Alan Bloom has built up a collection of around 5,000 species and varieties. This collection is certainly the largest of its kind in Britain and it includes many plants which are the result of hybridisation or selection on his adjoining nursery. The garden covers 6 acres (2.4ha) and the planting incorporates many alpines, ornamental grasses, bog plants and aquatics, for which pools were constructed at the lowest point. A more recent addition has been a smaller area devoted to heathers and conifers. The garden is completely informal in style, with the plants growing in large island beds of curving outline on a gently undulating site, the contours being cleverly exploited by the placing of the beds and the retaining of banks by low walls of Norfolk flint. The design is particularly successful where the beds occupy most of the space and the grass is reduced to broad curving paths. The views are enormously enhanced by the presence of magnificent native trees to which have been added many introduced species, especially conifers.

2½ m W of Diss on A1066

TM 0780 (OS 144)

Open Su May to end Sept; Th June to 2nd Th in Sept; W Aug; Easter Su and Bank Hols 1100-1800

Peak months June to August

Mannington Hall Gardens NORFOLK

The Hon Robin and Mrs Walpole, Saxthorpe, nr Holt.
tel. Saxthorpe (026 387) 284

There is a great sense of tranquillity at Mannington Hall. It is derived from a combination of its peaceful, sheltered site, the smooth rich green lawns, and the still waters of moat and lake in which are reflected fine trees and the handsome 15th-century brick and flint house. With the exception of some old rhododendrons planted under oaks, most of the ornamental planting has been undertaken in the past 15 years. The garden contained within the moat has been treated formally and includes a rose garden of modern bush and pillar varieties. A small yew-hedged enclosure contains elaborately shaped beds planted with herbs, sweetbriars and other plants to scent the air. Sheltered by a crenellated wall is an herbaceous border and near it a 'Sheraton' cherry in which a Japanese variety has been grafted on to the gleaming stem of *Prunus serrula*, while interesting climbers including campsis and the Banksian rose festoon the house. Outside the moat the style is informal with large island beds of mixed shrubs and many old varieties of roses. Beyond, on the edge of the lake, stands a Doric temple containing a statue representing Architecture. Worthy of notice are the attractive terracotta plant labels used throughout the garden.

15 m NW of Norwich on B1149 turn NE at Saxthorpe to Little Barningham and Matlaske

TG 1432 (OS 133)

Open May Su 1400-1700; June, July and Aug W, Th and F 1100-1800

P WC ♿ D (guide dogs only) 🍽 ⛱ 🐕 ★ ⚲

Oxburgh Hall NORFOLK

The National Trust, Oxborough, nr King's Lynn.
tel. Gooderstone (036 621) 258

The glory of these gardens is the large intricate parterre which decorates a
sunken lawn to the east of the fortified house, and which is probably unique in
British gardens. It was created about 1845 by the Beddingfield family,
descendants of the original builders of the house, who copied one they had
seen in a garden near Paris. The original design has since been traced back to a
book on garden design written by Anton Joseph Dazallier d'Argeville in 1709.
The pattern is carried out in box-edged beds and panels of grass, set out on
gravel with clipped yew sentinels; the beds are filled with blue ageratum,
yellow tagetes, grey santolinas, ruta and stachys. Forming a background to the
parterre is a yew hedge, and behind this a classic herbaceous border planted
against the Gothic-style brick wall of the kitchen garden that supports
climbing roses, honeysuckles and clematis. To the south of it is a shrub border
containing a standard pink *Wisteria floribunda*. The walled garden contains a
young orchard of plums, quinces and mulberries. Near the chapel, which
stands in the grounds, are traces of a Victorian 'wilderness' which it is hoped to
restore.

7 m SW of Swaffham
turn N of A134 at Stoke
Ferry

TF 7401 (OS 143)

Open early Apr and
May to end Oct M-W,
S and Su 1400-1800;
reduced rates for
parties of 15 or over
by appt

Peak months summer

WC ⊖ (limited) ⊟ ⬤
⚘ ★ ⛺

Sandringham House and Gardens

NORFOLK

H.M. The Queen, Sandringham.
tel. King's Lynn (0553) 772675

The spacious grounds of Sandringham bear the imprint of successive royal owners since it was first occupied by Edward, Prince of Wales, in 1862. The house is surrounded by enormous lawns and magnificent trees. From the public entrance a path runs through a woodland glade with shrubberies in which colour is provided by the camellias, cultivars of *Erica carnea* and massed daffodils of spring to the autumn berries of sorbus and cotoneasters. For the months between there are rhododendrons and azaleas, philadelphus and lavenders, hydrangeas and lilies. (Most of the plants are labelled.) This exemplary modern planting was carried out under the direction of T. H. Finlay of the Savill Gardens. Completely different in style is the formal garden adjoining the house, designed by Geoffrey Jellicoe for King George VI. Enclosed by pleached limes, box hedges create a number of enclosures, some containing small lawns, others hardy plants and roses. At the end is a statue of Father Time, purchased by Queen Mary. Near the south-west corner of the house are two lakes fed by water from natural springs which flows through rock outcrops planted with moisture-loving subjects. A further rock garden is planted with dwarf conifers and heathers.

8 m NE of King's Lynn on B1440

TF 6928 (OS 132)

Open Apr to late Sept M-Th 1030-1700 Su 1130-1700; closed late July and early Aug

P WC ⊖ 🖶 ➡ 🚻 🐕 ✿
★ 🏛 🕭

Sheringham Hall NORFOLK

Thomas Upcher, Esq., Upper Sheringham.

Sheringham Hall was among the last works of Humphry Repton, the Red Book showing his proposals being produced in 1812. He regarded it as his masterpiece. It is fitting that his crowning achievement should have been created in the county in which he grew up and in which he chose to be buried. Besides the park, Repton and his eldest son designed the Neo-Classical house for Abbot Upcher, ancestor of the present owner. Repton decided to place the house in the shelter of a wooded hill facing south and to forego views of the sea. Instead, it looks out on to rising, undulating land with the hilltops crowned by woods – a prospect of great beauty. The kitchen garden with a small formal rose garden was set at some distance from the house. In recent years a temple to Repton's design has been built overlooking the park. In the mid-19th century the woods were thickly planted with rhododendrons raised from seed collected by Wilson. During the 1950s the land between the house and walled garden was developed with a small lake, lawns, flowering trees and informal borders of shrubs, while the woods behind the house were planted with well-chosen camellias, azaleas and rhododendrons.

1½ m SW of
Sheringham on B1157

TG 1342 (OS 133)

Open May and June
M-S 1000-1300 and
1400-1800; last 2 Su
in May and 1st 2 Su in
June in aid of Church
1400-1800

Peak months mid May
to mid June

⊖ D ⯑ ⯑

Talbot Manor NORFOLK

Maurice Mason Esq., Fincham, King's Lynn.

This is the garden of one who has, in his own words, an 'apparently insatiable urge to put plants into the ground', with the result that beginning with a few borders around his house in 1940 the garden steadily extended over the adjoining open farmland so that now it covers 35 acres (14ha) and probably comprises the largest collection of hardy plants, from trees to alpines, in private hands in Britain. Even the swimming pool has been given over to water-lilies! Many of the plants have been brought back by the owner from plant-hunting expeditions in five continents. The site is flat, the soil a rich medium loam with a ph between 7 and 8. This rules out lime-hating plants, but camellias and tender rhododendrons are grown in a cool greenhouse. Other glasshouses contain cacti and succulents, citrus fruits, pelargoniums, begonias, ferns and a spectacular collection of bromeliads. Most of the garden is informal and there is no strong plan, but there are formal sections within it, such as a yew-hedged enclosure for a bowling green and a circular pool, and another for herbaceous borders. Numerous peacocks roam free and add their own splendour to this remarkable garden.

5 m NE of Downham Market on A1122

TF 6806 (OS 143)

Open 5 Su in June and early July 1400-2000

P WC 🚻 D 🍴 (in village hall)

219

Akenfield SUFFOLK

Mrs Peggy Cole, Charsfield, nr Woodbridge.

This is an object lesson for all who have small gardens, for packed into a quarter of an acre (0.1ha) is more of interest, use and beauty than is found in the majority of gardens many times this size. Every inch is used to good effect and there is no feeling of overcrowding, largely due to the high standard of maintenance. Twenty-five years ago Mrs Peggy Cole and her husband moved into what was then a council house and had to scythe a path down the garden, yet within seven years they were opening it to the public! Since her husband's death Mrs Cole has had the help of her brother and has taken over part of her neighbour's garden to grow flowers for cutting or drying. The front garden is devoted mainly to roses, while the roadside bank is bright with bedding plants. Behind the house is a small yard with innumerable pots and tubs. A path divides the back garden, one half being devoted to vegetables and chickens, the other to a series of small linked enclosures with mixed borders, two tiny rectangular pools, one with a cascade and diminutive water-wheel, and two greenhouses in which there is a cottage garden mixture of the ornamental and the edible.

3 m W of Wickham Market on B1078 turn N to Charsfield

TM 2556 (OS 156)

Open May to Sept daily 1000-1900

Peak months July to Sept

🚻 (by appt only) D

Beares SUFFOLK

S. A. Notcutt Esq., Saxtead, Framlingham.
tel. Framlingham (0728) 723232

Beares is a delightful plantsman's garden created by the present owners over a period of 20 years. It covers some 2½–3 acres (1ha) on a southern slope around an old farmhouse and its ponds. The soil is alkaline clay improved with pulverised bark, sharp sand and compost. The design grew around the existing paths, hedges and mature trees; only the raised terrace with its mixture of paving, lawn and beds was planned on paper. The rural nature of the site has been preserved by the informality, the retention of ditches, even when these cut across the garden, and in the cottage garden style of planting. The one element providing strong contrast is a wide, straight grass path, flanked by deep borders, running the full depth of the garden. Over 1000 varieties of trees, shrubs and plants are grown and all are labelled. A varied selection of evergreens forms a background for lilacs and hibiscus and for the autumn colours of rhus, photinia, acers and sorbus. Unusual trees include *Aesculus neglecta* 'Erythroblastos' with brilliant pink young leaves, and paulownia which regularly sets buds but flowers only in a good spring. Plants and alpines have been chosen for their ability to provide ground cover. The house is clothed with fremontodendron, carpenteria and *Abutilon* 'Kentish Belle.'

1 m NE of Saxtead
Green on A1120

TM 2566 (OS 156)

Open infrequently in
summer, frequently in
autumn, write for
details

Peak months June to
July, Sept to Oct

▣ 円 D 只 ⊛

Great Thurlow Hall SUFFOLK

Ronald A. Vestey, Esq., Haverhill.

This handsome Georgian house is set in a fine, immaculately maintained 16-acre (6.5ha) garden. When purchased by the present owners hardly anything existed except the old walled kitchen garden. Development began in 1947 to the designs of Vernon Daniel. In the best tradition of English mid-20th century gardens it has wide lawns, terraces, yew-hedged enclosures, interesting shrubs and trees, a profusion of flowers, with formality around the house melting gradually into natural lines. On the west side of the house flows the River Stour, and the land between has been stepped down to it. The top terrace is occupied by a rose garden while the lower levels contain excellent herbaceous borders. A timber bridge along which is trained wisteria and honeysuckle provides access to a stone-columned pavilion. There is a goldfish pond with fountain statue in an enclosure to the south of the house, and beyond a big open lawn ending at a ha-ha with views of unspoilt countryside. Between the two main axes, grass paths lead to the upper reaches of the river and a newly made trout lake. This part of the garden is delightful in April, being planted with great drifts of modern varieties of daffodil.

2 m NE of Haverhill on A143 turn NW onto B1061

TL 6850 (OS 154)

Open frequently between spring and autumn, write for details

D ☕

Lime Kiln Rosarium   SUFFOLK

Humphrey Brooke, Esq., Claydon, Ipswich.
tel. Ipswich (0473) 830334

This is a romantic garden devoted to the preservation of old and rare roses and
possessing at present a collection of over 500 varieties. The garden was started
by Countess Sophie Benckendorff who, in the 1920s, designed an intimate
formal garden with stone and brick paths around a mulberry and Irish yews.
This contains mainly Victorian hybrid-perpetual roses and a few later varieties
underplanted with hardy geraniums, Welsh poppies and hemerocallis. From
1956 the present owner extended the planting using the vegetable garden, the
verges of the drive and a large lawn where there are collections of rugosa and
wild roses. All the shrubs are allowed to reach a natural size; the only pruning
consists of removing dead wood. As a result many have grown enormously
large in spite of the chalky subsoil. This has influenced the character of the
garden, which resembles in places that of Sleeping Beauty! The wildness will
not appeal to everyone. Others will be enraptured by billowing masses of soft-
coloured flowers tumbling over walls, trees, pillars and paths. None could fail
to enjoy the intense rose fragrance, augmented here and there by honeysuckles
and philadelphus. The garden is naturally at its best around mid-summer.

3 m N of Ipswich on A45
turn NE onto B1113
then S

TM 1349 (OS 169)

Open mid May to mid
July daily 1400-1900

Peak month June

(by appt only)

Somerleyton Hall SUFFOLK

Lord and Lady Somerleyton, nr Lowestoft.

These gardens are contemporary with the ornate mid-19th century house and contain several interesting examples of Victorian gardening taste and technology. The designer employed was the fashionable W. A. Nesfield who constructed a large terrace which he decorated with an elaborate parterre. This has been replaced by simple rose beds, though an equatorial sundial and Irish yews remain from the earlier design. Fortunately, another feature has survived unaltered; this is a large maze of symmetrical plan with a pergola-like shelter on a grassy mound in the centre. Attached to the house is a big aviary, and near this a sunken garden enclosed by arcaded colonnades which are extended by clipped yew arches. Beyond these the garden changes in character. Here on rising ground there are curving borders of rhododendron and azaleas and other shrubs beneath interesting trees, both old and newly planted. At the top of the slope stands the kitchen garden, entered through a pillared portico which is flanked by glazed timber cases designed for cultivating camellias. Much of the kitchen garden has been grassed over but herbaceous borders line the centre path, while on the south-facing wall there are most unusual lean-to greenhouses designed by Paxton, which have ridge and furrow sliding roofs.

5 m NW of Lowestoft on B1074

TM 4997 (OS 134)

Open Easter Su to end Sept daily exc S 0900-1730

Peak month June

P WC ⊖ (1½ m walk) ⊟
⏹ ⛺ ✳ ★ ▥ ⚄

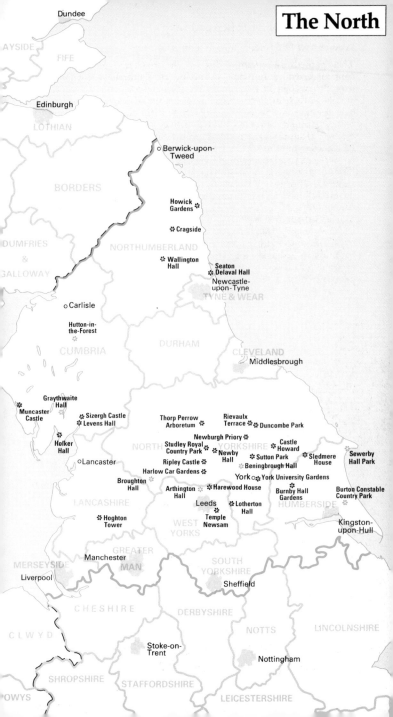

The North

Dundee

AYSIDE
FIFE

Edinburgh

LOTHIAN

BORDERS

DUMFRIES
&
GALLOWAY

○ Berwick-upon-
Tweed

Howick
Gardens ❊

❊ Cragside

NORTHUMBERLAND

❊ Wallington
Hall

Seaton
Delaval Hall
❊ Newcastle-
upon-Tyne
TYNE & WEAR

○ Carlisle

Hutton-in-
the-Forest

CUMBRIA

DURHAM

CLEVELAND

Middlesbrough

Graythwaite
Hall

❊ Muncaster
Castle

❊ Sizergh Castle
❊ Levens Hall

Thorp Perrow
Arboretum ❊

Rievaulx
Terrace ❊❊ Duncombe Park

❊ Holker
Hall

Newburgh Priory ❊
Studley Royal ❊ Castle
Country Park ❊ Newby Howard
❊ Hall
NORTH ❊ YORKSHIRE
Ripley Castle ❊ ❊ Sutton Park ❊ Sledmere
Beningbrough Hall House ❊ Sewerby
Hall Park

○ Lancaster

Harlow Car Gardens ❊

Broughton
Hall ❊

Arthington ❊ ❊ Harewood House
Hall

York ○❊❊ York University Gardens

Burnby Hall
Gardens ❊

Burton Constable
Country Park

Leeds
❊ Lotherton
Hall

HUMBERSIDE

❊ Hoghton
Tower

LANCASHIRE

Temple
Newsam

WEST
YORKS

Kingston-
upon-Hull

GREATER
MAN

MERSEYSIDE

Manchester

Liverpool

SOUTH
YORKSHIRE

Sheffield

CHESHIRE

DERBYSHIRE

NOTTS

LINCOLNSHIRE

CLWYD

Stoke-on-
Trent

Nottingham

POWYS

SHROPSHIRE

STAFFORDSHIRE

LEICESTERSHIRE

Holker Hall CUMBRIA

Mr and Mrs Hugh Cavendish, Cark-in-Cartmel, Grange-over-Sands.
tel. Newby Bridge (0448) 53328

Set between Morecambe Bay and the Lakeland hills, both of which can be seen from this 22 acres (9ha) of formal Victorian garden and woodland, the present design is largely by Paxton, for this is a Cavendish home. Paxton is also said to have suggested the formal Italianate steps descending between ilex hedges to a central pool and fountain. The gardens have been altered over the years several times from the early Dutch design; the formal gardens to the south of the house were laid out in 1875–6. A long walk meanders through herbaceous borders and a wide-ranging selection of shrubs and trees including azaleas and rhododendrons, magnolias and one of the first four monkey puzzle trees to be planted in England by Paxton for the 6th Duke of Devonshire. Also relishing the mild climate here are specimens of *Catalpa* (Indian bean tree), the tulip tree, *Gingko biloba*, *Hoheria lyallii*, a cut-leaf beech, a tree-sized *Magnolia acuminata*, *Drimys winteri*, *Embothrium*, *Paulownia*, *Staphylea holocarpa*, *Osmanthus yunnanensis* and *Myrtus luma*. In the spring daffodils and cherries brighten the scene and a double Banksian rose climbs the house wall. A paved sunken garden with a shelter and pergola designed by Thomas Mawson in 1912 is home for many species and old-fashioned roses including gallicas, cabbage, damask and noisette. Heather beds by the west wing are of 1769 planting.

5 m W of Grange-over-Sands on B5277, then B5278

SD 3577 (OS 96)

Open Easter to end Oct daily exc S 1030-1630; reduced rates for parties

Peak months spring and early summer

WC ⊖ (1 m walk) 🚻 D
🍽 🎪 ♨ ★ 🎁 (inc Motor Museum) Special events throughout summer season

Levens Hall CUMBRIA

O. R. Bagot, Esq., Kendal.
tel. Sedgwick (0448) 60321

No topiary garden in the country has a finer display than at Levens where the garden and the topiary were laid out for Colonel James Grahme in 1692 by M. Beaumont, a pupil of Le Nôtre. Most of the original topiary work still exists in box and yew, massive and in all manner of unusual shapes, set in truly Stuart-style box-edged parterres. The beech hedge, 20ft (6m) high, and the lime avenue, one of the earliest, at the end of the garden were planted by Beaumont. A circle of beech encloses a carpet of grass, and herbaceous borders line grass walks to one of the early ha-has, while the brightest of flowers are underplanted in the topiary garden and there are more flowers in beds in the old orchard. Across the road from the garden is the old park taking in the gorge of the River Kent where the 1890 design is intact, although the park was on estate plans in 1170. There are deer here, and an oak avenue, probably planted by the Countess of Suffolk and Berkshire in 1740, is in its prime and stone seats by the path give on to lovely vistas of the winding Kent. The house near the stable block was built for M. Beaumont.

5 m S of Kendal by
Levens Bridge on A6

SD 4985 (OS 97)

Open Easter Su to end
Sept Su-Th 1100-1700;
parties at other times
by appt; reduced rates

P WC ⊖ 🖪 🍽 ⛄ ⚘ ★
🏛

Muncaster Castle CUMBRIA

Patrick Gordon-Duff-Pennington, Esq., Ravenglass.
tel. Ravenglass (065 77) 614

Muncaster Castle is noted for one of the largest collections of rhododendrons which almost fills 300 acres (121ha) on a site of great natural beauty. The castle itself, parts of which are as early as the 13th century, is placed on a hilltop looking across to the rhododendron-filled valley and hillsides of the Esk. After the First World War, Sir John Ramsden first planted and bred many of the present collection, so there are 'Muncaster Bells', 'Trumpet', 'Blue Haze' and 'Ember Glow'. A most notable feature at Muncaster is the mile-long (1.6km) grass terrace of *c.*1780 fronted by a clipped box hedge battlemented with yews from where one views the flower-filled Esk vale and its hanging hillsides. Although it is so far north, the Hooker Himalayan large-leaved rhododendrons are happy here and include *R. macabeanum, falconeri, sinogrande* and *arboreum*. To keep up the colour scene the back of the terrace is planted with ornamental trees and flowering shrubs including many maples, *Eucryphia cordifolia* and *Nothofagus procera*. A more formal garden near the castle is planted up with shrubs, evergreen azaleas and herbaceous perennials.

1 m E of Ravenglass on A595

SD 1096 (OS 96)

Open Good Fri to 1st Su in Oct daily exc F 1200-1700; reduced rates for parties

🅿 WC ♿ (1 m walk) 🚻 D 🍴 ⚘ ★ 🎁 (limited opening) 🐕

Sizergh Castle CUMBRIA

The National Trust, Sedgwick, nr Kendal.
tel. Sedgwick (0448) 60070

Probably the largest collection of hardy ferns in the country is at Sizergh, a
lovely old mansion built round a pele tower of *c.*1350. The present garden layout of lawns, lake and limestone rock garden was designed and executed by
the noted nursery of nearby Ambleside, T. R. Hayes and Son, in 1926. An
approach garden of ancient yews, island beds of shrub roses, lilac and colourful
underplanting of lilies and many different geraniums leads to old gate piers.
Here a steep walk climbs to a high terrace and sheltering wall. The wall and
bed beneath hold *Osmanthus, Olearias, Solanum crispum, Ceratostigma* and
Caryopteris. From the house front a lawn leads to a small lake and a tree-filled
island. On the far side the sloping lawns are flowery meads, in spring a cloud of
pheasant's eye narcissus and later alive with wild orchis and other flora of the
limestone soils. The ¾-acre (0.3ha) sunken rock garden, which contains over
100 different species and varieties of ferns, is surrounded by surprisingly large
'dwarf' conifers. Japanese maples give their spring and autumn colour to the
evergreens, and a great variety of alpines, bog plants and marginals are planted
in and among the ferns which include many varieties of the royal fern, unusual
polypodias, blechnums, dryopteris and many more.

3½ m S of Kendal on
A591

SD 4987 (OS 97)

Open Apr to end Oct
Su, M, W and Th 1230-
1745

⚿ WC ⊖ 🚻 ⚹ ★
🏠 (limited opening)

Burnby Hall Gardens HUMBERSIDE

Stewart's Burnby Hall Gardens and Museum Trust, Pocklington.
tel. Pocklington (07592) 2068/2113

In 1904 after extensive world travels, Major P. M. Stewart made out of two ploughed fields at his home in Pocklington a pool, the Upper Water, for private fishing and swimming some 205yd (187m) long and 66yd (60m) wide and, in 1910, built a second pool, the Lower Water, with running water and cascades joining the two. In 1920 the Upper Water was extended to cover 1½ acres (0.6ha) and more trout were given a home. But in 1935 the whole project was changed and the Major started to build up a water-lily collection in his two pools, so that by 1950 some 5,000 plants in 58 species and varieties filled the Burnby Hall water with summer glory. Many other species and varieties were tried out but would not stand the northern climate, so now Burnby Hall has 5,000 blooms to show every day in July, though there are lilies to see from May to mid-September. The lakeside and walk by the stream, with pleasing glimpses of the Wolds in the distance, have been planted with hundreds of different marginals and bog plants, while rock gardens by the wayside display alpines and rock plants. There are decorative trees and shrubs, too, and 'tame' ornamental fish which almost eat out of the hand. In the grounds is a museum housing the Major's big-game successes and ethnological exhibits from many countries, all given to Pocklington along with the gardens after Major Stewart's death in 1962.

11 m E of York on
A1079 turn E onto
B1246 to Pocklington

SE 8048 (OS 106)

Open Easter to end
Sept M-F 1000-1900 S,
Su 1200-1900; reduced
rates for parties

Peak months late June
to mid Sept

⬛ WC ⊖ 🚻 D 🍴 (pm
only) ⛱ 🚭

Sewerby Hall Park HUMBERSIDE

East Yorkshire Borough Council, Bridlington.
tel. Bridlington (0262) 673769

At Sewerby is a garden on the very cliff top overlooking the North Sea. Here a hall or manor has stood since Norman times, and Anglo-Saxon and Roman remains have been found in the park. There are 50 acres (20ha) of garden and woodland where tender trees and shrubs defy the North Sea gales. Much of the present layout is basically the work of Mr Yarbrugh from 1841 onwards. In front of the 1715 house is a balustraded lawn on which is the three-coloured laburnum, *Laburnocytisus adamii*, a fine stand of copper beech and *Acer negundo*. Turning left from the house front the formal garden is dominated by six massive monkey puzzle trees and steps leading to an open temple, and planted around, giving a sub-tropical effect, are yuccas, fatsias, the palm, *Chamaerops humilis*, foxtail lilies and lovely weeping birch (*Betula pendula* 'Youngii'). Under the woodland border to this lawn appears a succession of flowers. A path through the trees comes to a principal feature of Sewerby, the old English garden, where topiary-worked yew hedges and box-edged, geometrically shaped beds give the formal parterre effect even when bright with cottage garden flowers during the summer. There is a Georgian conservatory full of flowers and colourful foliage, and through a wrought-iron gate is a walled rose garden planted in ornamental box-edged beds. A walled walk on the outer wall protects many tender hebes, pittosporums, cistus and olearias.

2 m NE of Bridlington
on B1255 turn S at
Marton

TA 2069 (OS 101)

Open throughout year
daily 0900-dusk

Peak months May and
late Aug to early Sept

🅿 WC ♿ 🚻 D 🍽 (limited
opening) 🎪 ⊛ ⚜ ★ 🏛
🚶

Sledmere House HUMBERSIDE

Sir Tatton Sykes, Bart, Sledmere, Driffield.
tel. Driffield (0377) 86208

An exemplary Brownian landscape is the setting for this Georgian house of
1751–83 with its magnificent Joseph Rose Greco-Roman style interiors and its
library modelled on the baths of Diocletian. Brown's plan for the whole estate
of 2,000 acres (809ha) hangs there. Under Sir Christopher Sykes the old village
was removed, a model village and the famous racehorse stud stables built, all
part of the surrounding house scene. The entrance is by way of the cupola-
topped stable block onto lawns flanked by colourful herbaceous borders and
climbing plants on the mellow brick walls, and dotted with chestnuts well
over 200 years old and stately cedars through which glimpses of the village
church are seen. In 1911 an Italian garden was created in a recess adjoining the
house with water, stone urns and statuary. Walls on the three sides are covered
with climbers. From the south front of the house the view is of a typical
Brown landscape: lawns marching up to the house foundations and sloping
away to rise again by a later added pool and fountain to rolling landscape
dotted with fine beech, elm and oak into the far distance where Brown's
signature, a belt of trees, closes the view. Left from the house through
woodland paths is a kitchen garden containing old glass and by its side an odd-
shaped rose garden and a walk of flowering trees, shrubs and wall climbers

3 m NW of Great
Driffield on A166 turn
NW onto B1252

TA 9364 (OS 101)

Open Easter weekend
(Good Fri-T); Apr Su;
May to late Sept daily
1330-1730

Peak months June to
Sept

P WC ⊟ D ● ⚘
★ ⛺

Hoghton Tower LANCASHIRE

Hoghton Tower Preservation Trust, nr Preston.

There can be few stately homes with the long-ranging vistas one gets at Hoghton, the seat of Sir Bernard de Hoghton. This 16th-century fortified mansion is on a hill top 700ft (213m) above sea level, and from the terraced walk which encircles the house can be seen the Welsh and Lakeland mountains, Morecambe Bay and the River Ribble running out to sea in its Lytham estuary. Three walled gardens keep up the old English gardening tradition. One is an old English rose garden, the second, the ramparts, so called because of the sentry walk in far-off days, is grassed, with highly coloured herbaceous beds, and the third, the wilderness, was once the formal garden which, once let go, became a wilderness. Now its large lawn is set off by flowers in great variety. Woodland of mature trees surrounds the Tower, through which walks are, in spring, among massed rhododendrons and carpets of daffodils. Later there are roses in the walled gardens. Hedging in the lower drive is of specimen trees and hybrid rhododendrons chosen for their high colour effect. In the house the outstanding panelling is made from the park's timber and the banqueting hall is where James I knighted the loin of beef in 1617.

5 m W of Blackburn on A675

SD 6226 (OS 103)

Open Easter weekend to end Oct Su and Bank Hol M, also S in July and Aug 1400-1700; parties at other times by appt

Peak months Apr to June

P WC ⊖ 🖥 D 🍽 🚻 ♨
★ ☎

Cragside NORTHUMBERLAND

The National Trust, Rothbury, Morpeth.

Cragside, the romantic, almost fairy-tale castle built for Lord Armstrong by Norman Shaw on a high bluff, is surrounded by craggy moorland, a natural garden for thousands of rhododendrons and placid lakes in a deep ravine of Debdon Beck. From the house platform, high above soaring conifers, whether one looks up or down, in the right season the hillsides are painted with colours, the result of smothering the rocky outcrops with a varied selection of rhododendrons and azaleas, though in the 940 acres (380ha) encircled by a hilly drive, everywhere one looks it is *Rhododendron ponticum* and sweet-smelling *R. luteum* colouring the landscape. In the dell below the house the way is through woodland over which a graceful suspension bridge sways. Woodland walks may be taken by the stream, now placid, then in a deep gorge, and by waterfalls, to view on the way the North American conifers which have reached record heights, many over 140ft (43m). To be seen are the Western hemlocks, Douglas firs, and other spiring giants – the noble, red and great firs, Colorado spruce, the ornamental tiger tail spruce, the Swiss arolla pine and *Abies concolor* and *A. magnifica*. Banks of heather offer light relief under large stands of beech and birch. As has been said of Cragside 'It is not so much a garden as a rhododendron and azalea drive', or a long 30-mile (48-km) hike.

11 m SW of Alnwick on B6341

NU 0702 (OS 81)

Open Apr to Oct daily 1000-1900; Nov to Mar S and Su 1000-1600; reduced rates for parties of 20 or over

Peak month June

⚑ WC ⊖ (1 m walk) ⛺ (by appt only) D 🍴 ⛱
♨ ★ 🏫 (limited opening) ♿

Howick Gardens NORTHUMBERLAND

Howick Trustees Limited, Howick, Alnwick.
tel. Longhoughton (066 577) 285

Despite Howick being only a mile from the icy blasts of the North Sea,
woodland shelter enabled Lord and Lady Grey from 1917 onwards to build up
this apparently West Coast garden of tender plants which has been carried on
by their daughter Lady Mary Howick. Rhododendrons, even the large-leaved
kind, have grown profusely here, such species as *R. cinnabarinum roylei,
sinogrande, davidsonianum* and *crassum*. As if to assert the 'western' effect
camellias and magnolias flower well, among the magnolias being *M. wilsonii,
campbellii* and *sinensis*. Other shrubs one does not expect to find here are
Corokia cotoneaster (the wire-netting bush), *Hydrangea villosa, Disanthus,
Eucryphia* and *Hoheria*. In the early part of the year bulbs of all kinds, among
which are a profusion of narcissus, add their bright colours to masses of
primula followed by meconopsis and trilliums among many cherries. A
September sight is massed *Kniphofia* 'Lord Roberts' inside a clipped yew hedge
accompanied by *Cedrus atlantica*. Both spring and autumn colour comes from
a collection of acers of which *A. griseum, rufinerve, davidii, capillipes* and *henryi*
also attract by the texture and colouring of their barks. On the house terrace
agapanthus of differing shades of blue do well and there are raised beds for
alpines and, in the park, many fine old trees.

3 m E of Alnwick on
A1068 turn E at Lesbury
onto B1339 to Howick
Grange 4 m N

NU 2417 (OS 81)

Open Apr to end Sept
daily 1400-1900

Peak months Apr to
June

P WC ⊖ ⊟

Wallington Hall NORTHUMBERLAND

The National Trust, Cambo, Morpeth.
tel. Scots Gap (067 074) 283

A garden's progress through the years can be seen at Wallington both on the ground and in plans to be seen in the house. Both parkland and gardens, like the house, are largely the work of Sir Walter Calverley Blackett from 1728 to 1777. Both west wood and east wood were planted by him, west wood with its middle pond and boat house pond, ice house and wishing well, and east wood with the China pond, called after a Chinese building which adorned it, and garden pond, with its Portico House by Garrett of 1740 still standing. Brown helped with the tree planting in the park and designed a grotto and a teahouse. A long pathway through native woodland leads to the Neptune Gate into the walled garden, first made by the Blacketts in 1760 but altered by the Trevelyan family. In 1938 Lady Trevelyan created the viewing platform above a fountain pool from where a flower-edged stream winds into a shrubbery at the far end. From the terrace is an even better view across the garden and the rolling countryside. There are lead statues on the parapet wall of 18th-century origin, and at the rear of the terrace a large conservatory, overlooked by the Owl House of 1765, housing a giant fuchsia and heliotropes. The walled garden contains a rose pergola, yew hedges, ornamental trees, honeysuckles, climbing old roses and ornamental shrubs.

12 m W of Morpeth on B6343 turn S onto B6342

NZ 0284 (OS 81)

Open daily Apr to Sept 1000-1900; Oct 1000-1800; Nov to Mar 1000-1600; reduced rates for parties of 20 or over

Peak months June to Aug

P WC ⊕ ⊟ (by appt) D
♥ ⋔ ⋇ ★
🎫 (limited opening) &

Seaton Delaval Hall

TYNE AND WEAR

Lord Hastings, Whitley Bay.
tel. Seaton Delaval (0632) 371493/373040

One of Vanbrugh's masterpieces is Admiral George Delaval's mansion Seaton Delaval, built in the early 1700s. This great theatrical pile was gutted by fire but still rises above its garden and parkland to dominate the scene. From the front the view is down to the distant port of Blyth and the North Sea, from the south it is over rolling parkland to ruined Tynemouth Priory. The garden on the west side of the house, designed by James Russell in 1950, was purposely made reminiscent of the original. It is a sunken one reached from a balustraded platform by two flights of wide steps, from where is seen, as it was meant to be, the patterns of the box parterres. At the far end behind a recessed seat is a David and Goliath statue by Baccio Bandinelli. During 1959–62 a shrubbery was cleared from the east and west sides of the main block and lawns laid. At the end of the enclosed lawn is a box-edged rose garden. Rhododendrons and azaleas and other flowering shrubs were planted here in 1964 and another classical statue, of Samson and a Philistine, by Gian Bologna was moved here. Bays are formed into buttresses on the wall side of the rose garden with shrub roses, peonies and a large buddleia. Clipped hollies are on this level as well as an unusual hypericum hedge to the small enclosed garden and greenhouse.

2 m NE of Seaton
Delaval on A190

NZ 3276 (OS 88)

Open May to Sept W,
Su, Bank Hol M 1400-
1800

Peak months June and
July

P WC ⊖ 🖳 ⚡ 🏠

Castle Howard NORTH YORKSHIRE

The Howard family, York.
tel. Coneysthorpe (065 384) 333

The castle and its setting were Sir John Vanbrugh's first architectural and landscaping work, though the Earl of Carlisle was the presiding genius behind this elysium. The approach to its 45 acres (18ha) of formal gardens is through a 5-mile (8-km) avenue, mainly of limes, planted in 1709 with some of the original planting still standing near the house, and Vanbrugh's martial outerworks of fortified walls and towers. To the front of the house is the north lake while the garden front looks over what was once Nesfield's great parterre, now trim lawns, and the Atlas Fountain brought by Nesfield from the 1851 exhibition. Ray Wood, to the left of the house, now being underplanted with rhododendrons, flowering shrubs and exotic trees, is historic in that George London's plans for a great star of interconnecting rides which would have destroyed the ancient woodland, were dismissed for Switzer's waterworks of basins, cascades and fountains under the old tree cover – said to be a turning point in English landscape history. Down what was once Henderskelfe village street is the terrace walk to Vanbrugh's beautiful Temple of the Four Winds, the Roman Bridge and Vanbrugh's and Hawksmoor's great mausoleum. The south lake overflows down a many-stepped cascade to the Roman Bridge, and in the 11-acre (4.5-ha) walled garden, with its Satyr Gate by Vanbrugh, is being built up an important collection of old-fashioned and shrub roses.

11 m NE of York on A64
turn N at Barton Hill

SE 7170 (OS 100)

Open late Mar to end
Oct daily 1030-1700;
reduced rates for
parties by appt

P WC ⊟ D ➤ ▩ ⚘
★ ⌂

Duncombe Park NORTH YORKSHIRE

Duncombe Terrace is the attraction here in a landscape with Bridgeman/Switzer overtones where, created for Thomas Duncombe *c.* 1715, it sweeps for half a mile (0.8km) of lawn in a great concave curve above the valley of the River Rye. At one end is a Vanbrugh-designed Ionic domed rotunda of 1718 above a serpentining wall, one of the earliest of ha-has. Terminating the far end of the terrace is a closed circular Doric temple of a slightly later date. Through woodland planted on the river valley side are views down to the meandering river and its cascades. From the open rotunda the peep is over the pantiled roofs of Helmsley. Formality came from the straight-sided yew hedges, etoiles and avenues on the far side of the terrace. The walk to the terrace from the Vanbrugh-inspired, but Wakefield-built house, now a school, is by way of a square lawn, said to be by Barry, to a life-size Van Nost lead Father Time sundial. Walks on the far side of the terrace give on to a secret garden and an old ruined orangery. To the west of the terrace, from the Tuscan temple along another escarpment, a walk turns off into the Terrace Bank Wood wherein is the tallest lime (154ft, 47m) and the tallest ash (148ft, 45m), in this country.

1 m SW of Helmsley on minor road S of castle

SE 6083 (OS 100)

Open May to end Aug
W 1000-1600

♿ (1 m walk)

Harlow Car Gardens NORTH YORKSHIRE

Northern Horticultural Society, Crag Lane, Harrogate.
tel. Harrogate (0423) 65418

Harlow Car Gardens, of some 60 acres (24ha), set out to be the 'Wisley of the North' when started upon by the Northern Horticultural Society in 1948, when only the roughest of pasture and overgrown woodland and an old hydropathic mineral spring establishment were there. Today it ranks as one of the finest of post-war garden creations. Apart from its native woodland, underplanted with rhododendrons, and its arboretum with its nature trail, wild life pond and hide, the garden acts as a touchstone for northern gardeners for almost every department of gardening. There are trials of heathers, delphiniums, annuals, perennials, roses and vegetables. The gardens accommodate the national collection of hypericums, a replica one of pyracanthas, one of the four 'vegetable sanctuaries' for endangered kinds. There are both vegetable and fruit plots and display collections of cane fruits, strawberries, and the national collection of rhubarb. Its model suburban gardens and collections of hostas, bergenias, hellebores, its peat garden and both limestone and sandstone rock gardens are object lessons in growing, as are the hedging and ground cover trials and the bog garden by the streamside. A most colourful display house gives shelter for a rare collection of alpines with an eclectic collection of greenhouse plants.

On SW outskirts of Harrogate on B6162

SE 2854 (OS 104)

Open throughout year daily 0900-dusk

P WC ⊖ ⊟ ● ⊼ ⌘ ⚹ ★

Newburgh Priory NORTH YORKSHIRE

Capt. V. M. Wombwell, Coxwold
tel. Coxwold (034 76) 435

Gardening has gone on here since 1145, when an Augustine priory was built on the site, of which old stew ponds still tell their historic story. The outstanding feature of the entrance drive are vast topiary yews cut into the shape of an earl's coronet, created before 1803 when the last Earl Fauconberg died. Topiary continues on the house front interspersed with flower beds. By the side of the house leading the eye over the lake, man-made in 1780, is an avenue of topiary peacocks, birds and dogs. Straight ahead from the house front is a cherry avenue, and to the right is a tree-lined avenue to the Wild Water Garden, a grand conception of Captain V. M. Wombwell created in 1938. Different trees of the avenue are marked by plaques to show they were planted by royalty. The water garden on a sloping hillside is filled with rhododendrons, azaleas, bamboos, astilbe, acers, flowering trees and shrubs. On level ground at the foot of the slope are many variously shaped stone troughs and containers of rare and unusual alpines. In a roofless building by the house are lawns surrounded by narrow borders containing figs. A walled kitchen garden still holds vegetable and fruit and walls filled with both fruit and climbers. In the house are two oil paintings of the garden as it was in the early 1700s, and a vault holding Cromwell's headless body.

3½ m SE of Thirsk on A19 turn E to Coxwold and Newburgh Priory

SE 5476 (OS 100)

Open mid May to end Aug W also Su in Aug 1400-1800; parties of 20 or over on other days by appt

🅿 WC ♿ D ☕

Newby Hall NORTH YORKSHIRE

R. E. J. Compton, Esq., Ripon.

Gardening has gone on here since Sir Edward Blackett built Newby in 1705, extended by Robert Adam in the mid-1700s. Early drawings show a square and compass layout. Remaining from those days is the 18th-century east to west walk edged by 17th-century Venetian statuary against yew and purple plum, and the elegant balustrading on the south front. It was the late Major Edward Compton who took over a Victorian garden in 1921, including the stepped and water-coursed rock garden attributed to Ellen Willmott, and the long (1,050ft, 320m), wide sloping border from the house down to the River Ure. In 1929 he converted croquet and tennis lawns into a species rose, a July and an autumn garden. In what was a period sunken rose garden he created Sylvia's garden, planted with his late wife's favourite flowers. Near what was once an iris walk is the long, winding pergola walk. A tropical garden near the river shelters behind its high walls many magnolias, *Azara microphylla*, *Xanthoceras sorbifolium*, *Embothrium lanceolatum* and *Carpentaria californica*. There is a 150-year-old tulip tree, *Liriodendron tulipifera*, and in sun-spangled woodland stand hydrangea, camellia, rhododendrons, many acers and a wealth of spring flowers. The large kitchen garden is now a children's playground and unobtrusively round the rockery edge runs a miniature train.

2 m SE of Ripon on
B6265 turn S at Bridge
Hewick

SE 3467 (OS 99)

Open Apr to end Sept
daily exc M but inc Bank
Hol M 1100-1730

P WC ♿ (1 m walk) 🚌
🍴 ⛲ 🎁 ✿ ★
🏛 (limited opening)
🚂 Miniature railway
and steam boat

Rievaulx Terrace NORTH YORKSHIRE

The National Trust, Rievaulx, Helmsley.
tel. Bilsdale (043 96) 340

Rievaulx Terrace of 1754 by Thomas Duncombe, son of the creator of Duncombe Terrace which, evidence shows, was to have been linked to Duncombe, is one of the outstanding achievements of 18th-century picturesque and romantic landscapes. Its serpentining half mile (0.8km) of grass lawn innovatively breaks away from any formal line-up and from this winding walk, high above Ryedale, are seen from the almost precipitous escarpment 13 differing bird's-eye views of the 1131-founded Rievaulx Abbey. Originally the wavy line of trees on the far side was interplanted with flowering shrubs and a gateway here was the entrance to the terrace off the estate road from Duncombe. At the terrace beginning is a Palladian Ionic temple, used as a banqueting house, with furniture by Kent, exquisite frescoes by Borgnis *c.*1760, and elaborately carved woodwork. At the far end is a domed Tuscan temple of 1758, circular and on a raised podium, its interior enriched by colourful Italian plasterwork. From its raised platform the view is into the valley of the Rye, the abbey, a medieval pack horse bridge and over moors, ridge and vale to the distant Cleveland Hills. Visitors so overcome by the sheer majesty of this imaginative conception have been known to walk the lawns in bare feet!

2½ m NW of Helmsley on B1257

SE 5784 (OS 100)

Open Apr to end Oct daily exc Good Fri 1030-1800

P WC ⊟ D ⚹ ★ ⛨

Ripley Castle NORTH YORKSHIRE

Sir Thomas C. W. Ingilby, Bart. Ripley, nr Harrogate.
tel. Harrogate (0423) 770152

This 14th-century castle lived in by the same family since 1250 looks over a mid-18th-century Brownian landscape, though Dorothy Stroud, his biographer, does not record it. But there is no doubt when one looks from the contemporary battlemented terrace to two serpenting lakes, islanded and stemming from a crystal cascade which divides a tree-studded park of beech and oak under which deer and cattle browse, this is definitive Brown. The lake disappears in a steep cascade under a pretty Victorian ironwork bridge. From the north-facing terrace a few steps and a path take one to the walled flower garden. The wall is terminated by two balustraded, stone-built summerhouses, contemporary with the 1820 orangery in the centre. Thick-stemmed wisteria and other climbers clothe the rest of the wall under which is a herbaceous border and on the two spacious lawns are roses in ornamental beds. The central path here makes for a short avenue of fastigiate yews and a wrought-iron gate to the reserve garden where trained fruit decorates the walls and a circular brick-pillared rose pergola, flanked by box-edged parterres, is terminated by a trimmed hornbeam hedge. A narrow sun-trap garden for early fruit and vegetables is reached through a wooden door. The orangery leads to a long woodland walk to a temple vista stop and under a stepped stone platform for a bird's eye view of garden and village.

3½ m N of Harrogate
on A61

SE 2860 (OS 99)

Open Apr to end Sept
daily 1100-1800;
reduced rates for
parties of 25 or over

Peak months July to
Aug

P WC ⊖ ⊟ D ☕ ✿ ⚘
★ ☎ (limited opening)

Studley Royal Country Park

NORTH YORKSHIRE

The National Trust, nr Ripon.
tel. Sawley (076 586) 333

If the South Sea Bubble had not burst this unique landscape would probably have never existed. For Chancellor John Aislabie retired here in disgrace and from around 1730 until his death in 1742 transformed the wild, rugged, steep-sided narrow valley of the River Skell into a shimmering formal garden set in magnificent greenery. The Skell was formed into a large lake running by grotto cascades into canals to form the Moon Pool and its two adjoining crescent-shaped pools. The water then runs over a formal rusticated cascade between two Venetian fishing houses into a large lake and a steep, hillside waterfall on its far side. Buildings both Gothic and classical adorn the grounds, a beautifully proportioned banqueting house by Colin Campbell of *c.*1727, the Temple of Piety, lead statues by the waterside and, over stepping stones by the last cascade, an uphill path leads to a steep, stygian, rocky tunnel grotto. This leads to a high viewing walk starting from an octagonal Gothic folly to Tent Hill, to Surprise View, where, through a door in a small building, in the distance by the Skell, stands Fountains Abbey. William, John's son, added a Chinese temple, no longer there, and the obelisk terminating a long avenue of trees aligned on the towers of Ripon Cathedral.

2 m SW of Ripon on B6265 turn S to Studley Royal

SE 2869 (OS 99)

Open throughout year daily exc 24 and 25 Dec; Oct to Mar 1000-1600; Apr, May, June and Sept 1000-1900; July and Aug 1000-2000

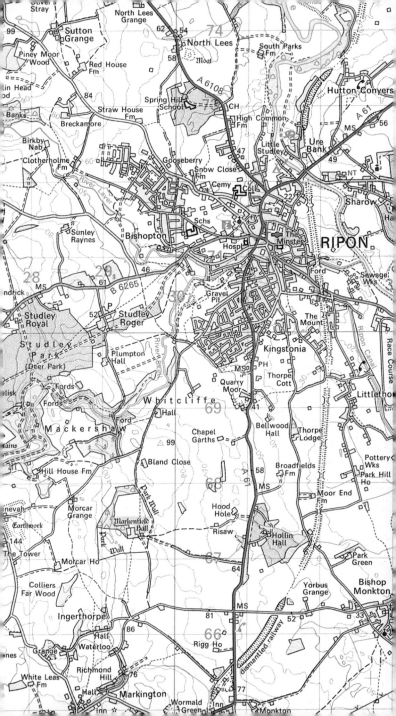

Sutton Park NORTH YORKSHIRE

Mrs N. M. D. Sheffield, Sutton-on-the-Forest, York.

Sutton Park is a 1962 creation by Percy Cane of a terraced garden using the original terracing and planted up in a most colourful and tasteful way by the owners since that time. The garden surrounds a medium-size Georgian house framed by lawns and a paved terrace with views over pastoral landscape said to be by Brown. The south garden side of the house has the spacious paved terrace, in York stone, punctuated with grass and beds. Wide stone steps lead to the first terraced rose garden with beds set in trim turf behind which are statues surrounded by the scented autumn-flowering *Clematis flammula*. The last terrace is marked by a lily tank and terminates in a high beech hedge shaped into a semi-circular niche for a white marble seat. There are delicate ironwork gazebos on one of the terraces and at the side of the house is a paved and pebbled area broken by beds of lavender and hydrangea in orange tubs, a present from Blenheim Palace. Glades on the east side of the terraced gardens lead to a woodland walk between forest trees, exotic and Japanese cherries to a temple, all created by the present owners. Columnar conifers most skilfully placed by the terrace walls add height to the picture, and planting has been carefully designed to give differing colour patterns, as on the paved terrace where mauve, grey and pink predominate.

8 m N of York on B1363

SE 5864 (OS 100)

Open Apr Su; May to end Sept Su, T; Bank Holidays 1330-1730; other times by appt; reduced rates for parties

Peak months Apr to July

P WC ⊖ 🍴 🍽 ⚹ ★ 🐕 ⛄

Thorp Perrow Arboretum   NORTH YORKSHIRE

Sir John Ropner, Bart, Park House, Bedale.

This is the finest arboretum in the north of England. It was started by the late Sir Leonard Ropner when his father gave him 40 acres (16ha) of rough fields about 45 years ago, which he continued to plant until his death. It is noted for rare trees, collections of species such as acers, oaks, walnut and conifers including cedrus, chemaecyparis and spruce. There is also a very fine cherry avenue. Both trees and shrubs have been so placed as to form contrasting glades, rides and avenues to depict the contrasting colours of foliage and differing outlines. Among the oaks are to be found *Quercus frainetto*, *phellos* and *camariensis* and an avenue of red oaks, *Q. rubra*. One of the features is the discerning planting of individual species to contrast with others, such as planes beside Camperdown elms, the wing nut tree beside balsam poplars, while *Acer saccharum* fights in autumn to out-colour *Betula maximowieziana*. A trout-filled lake separates the arboretum from formal lawns, topiary, shrub- and flower-filled borders on the house front. A large walled kitchen garden shelters trained wall fruits, greenhouses to bring on early pears and plums, and provides a standing ground for young trees and a garden plant sales area.

10 m NW of Ripon on
A6108 turn E onto
B6267 for 3 m turn N to
Well and Thorp Perrow

SE 2685 (OS 99)

Open Apr to mid Nov
daily 0900-dusk

Peak months Apr, May
Oct and Nov

P WC ⊟ D ⊼ ⚹

University of York Gardens

NORTH YORKSHIRE

Heslington, York.

A water garden on a grandiose scale has been constructed at York University; it has been created since 1950 yet is engagingly married to the Elizabethan Heslington Hall. The Hall's own garden is of massive topiary yews and a charming gazebo reached by steps, the old and new being cleverly linked by a canal pool and a small fish pool, part of a 19th-century landscape attempt, which now form the headwaters of a large lake around which many of the university buildings are grouped. The suggestion for this waterscape came from the late Frank Clark and was carried out by a committee. It is a most imaginative layout with Rialto-type bridges, covered walks above the water, stepping stones, fountains, a harbour side with slipways and bollards with buildings which in some cases hang over the lake, and in others rise from it in Venetian fashion. Trees and flowers, lily tanks and loggia promenades link the colleges and the waterscape, while wild fowl on the water and boating make for life and movement on the scene. A Henry Moore group of figures finds, surprisingly, an appropriate place on the edge of the topiary garden. It is interesting to note that the construction of the 14-acre (5.6-ha) lake and the waterways generally was the cheapest way to rid the site of boggy ground and surplus water.

In SE outskirts of York; university signposted off A64 to avoid city centre

SE 6250 (OS 105)

Open daily

Peak months May to July and late Sept to Oct

WC ⊖ ⊟ (by appt) D
⏻ ⏆

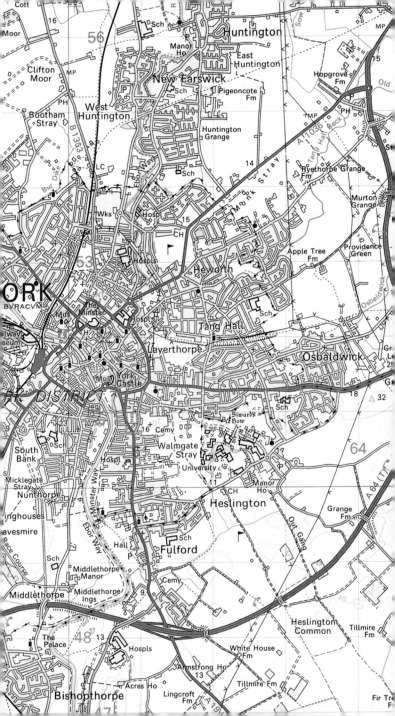

Harewood House WEST YORKSHIRE

The Earl of Harewood, Harewood, Leeds.
tel. Harewood (0532) 886225

'One of the most delectable of landscapes' wrote Dorothy Stroud of Brown's work at Harewood carried out for the 1st Earl in 1772. Here he enlarged the lake, moulded the rough farmland into an undulating park to match scenic Wharfedale, planted trees and banished the pleasure grounds to beyond the lake. A change of character came in 1843–48 with the Barry terrace on the south front of the house from where the view is still of Brown at his best. This balustraded terrace with its statuary and fountains is now being restored to its Victorian parterred splendour. The side lawns and walk under the terrace are planted with specimen trees, climbers, rhododendrons and flowering shrubs. A path passing the Carr stable block and bird garden goes downhill through thick woodland to the cascade bridge at the far end of the lake which overlooks a sunken garden – a bowl of rhododendron and azalea colour with a Japanese look stemming from the rocky stream, lined with gunneras, primulas and astilbes, and its oriental-style summerhouse. The path then leads through mature woodland underplanted with rhododendrons, many bred at Harewood, to the pleasure and rose gardens. The roses, mainly large and cluster flowered, are in two terraces. On the lawn overlooking the lake is a period summerhouse built into the wall by ancient mulberry trees and more rose beds.

8 m N of Leeds at junction of A659 and A61

SE 3144 (OS 104)

Open Apr to end Oct daily; Feb, Mar, Nov Su 1000-dusk; reduced rates for parties

Peak months late May to Oct

P WC ⊕ (1 m walk) ⊟ D ● ⇷ ⊛ ⚹ ★ ⛺ Bird garden

Lotherton Hall WEST YORKSHIRE

Leeds City Council, Aberford.

The skilful use of sun-orientated walls and shelter belts of trees has made this 10-acre (4-ha) garden in the Plain of York a congenial home of tender trees, shrubs and climbers rare in the North. It is the creation of the late Mrs L. G. D. Gascoigne in the early part of this century, very probably advised by her great friend Miss Ellen Willmott of 'Genus Rosa' fame. Both house and garden were given to Leeds Corporation in 1968 by her son, Sir Alvary. A formal rose garden in box-edged parterres is on the garden front where a border under a sheltering wall is a study in blue. At right-angles to the rose garden an avenue of Victorian pyramidal yews leads the eye to a vista stop of a white period summerhouse. Through the stolidly buttressed yew hedge is the walled sun-trap garden where flower, surprisingly, a range of slightly tender shrubs. Roses and heliotrope in box-edged borders scent the garden in high summer. Through a wrought-iron gate a William and Mary sunken garden is reached, with spiral box, classical urns and a lily pool. Beds around are full of herbs, and walls give shelter to plants which are rare for these parts. The ha-ha, now filled in, is a mecca for primula, astilbe and meconopsis and the giant hogweed. A rockery glen of 1912 with its mature accompanying acers is an 'up-and-down' walking experience, and nearby is one of the earliest of brick-on-edge tennis courts. There are working shire horses and a large aviary.

3½ m NE of Garforth on B1217

SE 4436 (OS 105)

Open throughout year daily 1030-dusk

Peak months spring and late summer

P WC 🚻 D ♥ 🏛 ★ ☎

Temple Newsam House WEST YORKSHIRE

Leeds City Council, Leeds.
tel. Leeds (0532) 645535

The gardens surrounding this Elizabethan mansion were first mentioned in a letter dated 1535 and there is a Knyff drawing of 1699 showing formal avenues and geometrically laid out formal gardens near the house. Today the long walk to the kitchen gardens is hedged in by massed rhododendrons and azaleas backed by laburnums, and mature forest trees. On the way note the Sphinx Gate, of 1768, designed by Lord Burlington and erected by Brown. As the visitor finally reaches a wooden bridge over a small lake, there are again, banked high on the far side, massed rhododendrons and azaleas beautifully reflected in the water. A steep uphill walk through woodland comes to the walled garden where in spring thousands of polyanthus are bedded out to be followed by annuals. This leads to the well-stocked rose garden and long lean-to greenhouses. From the three-sided square of the house, with its recently created brick maze, the view is over the rolling Capability Brown landscape to an open temple on a hilltop. Beyond is the long straight woodland walk to the village of Carlton, designed with bridge, three lakes and cascades, now silted up, by William Etty between 1712 and 1715. In front of the house a Jacobean garden of formal parterres, a water feature and pleached lime avenue have recently been laid out. On the far side of the house are two laburnum arbours. There is a model farm and unusual cattle and deer graze the park.

2½ m E of Leeds on A64 turn SE onto A63 turn S after 1 m at Halton

SE 3532 (OS 104)

Open throughout the year T-Su (and Bank Hol M) 1030-1815 (dusk if earlier); May to Sept W 1030-2030

P WC ⊞ ⏹ ⛩ ⚘ ★ ♨

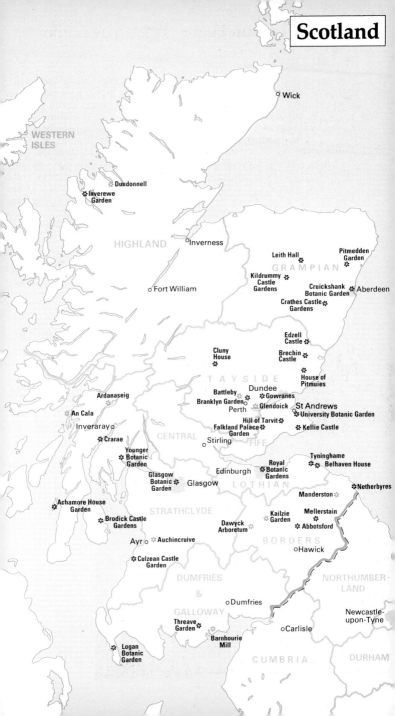

Scotland

Wick

WESTERN
ISLES

Dundonnell
Inverewe
Garden

HIGHLAND   Inverness

Fort William

Leith Hall   Pitmedden
Garden

GRAMPIAN

Kildrummy
Castle
Gardens   Cruickshank
Botanic Garden   Aberdeen

Crathes Castle
Gardens

Edzell
Castle

Cluny
House   Brechin
Castle

TAYSIDE   House of
Pitmuies

Ardanaseig   Dundee
Battleby   Gowranes
Branklyn Garden   Glendoick   St Andrews
An Cala   Perth   University Botanic Garden

Inveraray   Hill of Tarvit   Kellie Castle
Falkland Palace
Garden   FIFE

Crarae   Stirling

CENTRAL

Younger
Botanic
Garden   Tyninghame
Royal
Botanic   Belhaven House
Glasgow   Edinburgh   Gardens
Botanic   Glasgow   Manderston
Garden   LOTHIAN   Netherbyres

Achamore House   Kailzie
Garden   Mellerstain

Garden   STRATHCLYDE   Dawyck   Abbotsford
Brodick Castle   Arboretum
Gardens   BORDERS

Ayr   Auchincruive   Hawick

Culzean Castle
Garden

DUMFRIES   NORTHUMBER-
LAND

&

GALLOWAY   Dumfries   Newcastle-
upon-Tyne

Threave   Carlisle
Garden
Logan   Barnhourie   CUMBRIA   DURHAM
Botanic   Mill
Garden

Abbotsford BORDERS

Mrs P. Maxwell-Scott, Melrose, (Roxburghshire).
tel. Galashiels (0896) 2043

It would be quite intolerable to believe that a property which was at one time the home of Sir Walter Scott could have an indifferent or characterless garden. Sir Walter's love of trees is widely appreciated, and his devotion to his garden is no less apparent. The house was built between 1817 and 1821 on a terrace above the right bank of the River Tweed. To the south of the house a formal garden has been developed as a combination of precisely trimmed yew hedges and historic sculpture, such as the five medallions which came from the old Mercat Cross in Edinburgh and which are inset in the hedge. The bowl of the centrally positioned fountain in the garden was also a part of the same Mercat Cross, and the formality is maintained with four yews planted one at each corner of the fountain lawn. At the other side of the house the garden drifts into the beautiful countryside associated with this stretch of the River Tweed; with the river itself, so beloved by Scott, passing close to the house. Beyond the river are pleasant groups of trees, many of which are reputed to have been planted by Scott himself. On either side of the south entrance one encounters plants of viburnum, old shrub roses, azalea and rhododendron. There is also an early 19th-century fernhouse with begonias, orchids and pelargoniums as well as ferns.

2½ m W of Melrose on A6091 turn SW onto B6360

NT 5034 (OS 73)

Open mid Mar to end Oct M-S 1000-1700 Su 1400-1700; reduced rates for parties

WC ⊖ 🅿 🍴 ⌂ ♿ ★ 🚻

Mellerstain House BORDERS

Lord Binning, Gordon, (Berwickshire).
tel. Gordon (057 381) 225

The formal landscape garden is a rarity in Scotland and therefore likely to
make a greater impression than it would south of the border. Kinross House is
a good example of this form of art. Mellerstain, I believe, is superb. Surprisingly enough, the landscape is a fairly recent creation, having been laid out as late as
1909 by Sir Reginald Blomfield. It relies almost entirely upon architectural
features, starting with a balustrade-topped terrace to the immediate south of
the house, with ornate stairways leading to an area formerly of intricate
parterres, now planted with roses, then to a broad grass walk with a lake in a
woodland setting. The Cheviot Hills make a focal point in the far distance. In
early summer colour is brought to the woodland by azaleas and
rhododendrons. A very appropriate addition to the property has been made
by Lord Binning's mother, the Countess of Haddington, whose love of roses
has manifested itself in a splendid collection of shrub roses to the west of the
house. Mellerstain is a remarkable monument to that great Scottish architect,
Robert Adam, with the setting for the masterpiece wonderfully achieved by
Blomfield. It is, and will, remain one of the treasures of Scotland.

8 m NW of Kelso on
A6089 turn SW

NT 6439 (OS 74)

Open Easter weekend
and May to end Sept
daily exc Sat 1230-1700;
reduced rates for
parties by appt

Peak months July to
Aug

P WC ⊖ ⊟ D ⬤ ★ 🏛

Netherbyres BORDERS

Lt. Col. S. J. Furness, Eyemouth, (Berwickshire)
tel. Eyemouth (0390) 50337

In the 40 acres (16ha) of Netherbyres parkland one can find a walled garden
with several unique features. The surrounding walls are unusual in being
elliptical, and possibly more so in being lined with bricks which originated in
Holland, and may well have found their way to this country as ballast in ships
returning from exporting linen and wool to the Low Countries. The garden
walls were constructed by William Crow, a former owner of Netherbyres,
who being a gentleman with a flair for things mathematical, doubtless
designed his garden with specific objectives in mind, although it is now
difficult to determine exactly what these may have been. About 1822 the
property passed into the hands of Captain Sir Samuel Brown, who may have
been responsible for the fine conservatory which is still extant. Finally, it was
bought by the family of the present owner. Annuals play an important role in
the present garden, together with an interesting and equally colourful
selection of shrubs and roses with vegetables to maintain the appearance of a
traditional Scottish walled garden. The fact that the particular one at
Netherbyres is unusually shaped only adds to the fascination of the property.

¼ m S of Eyemouth on
Berwick side of bridge
on A1107

NT 9463 (OS 67)

Open few times each
year under Scotland's
Gardens Scheme; other
times by appt

Peak months Apr and
July to Aug

🅿 WC ♿ 🍴 (by appt) D
🐕 ✿

Logan Botanic Garden

DUMFRIES AND GALLOWAY

Dept. of Agriculture & Fisheries for Scotland, Port Logan, by Stranraer (Wigtownshire)

Of all the gardens on Scotland's western seaboard, Logan must have the most climatically favourable position. It lies on a narrow peninsula of land reaching to the south on the western side of Luce Bay, and although greatly exposed to prevailing winds, it is nevertheless relatively free of all severe frost. The potential of the garden to grow a range of less hardy plants was recognised early this century; it is now used by the Royal Botanic Garden, Edinburgh, as an annexe for more tender plants. Logan has the appearance of being a far more exotic garden than in fact it really is. The idea is suggested by cordyline, trachycarpus and dicksonia and the tall blue spikes of *Echium pinniana* in which the garden is abundant. The more familiar sight of primula and rhododendron in the woodland remind one of the other well known attractions of the garden, which can claim to be the first to have produced the now widely accepted style of garden known as peat walls. Throughout its 14 acres (6ha) the garden is a pleasure to explore, both for its established plants and the range of more exotic subjects. For colour it is essentially a spring garden, but for the plantsman, and one is tempted to say the cool glasshouse enthusiast, Logan will provide a new adventure.

10 m S of Stranraer on A716 turn SW onto B7065

NX 0942 (OS 82)

Open Apr to end Sept daily 1000-1700

Peak months Apr to Sept

P WC ⊖ ⊟ ☞

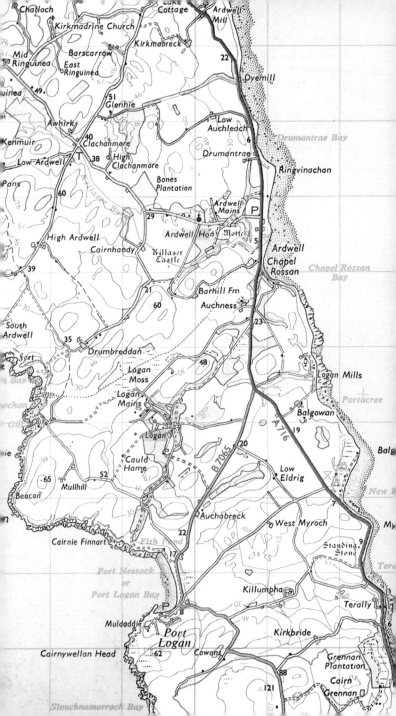

Threave Garden DUMFRIES AND GALLOWAY

National Trust for Scotland, Threave House, Castle Douglas,
(Kirkudbrightshire).
tel. Castle Douglas (0556) 2575

When Major Alan Gordon presented the Threave Estate to the Trust in 1948, the thought of establishing a school of gardening there almost certainly had been discussed, but no one could have imagined the large, varied and extremely interesting garden that would result. The School began in 1960 with the first six residential students. They, and those who succeeded them, have had the task of developing and extending the garden, and to them also has fallen a large measure of the maintenance of the 80 or so acres (32ha) of grounds. Essentially a teaching establishment, Threave has gradually acquired a wide collection of plants, as well as several types of garden embracing rock, water, woodland, rose and peat gardens, all built around the old walled garden, retained largely in the Scottish tradition of vegetable plots, or breaks dissected by paths and backed by flower beds. The walls support fruit, and several large, modern glasshouses include some designed for display and instruction. In addition to all of this, Threave has become an attraction to thousands of visitors each year. It is doubtful if even the imaginative Alan Gordon could have seen his home converted so successfully to a hostel for young people, or foreseen the immense pleasure his fields of wheat and barley would eventually provide for those who enjoy horticultural delights.

1 m SW of Castle
Douglas on A75 turn S
to Kirkland

NX 7560 (OS 84)

Open daily 0900-1700;
reduced rates for
parties

WC ⊖ D ☕ 卅 ⊛ ⚘ ★

Falkland Palace Garden   FIFE

National Trust for Scotland, Falkland Palace, Falkland.
tel. Falkland (0337) 57397

Although Falkland Palace and its garden are in the care of the National Trust for Scotland, it is a Royal residence and therefore a property of Her Majesty The Queen. During the Second World War the garden became a forest nursery and then in 1945 was again newly contrived by the then Captain, Constable and Keeper of Falkland, the late Major Michael Crichton Stuart, who commissioned Percy Cane to design a garden appropriate to the historical significance of the Palace of Falkland. Cane based his design upon a print of a former garden, modified to make the most of the relatively small 7-acre (3-ha) garden by creating seemingly long vistas over immaculately kept grass, with beds and borders around the perimeter to support the illusion of space. No attempt was made to select plants of a particular period, consequently the garden reflects the skilful ingenuity of Percy Cane seen in herbaceous borders, a wide selection of shrubs and trees, with a potentially large cut-leaved beech and a purple sycamore dominating the central grass walk. At the north end of the garden beyond a charming Victorian glasshouse, a later addition, the pool garden, is a complete contrast which is almost too severe, relying, as it does, upon foliage for effect. All the same, the Palace of Falkland makes a unique background for a most charming garden.

6 m N of Glenrothes on
A92 turn NW at Milltail
on A912 to Falkland

NO 2507 (OS 59)

Open Apr to end Sept
M-S 1000-1800 Su 1400-
1800; Oct S, Su 1400-
1800; reduced rates for
parties

Peak months June to
Sept

☉ ❋ ★ ☏

Hill of Tarvit FIFE

National Trust for Scotland, Cupar.
tel. Cupar (0334) 53127

Of the several gardens in Scotland which owe much to the inspiration and to the work of the late Sir Robert Lorimer, both Earlshall, at Leuchars, and Hill of Tarvit are especially good examples. While Earlshall incorporates the flair and exuberance of a young man bursting with ideas, Hill of Tarvit found in Lorimer the calmer, more rational man who more readily saw the attractions of the surrounding countryside and how they might be part of his landscape. It was in 1906 that Mr F. B. Sharp sought the help of Lorimer virtually to rebuild Hill of Tarvit House. At the same time Lorimer produced plans which would allow the house to fit comfortably into the pleasant and unspoiled countryside surroundings. The garden is divided by the approach drive into the upper and lower gardens. The lower garden, facing to the south, was designed in a very architectural way, with great use being made of horizontal and vertical lines provided by yew hedges, walls and a line of Irish yew. At either side of the house small, concealed rose gardens were planted, but great care was taken to ensure that these or any plants did not detract from the severe lines he had established in both the house and garden. Similarly, the upper garden has only a limited amount of colour, restricted and enclosed, and serving only as an interlude to one's enjoyment of magnificent views over the surrounding countryside.

2½ m S of Cupar on A916 turn E to Bridgend

NO 3811 (OS 59)

Open daily throughout year 1000-dusk

🅿 ⛱ 🚻 (limited opening) ♿

Kellie Castle FIFE

National Trust for Scotland, Kellie Castle, Pittenweem.
tel. Arncroach (033 38) 271

Robert Lorimer spent his boyhood at Kellie, which his father, Professor James Lorimer, had restored from a ruinous state. Here it was that Robert first developed his taste for garden design, and began by establishing the basis of creating a 'garden within a garden' seen in many gardens he subsequently made. In later years when he came to live at Kellie, his greater and more mature experience enabled him further to develop the garden, and in 1904 he received the accolade of an admirable account by Gertrude Jekyll following her visit to the garden. When the Trust acquired the property in 1970 it was a relatively simple matter to restore the garden with the help of Hew Lorimer, Sir Robert's son. Compared to gardens such as Brodick and Inverewe, Kellie is tiny, being just over 1 acre (0.4ha) in size, enclosed by a stone wall and situated on the north side of the castle, thus denying a quarter of this small area of land any direct sunlight. The object was to create a 'cottage garden'. The patterns for the new borders were gleaned from an article which appeared in the July 1906 edition of *Country Life*. Today the garden is all but complete, and seen in August is full of the colour and freshness of roses, herbaceous plants and many annuals, seemingly in gay disorder, with only the neat, regular rows of the vegetable plots and the primly cut box edging to remind one that it appears so by careful design and intention.

½ m W of Pittenweem
on A917 turn NW onto
B942 for 2¼m then
onto B9171 for 1¼m

NO 5205 (OS 59)

Open daily throughout
year 1000-dusk;
reduced rates for
parties of 20 or over

Peak months late June
to July

P WC ⊟ D 🎋 🐕
(occasional) ★ 🏛 (limited
opening)

University of St Andrews Botanic Gardens

FIFE

University of St Andrews, St Andrews.
tel. St Andrews (0334) 76161

Since its foundation in 1889, the University of St Andrews Botanic Garden has seen many changes and it was not until 1960, when 18½ acres (7.5ha) were set aside, that relative calm now prevails. The subsequent development of the garden has attracted visitors from all over the world. On offer to the discerning public are tree and shrub borders around the perimeter of the garden culminating in the central area of peat, rock and water features which contain a large number of species from all over the temperate world. There are plant order beds for the botany students to study the differences between families, and herbaceous and bulb borders for use in botanical teaching. In the early months of the year bulbs and spring-flowering shrubs provide considerable interest and this is followed by the early alpine plants drawn from mountain ranges from the four corners of the world. Peat-loving plants produce a floral display from early February commencing with rhododendrons and continuing with primulas, meconopsis, lilies, etc., and culminating with brilliant blue carpets of autumn gentians intermixed with startling autumn colours set against dark evergreens. It is a garden for all seasons for there are always plants in flower, from deepest winter to high summer.

Canongate in centre of St Andrews

NO 5016 (OS 59)

Open daily: summer 1000-1900, winter 1000-1600

WC ♿ ✤ (limited opening)

Crathes Castle Gardens GRAMPIAN

National Trust for Scotland, Crathes Castle, by Banchory (Kincardineshire).
tel. Crathes (033 044) 525

That the garden has been in existence for a great many years is clearly evident from the massive old yew hedges bordering the four small gardens on the upper level, but the present splendid display is the direct result of two people, the late Sir James and Lady Burnett of Leys. Fortunately, their skills and interests were complementary in that Sir James had a great knowledge of and love for trees and shrubs, and Lady Burnett, with a remarkable flair for colour combination, produced the outstanding herbaceous borders. There are eight small gardens in all, each with a specialised interest. The skills of both the former owners have enabled collections of several genera to be represented and a great many of the more uncommon or rare herbaceous perennials. Happily, most of these are dispersed throughout the garden, forming an important role in colour or foliage combinations rather than being grouped together as so often is the case. Sir James spent many years creating an arboretum in the policies, or parkland, but the majority of trees were destroyed in a severe gale of 1958; fortunately, several species of importance somehow managed to weather the storm. Crathes is one of the most interesting and colourful gardens on Royal Deeside, and a Mecca for the plantsman.

15 m SW of Aberdeen
on A93

NO 7396 (OS 38)

Open daily throughout
year 0930-dusk

🅿 WC ♿ 🍽 (limited
opening) 🚻 ⛽
★ (limited opening)
🎁 (limited opening)
🚶

Cruickshank Botanic Garden GRAMPIAN

The Cruickshank Trust and the University of Aberdeen, St Machar
Drive, Aberdeen.
tel. Aberdeen (0224) 40241 ext. 5247

The Botanic Garden was founded in 1898, to serve both as the University
Botanic Garden and as a place of leisure for the public. But apart from some
trees, the design of the garden dates from later. As a botanic garden, emphasis
is naturally on collections of plants for research and teaching, but the garden
also serves to present ideas in garden design and planting to the public. The
chief features are the sunken garden (conifers, rhododendrons, heathers), the
rock and water garden built in 1970 (alpines, bulbs, aquatic and marsh plants),
the woodland border (rhododendrons, meconopsis, hellebores, trillium,
gentians), the patio garden (wall, trough and paving plants) and the long
herbaceous border, with a rather 'botanical' emphasis. There is a small range of
glasshouses, open on application to the head gardener, with a large collection
of succulent plants. The garden, including a small young arboretum, covers
approximately 11 acres (4.5ha), with lawns, specimen trees and varied shrub
collections forming a frame to the special features mentioned above.

In Old Aberdeen, 1½ m
N of city centre off
Tillydrone Avenue

NJ 9507 (OS 38)

Open throughout year
M-F 0830-1630 also S
and Su; May to end
Sept 1400-1700

Peak months spring
and summer

⊖ 무 (by appt only) D 卉

Kildrummy Castle Gardens GRAMPIAN

Kildrummy Castle Gardens Trust, Kildrummy Castle, by Alford, (Aberdeenshire).
tel. Kildrummy (033 65) 264/277

In 1898 Col. James Ogston bought the Kildrummy estate and began by replacing the Lodge, the main house on the estate, with the present Tudor-style house, now the Kildrummy House Hotel. The gardens have been made in a quarry created by the production of stone for the 13th-century castle which forms a backcloth to the south of the garden. Col. Ogston made a new avenue to approach his house and then engaged a Japanese firm of landscape gardeners to transform a section of the burn passing under the bridge into a water garden. At the same time the alpine garden was made and planted by Backhouse of York in 1904. In all the garden extends to some 15 acres (6ha), of which less than an acre (0.4ha) is the rock garden, for which the property is best known. As a framework for the garden, trees (especially acer and ornamental conifers) planted in 1937 make a remarkable background for the many smaller shrubs and alpines, largely planted by Mrs Hylda Smith, the former owner and now honorary director of the gardens. As well as familiar friends it is possible to see *Corydalis cashmiriana*, celmisia or the tall Himalayan lily, *Cardiocrinum giganteum*, towering against a rocky background. The garden is delightful in spring and summer, as it is when the autumn colours of the acers create a picture which attracts many visitors.

16 m S of Huntly on A97 turn W

NJ 4516 (OS 37)

Open Apr to end Oct daily 0900-1700

Peak months May, June, Sept and Oct

🅿 WC ♿ 🚻 (by appt) D
🍴 (in car park only) 🐕
♨

Leith Hall GRAMPIAN

National Trust for Scotland, Kennethmont, Huntly, (Aberdeenshire).
tel. Kennethmont (046 43) 216 [Oct–Apr Udny (065 13) 2445]

The garden at Leith Hall owes its existence to the interest of two people, Mr and the Hon. Mrs Charles Leith Hay. It is very typical of many smaller gardens inspired by the combination of plentiful and relatively cheap manpower, plus an abundant amount of plant material which appeared in the early part of this century. Frequently the result could be bizarre, or at least nondescript, but occasionally such garden making did give rise to an end product which was as fascinating as it was individual, and such an example may be seen at Leith Hall. In all the east and west gardens extend to some 8 acres (3ha). That to the east is dominated by the two main features, namely a long serpentine herbaceous border and a rock garden. A border of roses links the rock garden with the herbaceous border, at its best in August. The west garden consists largely of a collection of shrubs, shrub roses and a few interesting trees, like *Acer griseum* and *Prunus serrula*. To the east of the house is the greater part of 236 acres (96ha) of land, presented with the property in 1949, which includes a loch and a lochside walk offering pleasant views of the surrounding countryside and considerable ornithological interest. The peace and quiet of the lovely Aberdeenshire countryside inspired the Leith Hays to make a garden here, and the same delightful unchanged atmosphere contributes in no small measure to an attractiveness quite disproportionate to the size of Leith Hall garden.

5 m S of Huntly on A97
turn SE onto B9002

NJ 5429 (OS 37)

Open daily throughout
year 0930-dusk

Peak months June to
Aug

🅿 WC ♥ ㅠ 🚻 (limited
opening)

Pitmedden Garden GRAMPIAN

National Trust for Scotland, Pitmedden, Ellon, (Aberdeenshire).
tel. Udny (065 13) 2445

Although the great garden of Pitmedden may have been a glorious and inspiring sight in its original conception by Sir Alexander Seton, a tragic fire of 1880 destroyed the house and with it any hope of knowing the designs which were used. In 1956 the National Trust for Scotland sought the help of the late Dr James Richardson to re-establish the garden. There are four parterre designs, three of which were adopted from contemporary patterns known to have existed at the Palace of Holyrood, Edinburgh; the fourth Richardson devised in the form of the Seton coat of arms. All are outlined in boxwood and filled each year with some 40,000 annual flowers, a historical inaccuracy necessary in the 20th century to attract visitors to the garden, and one, I believe, which preserves the original purpose to 'amaze and delight' those who saw it. The central walk of the 3-acre (1ha) garden is flanked by yews shaped in a contemporary style used by André le Nôtre, still to be seen at Vaux le Vicomte on the outskirts of Paris. 17th-century reproduction garden seats are being acquired to fill the yew buttresses, and suitable plants for the period are gradually being found. Pitmedden is as authentic a reproduction of a period garden as one can hope for with minimal labour and other financial restrictions. To the idealist it may be imperfect, but even they must agree that Scotland would be the poorer without it.

5 m E of Oldmeldrum
on A920

NJ 8828 (OS 38)

Open daily throughout
year 0930-dusk;
reduced rates for
parties

🅿 WC ♿ 🍽 🎋 ⚘
🏛 (Museum of Farming
Life, limited opening)

Inverewe Garden HIGHLAND

National Trust for Scotland, Inverewe House, Poolewe, (Ross and Cromarty).
tel. Poolewe (044 586) 200

In 1862, Osgood Mackenzie began to make Inverewe garden which, in the course of the next 100 years, established an international reputation for its plant content as well as the tremendous attraction it has for gardeners everywhere. High as the reputation of Inverewe may be, the gardens more than fulfil expectations. Mackenzie planted the whole area with pines, and waited for them to grow before clearing areas within the shelter they provided to grow many of the plants which now rank among the more valuable in the garden. On Mackenzie's death in 1922 his daughter, Mairi Sawyer, continued his work for a further 30 years before handing over the garden into the care of the National Trust for Scotland. Like Brodick, Inverewe owes much to a craze known as 'Rhododendron-mania' which commonly seized the country at the turn of the century. Species rhododendrons are now a feature of the garden. However, other collections are well established with primula, meconopsis, olearia and celmisia strongly in the forefront. Two extensive herbaceous borders offer a wealth of summer colour, together with a host of unusual bulbs, rare shrubs and trees, all contributing to that particular magic inside the garden, with unparalleled views of the Torridonian mountains adding to one's enjoyment.

6 m NE of Gairloch on A832 by Poolewe

NG 8582 (OS 19)

Open daily th'out year 0900-2100 (or ½ hour before dusk if earlier)

P WC ⊖ ⊟ D ☕ (limited opening) ⋔

Belhaven House LOTHIAN

Sir George Taylor (Director), The Stanley Smith Horticultural Trust, Dunbar, (East Lothian).
tel. Dunbar (0368) 63546

Belhaven is favoured by a climate which gardens on Scotland's western seaboard may well have cause to envy. It is extraordinary to find shrubs like *Colquhounia coccinea* and *Olearia semidentata* growing in an east coast garden, but they do grow, and extremely well. Belhaven House is now the home, and more importantly the garden, of Sir George Taylor, the former Director of Kew, and the Headquarters of the Stanley Smith Horticultural Trust. Sir George has added to the garden during the past 10 years or so to make it an outstanding and important collection of plants. At the front of the house one is greeted largely by dwarf rhododendrons. The garden continues around the side of the house into a more formal walled area devoted mainly to roses. An opening gives access to another walled garden, in this case used for many interesting ornamentals as well as culinary plants. A path leads to the highest point in the garden past *Eucryphia* × *nymansensis* and *E. cordifolia*, and where *Geranium wallichianum* 'Buxton's Blue' and a collection of silver-foliage plants make an unusual and interesting ground cover, to the even more sheltered downward slope. In fact this is a fascinating part of a fascinating garden. A much-prized *Abelia triflora* stands close to the foundations of former outbuildings, into which several troughs have been placed.

On A1087 in W outskirts of Dunbar

NT 6778 (OS 67)

Open once a year under Scotland's Gardens Scheme; other times by appt

Peak months Apr to May

&

Royal Botanic Garden, Edinburgh

LOTHIAN

Dept. of Agriculture & Fisheries for Scotland, Inverleith Row, Edinburgh.
tel. Edinburgh (031) 552 7171

The Royal Botanic Garden, Edinburgh, is one of three plant-taxonomic
research institutions run by the British Government. Plants are grown in
Edinburgh and at three outstations, the Younger Botanic Garden, Benmore,
Logan Botanic Garden and Dawyck Arboretum. Over 12,500 species are
cultivated from all parts of the world, but with an emphasis on plants from the
Himalaya and China. Nearly half the living plants are of known wild origin,
and the living collection is used for botanical research. The whole garden is
landscaped and plants are grown in a semi-naturalistic setting. The extensive
rock garden, with about 4,000 different species of plants, is world famous. The
exhibition plant houses which were opened in 1967 are also fully landscaped
and contain a large collection of tender plants including palms, orchids, ferns
and tropical economic plants. Two newer houses opened in 1978 display
research collections of several plant families including the *Ericaceae* (heath
family). The garden is known for its extensive collection of rhododendrons
(about 400 species). Other garden features include a wild garden, woodland
garden, arboretum, peat walls, annual and herbaceous borders, a
demonstration garden, heath garden and pond.

At Inverleith, with
access from Inverleith
Row or Arboretum Row

NT 2475 (OS 66)

Open throughout year
daily exc 25 Dec and
1 Jan M-S 0900-dusk;
Su 1100-dusk

WC ⊖ 🍴 ☕ (limited
opening) ♿ ★

Tyninghame LOTHIAN

The Rt Hon. The Earl of Haddington, KT, MC, Dunbar, (East Lothian).
tel. Dunbar (0620) 860330

Tyninghame is one of the few family estates in Scotland which has not diminished. Its tradition of gardening began in the early 17th century, and when the house was enlarged in 1828 the garden on the south side was redesigned and replanted. On the west side of the house, beyond a formal rose garden, Lady Haddington made an outstanding shrub rose garden, with a reproduction of an 18th-century folly with an Italian statue of Summer as a centrepiece. The excellent selection of roses is supported by colour combinations of clematis and herbaceous plants such as cimicifuga and bulbous plants like agapanthus. In contrast, a 4-acre (1.6-ha) walled garden has been greatly simplified by the removal of herbaceous borders, leaving only what were considered to be outstanding features. The 'apple walk' is such a one, first planted in 1891 as a pergola of closely planted trees and covering a distance of over 400ft (122m). Classical statues stand on well maintained grass against a yew hedge, replacing the borders formerly used to decorate this area of the garden. A woodland garden is rich with azalea, rhododendron, philadelphus and even embothrium. Beneath the light shade of large oaks grow sorbus and acer and the enormous spread of a large parrotia. Throughout drifts of primroses and wild hyacinths are yet another delight in this garden of so many different horticultural treasures.

4 m W of Dunbar on A1 turn N onto A198 for 2 m

NT 6179 (OS 67)

Open June to end Sept M-F 1030-1630

P WC ⊖ (1 m walk) 🚻 ♿

Scoughall

New Mains

Whitekirk Covert

Peffer Burn

Pefferside

Peffer Sands

83

Cairn

82

Tithe Barn

Whitekirk

Whitekirk Br

Lochhouses

9

11

Ravensheugh Sands

Frances Craig

St Baldred's Cradle

Tyninghame Links

Garleton Walk

8

Tyne P

60

61

Limetree Walk

62

63

P

64

Binning Wood

17

The Avenue

Tyne Sands

80

Gardens

Mon

Tyninghame Ho

Church

Sandy Hirst

Lawhead

P

Tyninghame

dside

36

5

B1407

Salt Greens Plantn

Heckies Hole

Hedderwick Hill

Firth Plantn

River A198

Preston Mains

14

Preston

78

Ford

Knowes

Kirklandhill

Weir

Standing Stone

Tynefield

MP

A 1 (T)

23

Beltonford

A 1081

Wes

Mill Weir

cot

Phantassie

NTS

Ninewar

Hedderwick

LC

North Belton

77

Howmuir

Biel Water

EAST LINTON

76

Beesknowe

Bielhill

Biel

Bielmill

Bielgrange

Sunnyside

Grangemuir

09

08

Pitcox

75

Ginglet

81

Meiklerig Wood

gate

Ruchlaw Mains

Church

Well

Meiklerig

Luggate Burn

P

Eastfield

Ruchlaw

Stenton

117

Achamore House Garden STRATHCLYDE

D. W. N. Landale, Esq., Isle of Gigha.
tel. Gigha (058 35) 253

Lying off the Mull of Kintyre in West Scotland, there are several small islands, including Colonsay, Jura and the smallest of all, the Isle of Gigha (pronounced Gia). Barely 3 miles (5km) long by no more than one mile (1.6km) at its widest point, it is nevertheless one of the most fertile of the Hebridean isles. Wild flowers in May are a marvellous sight. This small, windswept island was purchased in 1944 by the late Lt Colonel Sir James Horlick, Bt., who made Achamore House his home, and the land that surrounds it into a splendid and most remarkable 60 acres (24ha) of woodland garden. Sir James brought from his former Berkshire home laundry basketsful of rhododendrons, including many of his own hybrids, as the basis for his new garden. To these he added many more during the 29 years he continued to live on Gigha. It surprises many early visitors to find avenues lined with *Rhododendron ciliatum*, or carpets of candelabra primulas, the outstandingly vivid colours of the azalea garden, as much as the glades of wild hyacinths in more open woodland, amazingly sheltered from westerly winds. A walled garden serves both for vegetable growing and to house many outstanding treasures, such as *Rhododendron sinonuttallii*, *Metrosideros*, *Azara dentata* and a handsome and very uncommon *Abies delavayi* var. *delavayi*.

3 m off Mull of Kintyre; take ferry from Tayinloan, 17 m S of Tarbert on A83; gardens 1 m S of ferry terminal

NR 6447 (OS 62)

Open throughout year daily 1000-dusk

Peak months Apr to June

P WC 🚻 D 🍴 ⛱ ♿
★ (limited opening)
🚶

Brodick Castle Gardens   STRATHCLYDE

National Trust for Scotland, Brodick Castle, Brodick, Isle of Arran.
tel. Brodick (0770) 2202

Brodick Castle had been the home of the Dukes of Hamilton since 1503, and remained as such until the death of Mary, Duchess of Montrose caused the estate to be accepted in lieu of estate duty, at which time it was placed in the care of the National Trust for Scotland. The garden now has an almost international reputation for the remarkable collection of rhododendrons to be found there. Rather surprisingly, it is not old, having been begun by the late Duchess in the 1920s with a large initial stock from Muncaster, Westmorland, and Tresco, Isles of Scilly. Contributions from plant-collecting expeditions proved very rewarding and undoubtedly many of these provided the basis of the outstanding quality of the plants which now exist. The other notable part of the garden is the formal walled garden to the east of the castle, which has the date 1710 inscribed in the lintel of the north door. Formerly a kitchen garden, it was developed as a rose garden by the Duchess and has recently been restored to the Victorian style in which it was first conceived by her. There are many fine trees, which include exotic Chilean plants like the lantern tree (*Crinodendron*), and the magnificent *Populus lasiocarpa* and several *Nothofagus*. The woodland garden is a wonderfully fragrant place to be in spring, while the restored Victorian garden supplies ample colour during the summer.

1½ m N of Brodick on A841

NS 0137 (OS 69)

Open throughout year daily 1000-1700; reduced rates for parties

P WC ⊖ ⊟ D ⯑ (limited opening) ⯑ (limited opening) ⯑

Crarae Woodland Garden STRATHCLYDE

Sir Ilay Campbell Bart. (Trustee), Crarae Garden Charitable Trust, Inveraray, (Argyll).
tel. Minard (0546) 86633

Crarae is one of the delights of Scottish gardens. It was made in a glen down which the Crarae burn flows, having been started by Lady Campbell of Succoth in 1912, and expanded by the late Sir George Campbell who, by the time of his death in 1967, had created a garden which had become internationally known and respected. To wander through the 40-acre (16-ha) garden in spring is a pleasure one has to experience to appreciate fully. The path offers a dramatic view over the lower stretch of the Crarae burn to Crarae Lodge surrounded by acer and eucryphia, backed by a low hill clothed with azaleas, and the Lodge itself furnished with interesting plants such as *Hydrangea integerrima*. The path follows the course of the burn as it rises to over 100ft (30m) above the waters of the loch, past the impressive shape and size of the large-leaved rhododendrons, *R. macabeanum* and *R. hodgsonii*, and strategically placed plants of *Clethra delavayi* and *Disanthus cercidifolius* to the western limits of the garden. It is around this area that further expansion has been made to the garden in recent years to include more species of eucalyptus, several of the fragrant *maddenii* series of rhododendrons, set in a magnificent backcloth of pines and larch. This is an outstanding collection of plants in a beautiful and natural setting; it is undoubtedly one of Scotland's great gardens.

13½ m SW of Inveraray on A83

NR 9897 (OS 55)

Open Mar to end Oct daily 0900–1800

Peak months spring and autumn

P WC ⊟ D ⌘

Culzean Castle Garden and Country Park

STRATHCLYDE

National Trust for Scotland, Culzean Castle, (Ayrshire).
tel. Kirk Oswald (06556) 27

The south-west side of Culzean Castle is occupied by a formally designed fountain court garden, immediately in front of an attractive terrace built by Robert Adam, who was also responsible for the present design of the castle, as well as the home farm, now the country park centre. Throughout the woodland, areas have been selected for specialised treatment so that a pleasant country walk will unexpectedly give way to a colourful glade, such as that found around the camellia house, a Victorian Gothic-style building where magnolias, camellias and rhododendrons provide a variable interest in spring and early summer. Summer and early autumn are catered for in the extensive herbaceous borders and rose garden found in the walled garden. General plant interest is not lacking as one may see from long-established trees of libocedrus or *Pinus montezumae* and several eucalyptus or pittosporum. Since becoming a country park in 1969, financed by four local authorities, both the garden and countryside activities have given pleasure and relaxation to many thousands of visitors who find the castle, excluded from the country park, combines well with the several interests in the grounds to make an enjoyable day for the family.

4 m W of Maybole on
B7023, then off A719

NS 2309 (OS 70)

Open throughout year
daily 1000-dusk;
reduced rates for
parties exc July and
Aug

Peak months Apr to Oct

▣ WC ⊖ ⊟ D ➾ (limited
opening) ⌂ ⚹ ⚹
★ (limited opening)
🏛 (limited opening)

Glasgow Botanic Gardens   STRATHCLYDE

City of Glasgow Parks Department, Great Western Road, Glasgow.
tel. Glasgow (041) 334 2422

The gardens offer an extensive range of interest for visitors and act as a widely used resource centre. Links with the University of Glasgow date from their foundation in 1817 and they have been owned by the City since 1891. The Kibble Palace, just a few yards from the main gate, makes a good starting point for a visit. This large curvilinear iron glasshouse, named after John Kibble who had it erected here in 1873, is of special architectural merit. It contains a world famous collection of tree ferns and plants from warm temperate regions, arranged geographically. The entrance area has two wings, one with an exhibit on 'The Plant Kingdom' and the other a visitor centre (open every afternoon throughout the summer). The main range of glasshouses consists of eleven sections, each devoted to special groups of plants. Among those of major interest are the orchids (here there is an internationally recognised collection of orchid species); the begonias (the gardens have the national collection of begonias – non-tuberous); economic plants – those used in commerce, industry and medicine. Within the 40 acres (16ha) of grounds the areas of interest include a systematic garden, a herb garden, a chronological border and an arboretum.

On Great Western Road, junction of Byres Rd and Queen Margaret Drive

NS 5865 (OS 64)

Open throughout year daily 0700-dusk

WC ⊖ ⊞ (by appt only)
D ⌂ ⚘

Younger Botanic Garden, Benmore

STRATHCLYDE

Dept. of Agriculture & Fisheries for Scotland, nr Dunoon.

The estate of Benmore became the property of the nation in 1928. Since then the Younger Botanic Garden has served as an outstation of the Royal Botanic Garden, Edinburgh with help from the Younger Benmore Trust. Benmore is renowned for its collection of flowering shrubs and its extensive plantings of many species of coniferous trees. There are over 250 species of *Rhododendron* which flower from January to September, but the time to see the greatest number in flower is between the end of April and the beginning of June. The most spectacular of the conifers are the giant redwoods from California which were planted between 1865 and 1870 and form the entrance avenue. The climatic conditions at Benmore are excellent for conifers and many trees are among the largest in the British Isles.

6¾ m N of Dunoon on A815 turn W to Benmore for ½ m

NS 1385 (OS 56)

Open Apr to end Oct daily 1000-1800

Peak months May, June, Sept, Oct

P WC ● 日 D ● (exc S) 卅

Branklyn Garden TAYSIDE

National Trust for Scotland, Dundee Road, Perth.
tel. Perth (0738) 25535

It was in 1922 that John and Dorothy Renton built their home, Branklyn. In subsequent years their interest in ericaceous and alpine plants increased as their knowledge extended, and so their garden grew until it reached the present size of just under 2 acres (0.8ha). Dorothy Renton was undoubtedly a cultivator of great ability. Fortunately for them they lived at a period especially rich in the results of plant-collecting expeditions: their friends included, among others, George Sherriff. Specialities of the garden are numerous. Primulas and meconopsis are the backbone of an extensive collection, which includes rhododendrons, trees and shrubs, and an outstanding representation of alpine plants. To house all this there are two sections of rock garden, one recently rebuilt and extended, and a series of peat walls in various parts of the garden. At the far east end there are several large rhododendrons, of which *R. fictolacteum* and *R. baurevie* are especially good. Most of the well known meconopsis are represented, plus one or two rarer species, like *M. sherriffii*. The alpine for which the garden is particularly well-known is the fortunately now not so rare, *Paraquilegia anemoides*. It is indeed an outstanding plant with clear blue flowers and grey foliage. John Renton bequeathed Branklyn to the National Trust for Scotland in 1967. Today it reflects the interests of the Rentons and remains as a lasting memorial to two enthusiastic gardeners.

1½ m E of Perth on A912

NO 1222 (OS 58)

Open Mar to end Oct daily 1000-dusk

Peak months Apr to June

🅿 ⊖ ⚘

Brechin Castle TAYSIDE

Rt Hon. The Earl of Dalhousie, Brechin Castle, Brechin, (Angus).
tel. Brechin (035 62) 4566

By comparison with some other Scottish castles, Brechin is late, having been built by Alexander Edward in 1711. The garden and policies also have their origins from about that period. In all, there are now in the region of 40 acres (16ha) of garden, much of it being woodland, especially good to see in spring when rhododendrons are in flower. The walled garden consists of an upper level with attractive greenhouses, dating from the mid-19th century, as a centrepiece. The south-facing walls are used to grow plants of questionable constitution. On this level there are also trees and shrubs of particular interest including a curious rhododendron, *R.* 'Elizabeth Lockhart', with leaves which are almost purple, and obviously grown for foliage rather than floral effect. Divided from the upper level by bold yew hedges, the remainder of the garden to the south slopes gently towards a pool. A number of beds have been made to house meconopsis, primulas and a fascinating collection of mainly spring-flowering shrubs. Beyond, several trees of remarkable size provide shelter and a background of colour. Brechin's most notable plant must be *Rhododendron dalhousiae*, named after Lady Dalhousie, wife of a former Viceroy of India. It has distinctive lime-green flowers and pale green leaves, and because it is not reliably hardy in this part of the country is overwintered under glass.

In SW outskirts of Brechin on A94, N of R South Esk

NO 5959 (OS 54)

Open once a year under Scotland's Gardens Scheme; other times for various charities and by appt

♿ 🚻 (by appt only) ⚘

Cluny House TAYSIDE

R. S. Masterton, Esq., Aberfeldy, (Perthshire).
tel. Aberfeldy (0887) 20795

It was in 1950 that the Mastertons bought the house and then 6 acres (2.4ha) – now 9 acres (3.6ha) – of land around Cluny in Perthshire, and set about the awesome task of creating a garden from the overgrown woodland and a bankside which descends steeply to the banks of the River Tay. Today, what is considered to be one of the best collections of primula is grown there with the Petiolaris group especially outstanding. Meconopsis is another group of plants which do particularly well here. From a relatively open area in front of the house, paths wind through a woodland emerging occasionally into more open spaces where specimen trees such as *Prunus maackii* or *Magnolia sinensis* are planted to create interest. Here also one can find the 6- or 7-ft (2-m) stems of *Cardiocrinum giganteum* on the verge of the woodland, while in partial shade of the trees grow groups of trillium, fritillaria or erythronium. Spring and early summer are especially interesting times of the year, and so too is autumn when fruits and foliage of viburnum, cotoneaster, a good cercidiphyllum and several species of acer are equally rewarding. In 1982 Bobby Masterton was awarded the Scottish Horticultural Medal for outstanding service to gardening. This honour is ably reflected in the fascinating garden he has made with the remarkable collection of plants to be seen there.

½ m NW of Aberfeldy on B846 turn E for 2½ m then N to Edradynate

NN 8751 (OS 52)

Open Mar to end Oct daily 0900-1800

Peak months Apr to June and Oct

Edzell Castle TAYSIDE

Secretary of State for Scotland, Edzell, (Angus).
tel. Edzell (035 64) 631

Edzell Castle might well have remained just another ancient monument had
not the late Dr James Richardson, formerly Chief Inspector of Ancient
Monuments, sought to restore the former glory of the pleasance originally
created by Sir David Lindsay, Laird of Edzell. It was in 1604 that Sir David
returned to Edzell, having travelled widely, and set about the creation of a
beautiful early 17th-century garden. No expense was spared in securing
highly skilled stonemasons to embellish the walls with the seven planetary
deities, the seven liberal arts and the seven cardinal virtues. Overlooking the
square garden stood the castle at one corner, with a well house at the south-
west corner and a charming corner summerhouse in the south-east. In his
restoration Dr Richardson has used a centrally positioned circular yew on a
mound as a centrepiece, with four ball-shaped yews as guardians. A square
boxwood surround encloses four major parterre patterns, each with a
subsidiary triangular parterre set inside the boxwood corners. To fill the
designs, modern red and yellow cluster flowered (floribunda) roses have been
used to effect, whereas the white and blue Lindsay colours recreated with
alyssum and lobelia may raise an eyebrow. But this is one of very few period
garden restorations in Scotland, so we should applaud the achievement, as
much as admire the very high standard of maintenance of the garden.

7 m N of Brechin on
B966 turn W by Edzell
church

NO 5869 (OS 44)

Open Apr to end Sept
M, W, F, S 0930-1900,
Th and Su 1400-1900;
Oct to end Mar closes
1600; closed 25, 26 Dec
and 1 Jan

Peak months June to
Sept

P WC ♿ D 🪑 ♿ ★

Gowranes TAYSIDE

Professor and Mrs W. W. Park, Kinnaird by Inchture, (Perthshire).
tel. Inchture (0828) 86752

When the Parks acquired Gowranes in 1967 they faced the very formidable task of creating a garden from a run-down smallholding. The area of land is almost 2½ acres (1ha) in extent, roughly diamond shaped, and has a predominantly south-facing aspect. The attraction of Gowranes is that the garden the Parks have made is of a kind which most people would like to have. The plants do not include rarities, although they are interesting and one feels are the personal choice of the owners who have obviously given very careful consideration to the potential of various areas within the garden. The banks of the burn, which runs along the south side, have the bold foliage of *Gunnera manicata* as a background for primula, iris and willows, like *Salix lanata* and *S. wehrhahnii*. Foliage and colour contrasts are clearly important as one can see from plants of fothergilla, *Yucca flaccida* and that very graceful maple, *Acer pensylvanicum*. Somewhat surprisingly, there are also plants of desfontainea, pittosporum and crinodendron, certainly on the borderline of hardiness for this part of Scotland, as well as the unusual in abeliophyllum or koelreuteria. These are but a few of those plants which one may see in the wide selection grown in the immaculately maintained garden at Gowranes. The breathtaking views to the south over the Carse of Gowrie are a most delightful and welcome bonus to what will undoubtedly be a memorable visit.

10 m NE of Perth on
A85 turn N to Kinnaird

NO 2428 (OS 59)

Open few times each
year under Scotland's
Gardens Scheme;
phone for details; other
times by appt

Peak months May to
June; Sept to Nov

🅿 WC ♿ (by appt only)
🍽 (open days only)
🌼 (open days only)

House of Pitmuies TAYSIDE

Mrs Farquhar Ogilvie, by Forfar, (Angus).
tel. Friockheim (024 12) 245

The new House of Pitmuies is reputed to have been built in 1730 and at that time it was the possession of David Ogilvie. In 1919 the property was sold to a Major Crombie who was instrumental in recreating the garden, which by this time was in a neglected state. The Crombies were the first to plant delphiniums at Pitmuies, for which the property was later to be well known. In 1945 the property was purchased by Major and Mrs Ogilvie, and later came into the possession of Mr and Mrs Farquhar Ogilvie. Sadly Mr Farquhar Ogilvie died early in 1983. The fact that Mrs Farquhar Ogilvie, the present owner, is the daughter of Mr Gerald Annesley of Castlewellan may account for much of the excellence of the present garden at Pitmuies. At the height of the season, in June and July, one has the feeling of stepping into a garden overflowing with flowers. The main attractions are herbaceous perennials, largely contained in two borders, and roses including hybrid teas (large flowered) and polyantha as well as a delightful selection of shrub roses. To extend the season in the early part of the year there are shrubs, early-flowering perennials, meconopsis and foliage plants. All this and an avenue of lime trees as well as outstanding beeches and a Spanish chestnut, all planted prior to 1877, lend Pitmuies a long-established, and rather reverent character, which is a right and proper one for such a charming and very delightful garden.

6½ m E of Forfar on A932

NO 5649 (OS 54)

Open May to mid Aug daily 1400-1700; other times by appt

Peak months May and July

P WC 🚻 D 🐕 (by appt only) 🎪 🏵 ❄ 🎁 (by appt)

Gazetteer

London and Southern England

Folly Farm Mrs H. Astor, Sulhampstead, Reading, Berkshire (tel Reading [0734] 302326). 7 m SW of Reading on A4, turn SE to Sulhampstead. SU 6368 (OS 175). A very well preserved and maintained example of the Edwin Lutyens and Gertrude Jekyll partnership. The garden is on several levels, each with a different planting theme and character – herbaceous border, sunken rose garden, long pool garden, informal areas of trees and shrubs with bulbs naturalised in grass. Open once a year under NGS. ⓟWC ⊖ D

Jasmine House Mr and Mrs E.C.B. Knight, Hatch Bridge, Windsor, Berkshire (tel Windsor [075 35] 64726). 1 m W of Windsor on the A308. SU 9377 (OS 175). A cleverly planned ½-acre (0·2 ha) garden begun in 1962, with long vistas and secret corners created using specimen trees, shrubs, herbaceous plants, a bonsai collection, etc., for maximum effect. Open once a year under NGS.

Shinfield Grange University of Reading, Cutbush Lane, Shinfield, Reading, Berkshire. 3½ m S of Reading, 2nd turning E off A327 after M4. SU 7468 (OS 175). A teaching garden for students of horticulture at the University of Reading, with attractive lake, ornamental walled gardens, shrubs, annuals, herbaceous and bog plants. Open all year; also Su frequently from spring to autumn. Peak months May to Oct. ⓟ⊖🅷⛟🚻🐝

Bramdean House Mrs H. Wakefield, Bramdean, near Alresford, Hampshire (tel Bramdean [096 279] 214). 10 m E of Winchester on the A272. SU 6228 (OS 185). A delightful distillation of all the very best ingredients of an English country house and garden: a mellow brick early 17th-century house hidden behind high hedges and trees, vistas through wrought-iron gates in old walls, lovely floral borders, a productive kitchen garden and everywhere a sense of tranquillity and timelessness. Open a few times each year under NGS, other times by appt. Peak months May to July. ⊖ (limited).

Fairfield House Peter Wake Esq., Fairfield House, East St, Hambledon, near Portsmouth, Hampshire (tel Hambledon [070 132] 431). 10 m SW of Petersfield, on B2150. SU 6415 (OS 196). Two contrasting walled gardens have both been redesigned to great effect in the last 14 years. Contrasting trees and shrubs, and especially shrub roses, dominate the larger garden while the smaller second garden has roses and climbers, as well as effective herbaceous plantings. Open 8 days late June under NGS; other times by appt. Peak months Apr and June. ⓟWC ⊖🅷D⛟ (S and Su only) 🐝 (occasional)

Furzey Gardens Mrs M.A. Selwood (manager), Minstead, near Lyndhurst, Hampshire (tel Southampton [0703] 812464). 2 m N of Lyndhurst on A337, turn W to Minstead. SU 2711 (OS 195). An informal garden with some 8 acres (3 ha) open to the public, with winding paths leading through the massed rhododendrons, azaleas and numerous other shrubs, a water garden with many marginal plants, thousands of spring flowers, brooms and heathers to give interest during the summer, and autumn colour in the specially chosen trees. Open daily 1000-1700 all year; closed Dec 25, 26. Peak months Apr to June. ⓟ⊖WC 🅷⛟ (occasional) 🚻 ★ 🐝

West Green House The National Trust, Hartley Wintney, Basingstoke, Hampshire. 7 m SW of Camberley on A30 turn W at Hartley Wintney. SU 7456 (OS 186). The gardens of this 18th-century red brick house are in contrasting styles. The walled kitchen garden is of particular interest, part productive and part ornamental, with herbaceous borders, flowers and shrubs, herbs and climbers. The enclosures are otherwise terraced lawns, with orangery and rustic garden house. A nymphaeum and miniature Stourhead landscape have recently been developed. Open Apr to Sept W, Th, Su 1400-1800. ⓟ⊖ (1 m walk) ★ 🐿

Coldham Dr J.G. Elliott, Little Chart Forstal, Ashford, Kent (tel Ashford [0233] 84250). 1 m NW of Ashford on A20 turn SW to Hothfield and Little Chart Forstal. TQ 9646 (OS 189). The 1½ acre (0·6 ha) garden of this 16th-century farmhouse has been reclaimed since 1971 to create fascinating habitats for unusual plants, combining informality with a sense of order. Many rare plants are on sale on the open days. Open few times a year under NGS. Peak months June and July. ▉WC ✿ (limited opening) ▩

Crittenden House Mr B.P. Tompsett, Matfield, Tonbridge, Kent. 5 m NE of Tunbridge Wells on B2015, turn E at Coltshill for ½ m. TQ 6543 (OS 188). Particularly brilliant displays in late spring and early summer are a feature of this attractive garden. The flowering trees are also lovely, wild flowers grow naturally in the old orchard, and the ponds have been richly planted with waterside-loving plants. Open few times a year under NGS. Peak months Apr to Aug. ▉WC ⊖ (1 m walk) ⊟

Hall Place The Lord Hollenden, Leigh, Kent. 2 m NW of Tonbridge on B245, turn W onto B2027. TQ 5446 (OS 188). A garden of contrasting styles surrounds the Victorian mansion: formal gardens now planted with massed colour borders, an extensive rose garden, a Dutch garden with clipped yew hedges and topiary, and an attractive wild garden. There is also an 11-acre (4·5-ha) lake, rhodo-dendrons and azaleas, and many fine trees to add to the grandeur of the grounds. Open mid-May to late June, Su 1430-1830; some of time under NGS. ▉WC ⊖ (by appt) D✿

Hever Castle Broadland Properties Ltd., Edenbridge, Kent (tel Edenbridge [0732] 865224). 1½ m SE of Edenbridge on B2026, turn E. TQ 4745 (OS 188). A spectacular example of an early 20th-century garden and park on a large scale, the creation of the wealthy Waldorf Astor around the restored Hever Castle. Contrasting styles are a major feature, with the period gardens around the house, the moat studded with water-lilies, an Italian garden with Roman antiquities, cascade and pool, a pergola, rose garden, and massed azaleas and rhododendrons among many fine trees. Open Apr to early Oct, daily exc Th in Apr, May and Sept, 1200-1700, parties other times by appt. ▉WC ⊖ (1 m walk) ⊟ (by appt) D✿⊼ ★ ▩✿✿⚘

Waystrode Manor Mr and Mrs Peter Wright, Cowden, near Edenbridge, Kent. 4½ m E of East Grinstead on A264, turn N to Cowden. TQ 4540 (OS 188). A garden for all seasons, covering some 6 acres (2·5 ha). The style is mostly informal, with groups of shrubs and specimen trees set in lawns. A more formal paved garden is richly planted; there are also ponds and an arboretum. Open a few times annually under NGS; parties at other times by appt. Peak months May to July. WC ⊟✿⊼▩

Hyde Park Dept of the Environment, The Stove Yard, Hyde Park, London W2 (tel 01-262 5484). Off Knightsbridge, Park Lane and Bayswater Rd. TQ 2780 (OS 176). One of London's green 'lungs', occupying about 380 acres (154 ha), with easy access to the West End. It contains many hundreds of mature trees and seasonal bedding plant displays, and is almost bisected by the famous Serpentine lake, covering 32 acres (13 ha), which is used for swimming, fishing and boating. Open daily all year. Peak seasons spring and summer. ▉WC ⊖⊟ (by permit) D✿⊼▩

Kensington Gardens Dept of the Environment, The Stove Yard, Kensington Gardens, London W8 (tel 01-937 4848). Off Kensington High St, Kensington Grove, Bayswater Rd. TQ 2680 (OS 176). Covering some 275 acres (111 ha), the park has a number of avenues, sunken gardens, a lime bowery, and the stunning flower walk – almost a quarter of a mile (0·4 km) of mixed annual and perennial plants. It also contains the Round Pond, the beloved statue of Peter Pan, Henry

Moore's arch, and the Serpentine Gallery. Open daily all year. Peak seasons, spring and summer. **P**WC ⊖ 🖳D 💧 🚻 🐕

Chilworth Manor Lady Heald CBE, Chilworth, Guildford, Surrey (tel Guildford [0483] 61414). 3½ m SE of Guildford on A248. TQ 0247 (OS 186). The gardens are on several distinct levels, of which the highest, built by Sarah, Duchess of Marlborough in the mid 18th century, is the terraced kitchen garden. There are terraced grass walks between old fruit trees, a herbaceous border, lawns, a paved court, an ancient stew pond and an informal woodland garden especially colourful in May and June. Open a few times each year under NGS; other times by appt. Peak months Apr to Aug. **P**WC ⊖ 🖳 D 💧 (limited opening) 🚻 🐝 (occasional; boxes of seeds and plants available in last 2 weeks in May) 🐕 (by appt)

Ramster Mr and Mrs Paul Gunn, Chiddingfold, Surrey (tel Haslemere [0428] 4422). 4 m E of Haslemere on B2131, turn N to A283 for 1½ m. SU 9634 (OS 186). A fascinating, extensive woodland garden with many good specimens of unusual trees and shrubs and spectacular displays of rhododendrons and azaleas in late May and June. Open late Apr to early June, 1400–1830. **P**WC ⊖ 🖳 (by appt) D 💧 (weekends) 🚻 🐝 ♿

Vann Mr and Mrs Martin B. Caroe, Hambledon, near Godalming, Surrey (tel Wormley [042 879] 3413). 5 m S of Godalming on A283, turn E to Hambledon; Vann is 1 m to E. SU 9837 (OS 186). A particularly good example of a Gertrude Jekyll garden faithfully perpetuated in her style. The 4½ acres (1·8 ha) combine an attractive blend of formal and informal styles with woodlands, water gardens, orchards and vegetable garden. Open a few times each year under NGS; other times by appt. Peak months Apr to June. 🖳 (by appt) D 💧 (limited opening) 🚻 (by request) 🐝 ✿

Heaselands Mrs E.G. Kleinwort, Haywards Heath, West Sussex (tel Haywards Heath [0444] 458084). 1 m S of Haywards Heath Hospital on A273, turn W. TQ 3122 (OS 198). A remarkable garden of over 20 acres (8 ha) with streams, valley ponds, woodland gardens, rhododendrons and azaleas, walled and paved gardens all richly planted, in a particularly beautiful part of the Sussex Weald. Open a few times each year under NGS; parties other times by appt. Peak months May, July and Oct. **P**WC ⊖ 🖳 (by appt) 💧 ✿

The High Beeches The Hon. Edward Boscawen, Handcross, West Sussex. 4 m S of Crawley on A23 at Handcross. TQ 2629 (OS 187). A fine woodland garden laid out early this century, now with many large, mature specimens, including acers, magnolias, rhododendrons, azaleas, pines and others. Recently more formal gardens have been made round the house. Naturalised flowers are encouraged, and unusual conifers and trees are a special feature. Open a few times each year under NGS; parties other times by appt. Peak months Apr, May, June, Oct. **P**WC 🖳 🚻 🐝

Petworth House The National Trust, Petworth, West Sussex (tel Petworth [0798] 42207). 6½ m E of Midhurst on A272. SU 9721 (OS 197). One of the finest surviving Capability Brown landscape parks, a grand setting for the great house. Deer graze in the 750 acres (304 ha) of parkland, the lake covers some 13 acres (5 ha), and there are belts and groups of trees. The pleasure grounds contain Japanese maples, rhododendrons, many mature shrubs and some magnificent trees. Open Apr to end Oct, daily exc M and F 1400–1800 (also open Bank Hols). Peak months May to Aug. **P**WC 🖳 (by appt) D 💧 🚻 ★ ♿

West Dean Gardens The Edward James Foundation, West Dean, Chichester, West Sussex (tel Singleton [024 363] 301). 5 m S of Midhurst on A286, turn SE at West Dean. SU 8612 (OS 197). The gardens cover some 30 acres (12 ha), and have retained their informal 19th-century character. The trees are outstanding; there is also an impressive colonnaded pergola, a gazebo, a spring garden, a wild garden and a walled garden. Open Apr to end Sept, daily 1100–1800. Peak months May and July. ⛿WC ⊖⛨⛩ (from 1400) ⛩☙⚘ ★

The West Country

Chyverton Mr and Mrs Nigel Holman, Zelah, Truro, Cornwall (tel Zelah [087 254] 324). 8 m NE of Redruth on A30, turn N to Little Callestock. SW 7951 (OS 200). An 18th-century landscaped garden, covering about 15 acres (6 ha), and with a very large collection of trees and shrubs in a woodland setting. Open frequently March to end May by appt, and occasional Su for charity. Peak months March to May. ⛿D

Ince Castle Gardens The Viscountess Boyd of Merton, Saltash, Cornwall (tel Saltash [07555] 2249). 2 m W of Saltash on A38, turn S to Trematon and Elm Gate. SX 4056 (OS 201). Several carefully planned, separate gardens provide great interest in design and planting in about 12 acres (5 ha). The kitchen garden and greenhouses are in productive use; there are two secluded gardens, one white and cool, the other orange, red and hot. There is a small wooded area leading to a sunken garden, and throughout the garden the walls are covered with climbers and shrubs which accompany interesting plants in the beds and borders. Open a few times each year for local charities. ⛿ WC⛩D (on lead) ⛩☙

Moyclare Mrs Louis Reid, Lodge Hill, Liskeard, Cornwall (tel Liskeard [0579] 43114). S of Liskeard station on B3254. SX 2564 (OS 201). The garden was started by the present owner when the house was built in 1927, and it covers about an acre (0·4 ha). Trees, shrubs and other plants have been carefully grouped with numerous half-hardy, variegated and tender plants. There is colour and interest all the year

round. Open all year by appt. ⛿ (limited) WC ⊖⛩⛩☙ (occasional)

Trehane Mr and Mrs D.C. Trehane and Simon Trehane Esq., Probus, Truro (tel Truro [0872] 74282). 3 m N of Truro on A3076, turn E to Trehane Barton. SW 8648 (OS 204). Half of this 10-acre (4-ha) garden around a ruined Queen Anne mansion is woodland with bulbs, the remainder of the informal garden with plantings of many kinds, including a wide range of old and uncommon herbaceous plants. There is also a fine collection of camellias. Open Mar to Aug, monthly; parties at other times by appt. Peak times Mar to Aug. ⛿D ☙☙

Trengwainton The National Trust, near Penzance, Cornwall.2 m NW of Penzance on B3312, turn S at Madron. SW 4431 (OS 203). This 12-acre (5-ha) garden rising to 400 ft (122 m) above sea level is nevertheless sheltered. Its streams provide fine conditions for primulas, arums and other water-lovers; rhododendrons, especially the scented kinds, give spring colour, followed by eucryphias, myrtles and hydrangeas. The 2-acre walled garden contains even more tender plants, which are also grown in the 19th-century banked beds. Open March to end Oct, W–S and Bank Hol M 1100–1800. ⊖⛩D

Arlington Court The National Trust, Arlington, near Barnstaple, Devon (tel Shirwell [027 182] 296). 6 m N of Barnstaple on A39, turn E. SS 6140 (OS 180). A Regency house surrounded by parkland, with many impressive trees, and woods. Shrub borders surround the house and break up the expanse of lawn, and there is a terraced garden. One of the greenhouse conservatories has been rebuilt and planted with tender rhododendrons and other shrubs. Open Easter to end Oct, daily exc S, but including Bank Hol weekends, 1100–1800. Peak months May to June. ⛿WC ⛩ (by appt) D ☙⛩☙⚘ ★ ⛨ ⚕

Bickham House The Lord Roborough, Roborough, Plymouth,

Devon (tel Yelverton [0822 85] 2478).
6 m S of Tavistock on A386, turn W to
Lopwell. SX 4965 (OS 201). A series of
gardens with shrubs – rhododendrons,
azaleas, camellias and so on – much in
evidence; also a walled rose garden, a
pond with water plants, a developing
arboretum in an old wood, and
extensive views. Open Apr and May,
Su, May Bank Hol M and infrequently
in summer under NGS. Other times by
appt. Peak months Apr and May. ▣WC
❺ (1 m walk) ▤❀

Buckland Abbey The National
Trust, Yelverton, Devon (tel
Yelverton [082 285] 3607). From
Yelverton, take road to Milton Combe
for 2½ m. SX 4866 (OS 201). The
13th-century buildings, once a
monastery and later owned by Sir
Francis Drake, are now a naval and
folk museum. The gardens contain
venerable magnolias, trees, shrubs
and other flowering plants, and box-
edged beds filled with culinary and
nosegay herbs. Open Good Fri to end
Sept daily 1100-1800, Su 1400-1800;
winter W, S, Su 130-1630. Peak season
spring. ▣WC ❺ (not Su) ▤D
● (summer season) ▥❀⋇ ★ ▨

Tapeley Park Mrs Rosamund
Christie, Instow, Devon (tel Instow
[0271] 860528). 1½ m S of Instow on
A39. SS 4729 (OS 180). A 10-acre (4-
ha) garden laid out in Victorian-
Edwardian times with much of interest
today, including a steeply terraced
Italian garden, summer house, walled
kitchen garden, pines and palms giving
an exotic background for herbaceous
borders, shrubs and climbers. Open
Good Fri to Oct daily (exc M) but
including Bank Hol M 1000-1800; Nov
to Apr, daily daylight hours. ▣WC
❺ (¾ m walk) ▤ (by appt) D ●▥❀ ★ ▨

Woodside Mervyn T. Feesey, Higher
Raleigh Rd, Barnstaple, Devon (tel
Barnstaple [0271] 43095. Off A39 in N
outskirts of Barnstaple. SS 5634 (OS
180). A sloping, south-facing garden of
some 2 acres (0·8 ha) crammed with
plants, many of them rarities, from all
over the world. Open 4 times a year
under NGS. ▣WC ❺ (limited) ▤D

Forde Abbey M. Roper Esq., near
Chard, Dorset. 2 m S of Chard on
A358, turn E at Tatworth to Chard
Junction and Maudlin Cross. ST 3605
(OS 193). Originally designed in the
18th century, the largely informal
gardens cover some 25 acres (10 ha).
There are four ponds joined by
cascades, and surrounded by colourful
borders, trees and shrubs. Beyond the
park garden is the arboretum, with its
marvellous collection of rare trees and
shrubs. Open Mar, Apr, Oct Su 1400-
1630; Easter Su and M 1400-1800; May
to Sept Su, W and Bank Hols 1400-
1800. Peak months Apr to Sept. ▣WC ▤
D ●▥❀⋇ ★ ▨

Ivy Cottage Mr and Mrs N. A.
Stevens, Ansty, Dorchester, Dorset
(tel Milton Abbas [0258] 880053).
12 m NE of Dorchester off A354. SY
7698 (OS 194). Herbaceous perennials
and moisture-loving plants grow in a
setting of mature trees in this 1½-acre
(0·5-ha) garden, in which a woodland
setting and ditch garden have been
created. Open Apr to end Sept Th, and
a few times each year under NGS and
Gardeners' Sunday Organisation. ❀

Minterne The Lord Digby, Minterne
Magna, Dorchester, Dorset (tel Cerne
Abbas [03003] 370). 9 m N of
Dorchester on A352 at Minterne
Magna. ST 6604 (OS 194). A woodland garden since the 18th century,
where mature trees provide shade for
rhododendrons, azaleas and many
unusual shrubs, with moisture-loving
plants bordering the small waterfalls
and lakes. Open Apr to end Oct daily
1000-1900. Peak months Apr and May.
▣WC ❺ (limited) ▤D

Parnham House John Makepeace
Esq., Beaminster, Dorset (tel
Beaminster [0308] 862204). 6 m N of
Bridport on A3066. ST 4700 (OS 193).
Well-maintained terraced gardens and
woodland covering 14 acres (5·5 ha)
surround Parnham, and new plantings
have been made since 1976, when it
was bought by John Makepeace. In the
formal terraces that sweep down
towards the river, cascades and narrow
channels of water are bordered by

attractive clipped yews. Open Apr to end Oct, Su, W and Bank Hols; parties only T and Th 1000-1700. Peak months May, June, Oct. ▣WC ⊖🔒D ♥🔒★🔒 furniture workshops.

Brympton d'Evercy Charles Clive-Ponsonby-Fane Esq., near Yeovil, Somerset (tel West Coker [043 586] 2528). 4 m W of Yeovil on A3088. ST 5215 (OS 183). These once famous gardens have been steadily restored over the last 10 years, with herbaceous borders, shrub beds overlooking the large pond, and a very productive vineyard. Open Easter weekend (F-M) and May to late Sept S-W 1400-1800. Peak months May to July. ▣WC ⊖🔒D♥🔒🕸🌿★🔒

East Lambrook Manor F.H. Boyd-Carpenter Esq. (director), South Petherton, Somerset (tel South Petherton [0460] 40328). 7 m E of Ilminster on A303, turn N at South Petherton, continue until East Lambrook. ST 4319 (OS 193). Admirers of the late Margery Fish and devotees of ground-cover plants should visit the intriguing garden where she lived for many years. It is divided into several small gardens by narrow stone paths, walls and small hedges. There is hardly any lawn, just beds and borders filled with unusual plants. Open daily all year 0900-1700. Peak months March, late June. ▣WC ⊖ (2 m walk) 🔒 (by appt) ♥ (by appt for parties) 🔒🕸🌿🔒 (limited opening)

Hadspen House Paul Hobhouse Esq., Castle Cary, Somerset (tel Castle Cary [0963] 50200/50427). 2 m SE of Castle Cary on A371. ST 6631 (OS 183). A sheltered, south-facing, 8-acre (3-ha) garden, including the 19th-century walled garden, with many rare and unusual plants, herbaceous borders, climbing plants, and a sunken garden. Open T-Th 1000-1700; Su (Apr-Oct) 1400-1700; other times by appt. Peak seasons spring and summer. ▣WC⊖♥🕸🌿

Corsham Court The Lord Methuen, Corsham, near Chippenham, Wiltshire (tel Corsham [0249] 712214).

3 m SW of Chippenham on A4, turn S. ST 8770 (OS 173). The Methuen family bought Corsham Court in 1745, and employed Capability Brown to design the gardens. They include herbaceous borders, a secluded garden sheltered by walls and pleached hornbeams, and a fine broad avenue of *Prunus* 'Kanzan', *Prunus padus*, malus and imposing horse chestnuts. Open mid-Jan to mid-Dec, T-Th, S and Su 1400-1600; June, Sept and Bank Hols 1400-1800. Peak season spring. ▣WC 🔒 (by appt) D🔒🕸 (occasional) 🌿🔒

Heale House Mrs David Rasch, Woodford, Salisbury, Wiltshire (tel Woodford [072 273] 207). 5 m N of Salisbury on A345, turn W at High Post to Upper Woodford. SU 1236 (OS 184). Shrub roses and perennials are a prominent feature of the mainly informal layout of this 5-acre (2 ha) garden. A Japanese tea-house and bridge provide an oriental setting for the magnolias, acers and flowering cherries in the water garden, and the kitchen garden is attractively laid out with box hedges and a pergola. Open Good Fri to autumn, M-S, also first Su in each month. ▣WC ⊖🔒 (by appt) D🔒🕸 (occasional)

The Wansdyke Nursery and the Pygmy Pinetum D. and M. Van Klaveren, Hillworth Rd, Devizes, Wiltshire (tel Devizes [0380] 3008). W of A360 in centre of Devizes. SU 0061 (OS 173). The pinetum houses the largest collection in the British Isles of dwarf and slow-growing conifers – over 1200 varieties can be found growing in rock gardens, raised beds and borders. Open all year, M-F 0800-1300, S 0900-1230. ▣WC ⊖🔒🕸

Wales and Western Counties

Arley Hall The Hon. M.L.W. Flower, Northwich, Cheshire (tel Arley [036 585] 203/284. 7 m SE of Warrington on A50, turn S at High Legh to Arley Green. SJ 6780 (OS 109). An unusual 8-acre (3-ha) garden dating from the mid-19th century with double herbaceous borders housing buttressing yews, a unique ilex avenue, pleached limes, a scented garden and walled herb garden, 18th-century walled kitchen garden, fish garden and rose garden. Open Easter to early Oct, daily (exc M but including Bank Hols) 1400-1800. Peak months mid-May to Sept. ▣WC ⊖ ⊟ (by appt) D ● ⋒ ▧ ⋇ ★ ▪

Capesthorne Hall Lt-Col. Sir Walter Bromley-Davenport, Macclesfield, Cheshire (tel Chelford [0265] 861 221/439. 6½ m N of Congleton on A34. SJ 8472 (OS 118). A series of pools and fish-stocked lake surrounded by lawns with double herbaceous and shrub borders. The spring flowers of the woodland are followed by azaleas, rhododendrons and other shrubs, and there is a further blaze of colour in the autumn. Open July to Sept, daily (exc M and F) 1200-1800; May and June, S, Su and W only; Apr Su only. ▣WC ⊖ ⊟ D ● ⋒ ⋇ ★ ▪ ⋔

Dunham Massey The National Trust, near Altrincham, Cheshire (tel 061-941 1025). 2 m W of Altrincham on A56, turn W onto B5160 to Dunham Town. SJ 7387 (OS 109). Once a garden of impressive grandeur, of which the Elizabethan mill, an orangery, a deer house, obelisks and stone statues survive. The moat stream, woodlands and herbaceous borders on the house lawns have been refurbished with a bog garden, rhododendrons and other flowering shrubs and plants. Open Apr to end Oct daily (exc F) 1100-1800. ▣WC ⊖ ⊟ D ● ⋇ ★ ▪ (limited opening)

Little Moreton Hall The National Trust, Congleton, Cheshire (tel Congleton [02602] 272018). 4 m SW of Congleton on A34. SJ 8358 (OS 118). Since passing into the ownership of the National Trust in 1938, the gardens have been restored in keeping with the 16th-century black-and-white timbered house, with a box-edged knot garden and regularly set out borders planted with appropriate flowers and herbs. A small lawn is traditionally planted with an

assortment of apples, pears and quinces. Open Apr to end Sept daily (exc T and Good Fri); March and Oct S and Su, 1400-1800. ▣WC ⊖ (½ m walk) ● (for parties by appt) ⋒ ★ ▪ Open-air play in July; concerts.

Chirk Castle The National Trust, Chirk, Clwyd (tel Chirk [0691] 777701). 6 m N of Oswestry on A483, at Chirk turn W to New Hall. SJ 2638 (OS 126). A 4½-acre (1·8-ha) landscaped garden of woods and shrubberies originally created in the 18th century, with 19th-century topiary and a new shrub garden in which some tender shrubs flourish. Open Easter Su to end Oct; telephone for details. ▣WC ⊖ ⊟ ● ⋇ ★ ▪

Westbury Court Garden The National Trust, Westbury-on-Severn, Gloucestershire (tel Westbury-on-Severn [045 276] 461). 9 m SW of Gloucester on A48. SO 7113 (OS 162). An outstanding example of the formal late 17th-century water garden, with a long canal constructed in the early 18th century, and recently replanted in period with wall fruits, roses and, in a small walled garden, almost 100 species of plants known to have grown in England before 1700. Open Apr and Oct, S, Su and Easter Mon 1100-1700; May to Sept, W-Su and Bank Hols 1100-1800. ▣ ⊖ ⊟ (by appt) ⋒ ⋇

Llanfihangel Court Mrs Somerset Hopkinson, near Abergavenny, Gwent. 4½ m N of Abergavenny on A465, turn E at Llanfihangel Crucorney for ¼ m. SO 3320 (OS 161). Surrounded by woods containing many fine conifers and set among superb scenery, the garden includes a new shrub border in a glade backed by copper beech and thuyas, and one of the original guard towers, or possibly gazebos, splendid specimens of copper beech and the London plane in the stable yard, and an enclosed courtyard with lily pool. Open July and Aug daily 1430-1800; also Easter Su and Bank Hols; parties other times by appt. Peak months spring and early July. ▣WC ⊟ (by appt) ● ⋒ ⋇ ★

Penrhyn Castle The National Trust, Bangor, Gwynedd (tel Bangor [0248] 53084/53356). 2 m E of Bangor on A5, turn N. SH 6071 (OS 115). A 19th-century castle in a dominating position, with a walled garden on three levels: a Victorian parterre terrace, with lily ponds and loggia; a sloping lawn with shrubs giving year-round colour; and a wild garden below. Open Apr to late May and Oct daily 1400-1700; late May to Sept and Bank Hol weekends 1100-1700. ⓟWC ⊖⌂D◗⚹★⛫

Plas Newydd The National Trust, Llanfairpwll, Isle of Anglesey, Gwynedd (tel Llanfairpwll [0248] 714795). 2 m SW of Menai Bridge on A4080. SH 5269 (OS 115). There is a magnificent view of Snowdonia from this fine shrub garden within the shelter of trees planted according to Repton's suggestion. The climate is ideally suited to rhododendrons, camellias, eucryphias and embothriums. To the north of the house is an Italianate terrace garden. Open Apr, Sept and Oct, daily (exc S) 1400-1700; May to Aug and Bank Hols 1200-1700. Peak season spring. ⓟWC⌂◗⚹★⛫

Abbey Dore Court Mrs C.L. Ward, near Hereford, Hereford and Worcester. ½ m E of Abbey Dore on B4347. SO 3830 (OS 149). Reclaimed within the past 18 years, with a woodland garden beside the River Dore, a rock garden with a wide variety of plants and a herbaceous border also with a varied profusion of plants. There is an excellent nursery and plant shop. Open mid-Mar to end Oct, daily 1030-1830. Peak months June to Sept. ⓟWC⌂ (by appt) ◗⩏❀

Moccas Court R. Chester-Master Esq., Moccas, Hereford and Worcester (tel Moccas [098 17] 233). 10 m W of Hereford on B4352, turn N. SO 3543 (OS 149). Overlooking the beautiful Wye landscape, the garden has been designed very much with the river views in mind, and has Victorian terraced gardens converted

to mown grass, a stream garden full of the lush-leaved plants of wet places, and an enclosed woodland walk. Open Apr to Sept Th 1400-1800; parties at other times by appt. Peak season summer. ⌂ (by appt) D⩏⚹⛫

The Weir The National Trust, Swainshill, Hereford and Worcester. 5 m W of Hereford on A438, turn S to River Wye. SO 4341 (OS 149). A wild garden that tumbles down the steeply sloping banks of the River Wye, and in spring is a mass of daffodils, bluebells and other wild flowers. In the upper garden there is a superb view across the river, and there is a small rock garden. Open Apr to mid-May, daily (exc S and Good Fri); mid-May to end-Oct, W and Bank Hols 1400-1800. ⓟ⊖ (1½ m walk) D

Benthall Hall The National Trust, Broseley, Shropshire (tel Telford [0952] 882254). 3 m NE of Much Wenlock; 1 m E on B4376, fork NE onto B4375. SJ 6502 (OS 127). At its best in early spring, June or September, the garden contains many descendants of the crocuses of George Maw, author of *The Genus Crocus*, as well as many unusual and interesting plants in the raised terrace garden to the west of the Elizabethan house. Open Easter Sat to end Sept, T, W, S and Bank Hols 1400-1800. ⓟ⚹⛫

Dudmaston The National Trust, Bridgnorth, Shropshire. 4 m S of Bridgnorth on A442. SO 7488 (OS 138). A large pool was created from a series of smaller pools here during the 19th century, when the grass slope was also terraced. There is a rock garden at one corner of the lake, and at the other end an interesting bog garden. On rising ground to the south is a long rectangular border planted with American plants. Open Easter to end Sept daily 1430-1800. Peak months May to June. ⓟWC⌂ (by appt) D⩏❀ (occasional) ★⛫⩗

Weston Park The Earl of Bradford, Weston-under-Lizard, near Shifnal, Shropshire (tel Weston-under-Lizard [095 276] 207/385). 6 m E of Telford off A5. SJ 8009 (OS 127). A distinctive creation of Capability Brown, who devised the garden's three pools and the original plantings in Temple Wood. Formal bedding is still practised in the 19th-century terrace gardens, though this is primarily a garden for those interested in noble landscape or garden architecture. Open Apr, May and Sept, S, Su and Bank Hols; June to end Aug daily (exc M and F, but inc Bank Hols) 1100-1900. Peak months May to early June. ▯WC ⊖ ⊟ D ● ⚲ ⚲ ★ ▥ ⚲

Central England

Chicheley Hall Trustees of the Hon Nicholas Beatly, Newport Pagnell, Buckinghamshire (tel North Crawley [023 065] 252). 3 m NE of Newport Pagnell on A422. SP 9045 (OS 152). Fine specimen trees provide a mature parkland setting for the early 18th-century house and its 15 acres (6 ha) of gardens, which match the house in their relatively formal design. Open Apr to late Sept, Su, Good Fri and Bank Hols, also W in Aug, 1430-1800; parties at other times by appt. ▯WC ⊟ (by appt) D (guide dogs only) ● ⚲ ⚲ ★ ▥

Milton Cottage Milton Cottage Trust, Deanway, Chalfont St Giles, Buckinghamshire (tel Chalfont St Giles [024 07] 2313). 8 m SE of Chesham on A413, turn W to Chalfont St Giles. SU 9893 (OS 175). The three levels of this garden, probably created in the 17th century, form three separate intimate gardens for the cottage where Milton completed *Paradise Lost* in the 1660s. The top level is a tiny orchard and vegetable garden, the middle level features a rose pergola and cottage garden flowers and plants, and the lowest a lawn with cottage-style borders and edgings to set off a mulberry tree. Open Feb to Oct, T-S and Bank Hol M 1000-1300, 1400-1800; Su 1400-1800. Peak months June and July. ⊖ ⊟ (by appt) ● (limited opening) ★ ▥

Nether Winchendon House

Mrs Spencer Bernard, nr Aylesbury, Buckinghamshire (tel Haddenham [0844] 290101). 6 m SW of Aylesbury on A418, turn N to Cuddington. SP 7312 (OS 165). Since the 1950s an ornamental arboretum has replaced some of the elaborate formal gardens at this Tudor manor house, while the south and west gardens are on the older pattern of formal enclosures: one a lawn flanked by a yew hedge and walls with attractive planted borders, the kitchen garden accommodating a tennis court and a small rock garden. Open May to Aug, Th and Bank Hol weekends, plus other weekends in June and July 1430-1730; parties at other times by appt. ⊟ ⚲ ▥

Stowe School Allied Schools Limited, Buckingham, Buckinghamshire (tel Buckingham [0280] 813650). 2 m NW of Buckingham on A422, turn N to Dadford. SP 6737 (OS 152). William Kent and later Capability Brown altered Stowe's original formal gardens to create a vast classical landscape park of temples, monuments, wooded groves, serpentine lakes, classical bridges and rolling vistas. It provides a magnificent setting for the imposing mansion. Open Easter weekend, mid-July to early Sept F-Su and Aug Bank Hol M 1300-1800. ▯WC ⊟ (by appt) D ● ⚲ ★ ⚲

Haddon Hall The Duke of Rutland, Bakewell, Derbyshire (tel Bakewell [062 981] 2855). 2½ m SE of Bakewell on A6. SK 2366 (OS 119). The series of terraces and steps at Haddon Hall owe their present form to the 17th century, and offer one of the finest of terraced gardens. The house is on a broad terrace with a rose garden; the house lawn is bounded by a balustrade leading to the fountain garden. Below this the ground drops steeply down to the River Wye. The walls are planted with roses and climbers, while peonies, shrub roses and buddleias grow well between the buttresses of the lower garden. Open Apr to end Sept, T-S and Bank Hol M 1100-1800; Bank Hol Su 1400-1800. Peak months June, July. ▯WC ⊖ ⊟ ● ⚲ ★ ▥

Kedleston Hall The Viscount Scarsdale, Derby, Derbyshire (tel Derby [0332] 842191). 4½ m NW of Derby on A52, turn N at Kirk Langley. SK 3140 (OS 128). Robert Adam was responsible from 1758 onwards for the landscape, ornamental buildings and 22 acres (9 ha) of gardens at Kedleston, which include a river-like lake, a woodland walk bright with spring flowers, pleasure garden, paved garden and fountain. Open Easter weekend, then May to end Aug, Su, Bank Hol M and T, 1300-1700. Peak months May and June. ▣WC ⌂ D ➽ ★ ▣

Whatton The Lord Crawshaw, Loughborough, Leicestershire. 4½ m N of Loughborough on A6, turn W. SK 4924 (OS 140). An extensive and attractive garden, with an arboretum, spring bulbs and flowering shrubs, a long, well-planted herbaceous border, formal rose gardens and a large kitchen garden. The Chinese garden is unusual and intriguing, with Chinese and Japanese bronzes displayed in a dell garden setting. Open Easter to end Sept, Su and Bank Hol M 1400-1800; parties at other times by appt. ▣WC ⊖ ⌂ D ➽ ▩ ★

Deene Park, Edmund Brudenell Esq., near Corby, Northamptonshire (tel Bulwick [078 085] 287/361). 5 m NE of Corby on A43. SP 9592 (OS 141). A splendid panoramic setting, fine specimen trees, and a discerning choice of shrubs and herbaceous perennials throughout the garden make impressive surroundings for the imposing mansion. Open June to Aug, also Bank Hols Easter to Aug, 1400-1700. Peak months May to July. ▣WC ⌂ ➽ ⋔ ▩ (occasional) ★ ▣

Holdenby House James Lowther Esq., Northampton (tel Northampton [0604] 770786 or 770241). 6½ m NW of Northampton on A50, turn W. SP 6967 (OS 152). A timeless garden, recently restored and planted with herbaceous plants and shrubs available in 1580, when the original palace was built here. A new Elizabethan garden has been made, there is a double-sided scented border, rose plantings and a traditional kitchen garden, 16th-century fish ponds and pastoral views. Open Apr to end Sept, Su and Bank Hol M; also July and Aug Th, 1415-1715; parties at other times by appt. ▣WC ⌂ ➽ ▩ ☙ ★ ▣ (parties by appt) Rare farm animals; donkeys and train rides.

Lamport Hall Lamport Hall Trust, Lamport, Northamptonshire (tel Maidwell [060 128] 272). 9 m N of Northampton on A508, turn E onto B576. SP 7574 (OS 141). The gardens at Lamport date back to 1677. There are sweeping lawns, fine trees and noble vistas of the parkland beyond, with mixed plant borders, wall plants and a rose garden, a rock garden, and a box bower or arbour. Open Easter to end Sept, Su and Bank Hol M; also July and Aug, Th 1415-1715. Peak months May to July. ▣WC ⊖ ⌂ ➽ (limited opening) ⋔ ▣ ⚕

Flintham Hall M.T. Hilyard Esq., near Newark-on-Trent, Nottinghamshire. 17 m NE of Nottingham on A46. SK 7346 (OS 129). A 19th-century garden, with lake and woodlands, very fine roses, a unique conservatory c.1850, luxuriantly planted, a pheasantry, aviary, shrub and walled gardens and herbaceous borders. Open a few times each year under NGS. ▣WC ⊖ D ➽ ⋔ ▩ (occasional)

Broughton Castle The Lord Saye and Sele, Banbury, Oxfordshire (tel Banbury [0295] 62624). 2½ m SW of Banbury on B4035. SP 4137 (OS 151). Gertrude Jekyll may have had some involvement with the gardens of this partly fortified, moated old house. There are long, attractive herbaceous borders, open grassy meads, parkland, and a charming walled garden which has a knot in box, and circles filled with roses, lavenders and other 'period' plants. Open mid-May to mid-Sept, W and Su; July and Aug W, Th and Su, Bank Hol M, 1400-1700; parties at other times by appt. Peak months June to Aug. WC ⊖ ⌂ D ➽ ⋔ ▩ ☙ ★

Buscot Park The National Trust, Faringdon, Oxfordshire (tel Faringdon [0367] 20786). 2½ m NW of Faringdon on A417. SU 2496 (OS 163). An inviting landscape garden and designed parkland surround the 18th-century house. Three long vistas radiate from the house terrace, one leading to the formal water garden and the others forming green corridors through ornamental trees and young woodlands stretching down to the great lake. Open Apr to end Sept, W-F; also 2nd and 4th S and Su in each month, 1400-1800. Peak months Easter and June to Aug. ⓅWC🚻(by appt) ☛ (from 1430; parties by appt) ⚘ ⌂

Kingston Bagpuize House The Lady Tweedsmuir, near Abingdon, Oxfordshire. 10 m SW of Oxford on A420 at Southmoor. SU 4097 (OS 164). Three distinct periods of garden are displayed here: the formal 17th century around the house, with terracing, statuary and gazebo; the trees and shrubbery of the Victorian era; and the extensive woodland garden and its many interesting plant borders, developed after the Second World War. Open Apr to end June, S, Su and Bank Hol M 1430-1730; parties at other times by appt. Peak season spring. Ⓟ (limited) WC ⊖ (limited) 🚻 (by appt) ☛ ⌂ ❀ ★ ⌂ (no children under 5)

Kingstone Lisle Park Capt T.L. Lonsdale, Wantage, Oxfordshire. 5 m W of Wantage on B4507. SU 3287 (OS 174). Over 2000 new trees have been planted in the garden's 30 acres (12 ha) since the 1950s; the gardens include avenues, an arboretum, parkland and a series of lakes, and a circular rose garden. The walled garden and glasshouses are run as a commercial venture and plants are on sale to visitors. Open Apr to end Aug, Th and Bank Hol weekends 1400-1700; other times by appt. ⓅWC🚻D ☛ (by appt) ⚘ ⌂

Waterperry Horticultural Centre near Wheatley, Oxfordshire (tel Ickford [084 47] 226). 6 m E of Oxford on A40, turn NE at Holton to Waterperry. SP 6206 (OS 164). The extensive walled gardens are now run as nurseries and a garden centre. There are also alpine and rock gardens, and the main ornamental gardens include herbaceous borders, a series of more informal shrub and mixed borders, and a dell and bridge leading to the River Thames. Open daily throughout year (exc Dec 24 to Jan 1); Apr to Sept 1000-1800, Oct to Mar 1000-1600. ⓅWC ⊖ (1 m walk) 🚻 (by appt) D ☛ 🄰 ❀ ⚘

Wroxton Abbey Dr J.R. Seagrave (Director), Wroxton, Banbury, Oxfordshire (tel Banbury [0295] 73551). 2½ m W of Banbury on A422. SP 4141 (OS 151). The 18th-century designs of these 56-acre (23-ha) gardens are a unique example of the early picturesque style of gardening, laid out by Sanderson Miller to make use of flowing lawns, specimen trees and woodlands, natural-looking waters and eye-catching buildings. Flower borders were added in the 19th century. After many years of neglect, the gardens are now being extensively restored. Open Apr to end Sept; passes for garden can be obtained from Reception. Ⓟ🚻 (by appt) D ⚘ ⌂ (by appt)

Alton Towers J.L. Broome Esq., Alton, Staffordshire (tel Oakamoor [0538] 702449). 4½ m E of Cheadle on B5032, turn N. SK 0743 (OS 128). An important and eccentric fragment of garden history, this collection of ornamental garden architecture was created in the early 19th century – an unrepeatable rich man's folly. Open late March to end Oct, daily 0900-dusk. ⓅWC ⊖ 🚻 D ☛ 🄰 ⚘ ★ ⌂ ⚕

Chillington Hall Peter Giffard Esq., Codsall Wood, near Wolverhampton, Staffordshire (tel Brewood [0902] 850236). 6 m N of Wolverhampton on A449, turn W to Coven and Brewood. SJ 8606 (OS 127). An almost untouched park by Capability Brown, with triumphal arch, mile-long (1·6 km) avenue, and one of Brown's largest lakes – 75 acres (30 ha) in extent. The pleasure gardens round the house are pleasingly underplanted with azaleas and rhododendrons. Open May to mid-Sept, Th, Bank Hol Su and Su in Aug 1430-1730; parties at other times by appt. ▣ 🚻 (by appt) D 🚻 🏛

Clive Memorial Garden
Willoughbridge Garden Trust, Elds Wood, Willoughbridge, Market Drayton, Staffordshire (tel Pipegate [063 081] 411). 9 m SW of Newcastle-under-Lyme on A53, turn NW onto A51 for 2 m. SJ 7539 (OS 127). The woodland garden was first created in 1937; in 1961 work was begun on the adjacent sloping field. Pines, birches and oaks provide an effective background for the increasing range of interesting plants round a pool, in the scree garden and in the original woodland garden. Open Mar to end Nov daily 1100-1930. Peak months May, June and autumn. ▣ WC ⊖ 🚻 D 🚻

Farnborough Hall The National Trust, near Banbury, Warwickshire. 6 m N of Banbury on A423, turn NW. SP 4349 (OS 151). The house and its landscape have been altered little since their creation, and remain a splendid example of 18th-century taste. The grass terrace is a great achievement of the British landscape movement, with planned viewing points for the superb views, while visitors are enticed onwards by glimpses of the Ionic temple, the oval temple and the obelisk. Open Apr to end Sept W, S and May Bank Hol weekend, 1400-1800. Peak season spring. ▣ WC ⊖ (limited) 🚻 (by appt) D 🚻

Wightwick Manor The National Trust, Wightwick Bank, Wolverhampton, West Midlands (tel Wolverhampton [0902] 761108). 2½ m W of Wolverhampton on A454. SO 8698 (OS 139). The house is a Pre-Raphaelite shrine, and the garden was laid out in the same mood by Alfred Parsons RA. Yew enclosures lead towards the rose garden and downhill to the ponds. In the lawns are a number of trees planted by notables. The house and garden provide a powerful impression of the Pre-Raphaelite achievement. Open March to end Jan, Th, S, Bank Hol Su and M 1430-1730; parties at other times by appt. ▣ WC ⊖ 🚻 (by appt) D 🚻 ★ 🏛

Eastern Counties

Luton Hoo The Wernher family, Luton, Bedfordshire (tel Luton [0582] 22955). 2 m SE of Luton, entrance W off A6129. TL 1018 (OS 166). A landscape created by Capability Brown in the 1760s, with further tree planting in the 19th century. There are two terrace gardens, one an imposing Italianate rose garden, topiary and formal yew hedges, and an unusual rock garden in the park. Open Apr to mid-Oct, M, W, Th, S and Good Fri 1100-1745, Su 1400-1745. ▣ WC ⊖ 🚻 ▶ 🚻 🚻 ★ 🏛

Duxford Mill Mr and Mrs Robert Lea, near Cambridge, Cambridgeshire (tel Cambridge [0223] 832325). 9 m S of city on A1301. TL 4846 (OS 154). The River Cam winds through the garden, which contains over 2000 modern roses against a background of fine trees, and is landscaped to give pleasing vistas of the mill and other features. Open a few times each year under NGS; parties at other times by appt. Peak months end of June and July. ▣ WC ⊖ 🚻 D ▶ 🚻 🚻

Audley End Dept of the Environment, Saffron Walden, Essex (tel Cambridge [0223] 358911 ext 2245). 1 m W of Saffron Walden on B1383. TL 5238 (OS 154). The grounds designed by Capability Brown in 1763 have remained much as he planned them, with the River Cam widened to form a lake, and 7 acres (2·8 ha) of lawns between it and the house. A ha-ha ensures an uninterrupted view of the tree belts and clumps, and the temples, bridges and an obelisk by Robert Adam (who worked on the house) all remain. There is a small rose garden. Open Apr to Sept daily (exc M, but inc Bank Hol M other than May Day) 1200-1830. Peak season summer. ▣ WC ⊖ 🚻 D ▶ 🚻 🏵 🚻 ★ 🏛

Glazenwood D. Baer Esq., Bradwell, Braintree, Essex. 4 m E of Braintree on A120, turn S. TL 8022 (OS 168). Originally the garden of Samuel Curtis of *Curtis's Botanical Magazine* fame, this is now mostly an informal garden, with grassy walks between borders filled with flowering trees, shrubs, roses, particularly shrub varieties, and ground-cover perennials. Open a few times each year under NGS; parties at other times by appt. ▣WC ⊖ ⊟ D ● ⌂ ✿ ⁂

The Magnolias Mr and Mrs Roger Hammond, 18 St John's Ave, Brentwood, Essex. Turn S off Brentwood High St into Ingrave Rd; after 300 yds turn right at traffic lights, over railway and take 3rd turning to right. TQ 6093 (OS 177). Within a cleverly planned ½-acre (0·2-ha) town garden are to be found 80 varieties of hosta, 40 different magnolias, rare snowdrops and the national collection of arizaemas, pools, ponds, a Japanese pavilion and a wisteria-hung bridge. Open a few times each year under NGS; parties at weekends March to Oct 1000-1700 by appt. ▣ ⊖ ●✿

Benington Lordship Mr and Mrs C.H.A. Bott, Benington, Stevenage, Hertfordshire (tel Benington [043 885] 668). 3 m SE of Stevenage on A602, turn N to Aston and Benington. TL 2923 (OS 166). An intensely English garden, beautifully restored, with a lawn-framed formal rose garden, fish ponds, a rock and water garden, a superb double-sided herbaceous border, and a small, intimate dell garden. Open Easter Mon, May to July, W, Su and Bank Hols; 1st W and Su, and Bank Hols in Aug, 1400-1700; other times by appt. Also 'Snowdrop Sunday', end Feb or early March. Peak months May to July. ▣WC ⊖ (Su limited) ⊟ ● (Su and Bank Hol M) ✿ ⁂

Marston Hall The Rev. Henry Thorold, near Grantham, Lincolnshire (tel Loveden [0400] 50225). 4½ m NW of Grantham on A1, turn NE. SK 8943 (OS 130). The house and 4-acre (1·6-ha) garden have been owned by the same family since the 14th century, and the garden's ancient trees reflect this continuity. The present informal garden of trees and shrubs was designed by John Codrington. There is a rose garden surrounded by a yew hedge and a kitchen garden in the Scottish style, the four sections bordered by herbaceous planting. Open certain Su for local charities; other times by appt. ▣WC D ⌂ ⁂ ▥

Stody Lodge Mr and Mrs Ian MacNicol, Melton Constable, Norfolk (tel Melton Constable [0263] 860 254/572). 3 m S of Holt take Edgefield road off B1354 at Briston, after ½ m turn left through Breck Farm. TG 0634 (OS 133). A magnificent sight in May, this is an unusual garden for East Anglia, with over 2000 azaleas and rhododendrons in the woodland setting and a more formal layout with lawns and shrub borders near the house. Open mid-May to mid-June, Su 1400-1800; other times by appt. ▣WC ⊟ ● (Su and Bank Hols only)

Haughley Park A.J. Williams Esq., near Stowmarket, Suffolk (tel Elmswell [0359] 40205). 3 m NW of Stowmarket on A45, turn N at Haughley New St. TM 0062 (OS 155). A Victorian garden improved by the addition of a well-chosen selection of ornamental shrubs: borders of rhododendrons, viburnums and hydrangeas; a dell planted with mahonias, bamboos, Solomon's seal and other shade-lovers; while the park has good trees and there is a large wood. Open May to Sept T 1500-1800. Peak month May. ▣WC ⊟ (by appt) D ⌂ ▥ ⚹

Helmingham Hall The Lord Tollemache, Stowmarket, Suffolk (tel Helmingham [047 339] 363). 11 m N of Ipswich on B1077. TM 1857 (OS 156). A peaceful garden surrounded by a moat and set within an ancient deer park, and including a walled flower garden with box-edged beds, borders filled with roses, and an old-style kitchen garden where vegetables, fruit and flowers for picking are cultivated. Open May to end Sept Su 1400-1800; parties at other times by appt. Peak months June to Sept. 🅿WC 🖶D 💠🎋♨✿ ★

Heveningham Hall Gulfpark Property Management Ltd, near Halesworth, Suffolk (tel Ubbeston [098 683] 355). 4½ m SW of Halesworth on B1117. TM 3573 (OS 156). The imposing mansion is set within a park landscaped by Capability Brown, with lake and circular ice-house. The Victorian formal garden has been simplified; the orangery by Wyatt is well proportioned; the old, walled kitchen garden contains a rose garden and well-planned mixed borders. Open Aug daily 1000-1730. 🅿WC 🖶 💠🎋♨ ★ 🏛

Ickworth The National Trust, Horringer, Bury St Edmunds, Suffolk (tel Horringer [028448] 270). 2½ m SW of Bury St Edmunds on A143, turn W at Horringer. TL 8161 (OS 155). Though there are traces from the reign of Queen Anne in this garden, the main gardens were laid out in the 1820s to accompany the newly built mansion, and included terraces, lawns, hedges and flowerbeds. More evergreens were added during the 19th century, while this century has seen improvements in the flower borders. Open Apr to end Aug daily (exc M, but inc Bank Hols), Sept to mid-Oct daily (exc M and F), 1400-1800. 🅿WC 🖶 (by appt) D 💠 🎋♨ ★ 🏛 ♿

Magnolia House Mark Rumary and Derek Melville, Yoxford, Suffolk (tel Yoxford [072 877] 321). On A1120 in centre of Yoxford village. TM 3968 (OS 156). The immensely appealing half-acre (0·2-ha) garden of a distinguished garden designer, divided into four separate elements and containing trees, shrubs, hardy perennials and bulbous plants interrelated to provide interest and variety throughout the year. Open a few times each year; write for details. Peak months May to Aug. ⊖ (1 m walk).

The North

Graythwaite Hall Esthwaite Estate Company, Ulverston, Cumbria. 10 m NE of Ulverston on A590, turn W at Newby Bridge. SD 3791 (OS 96). One of the first of Thomas Mawson's landscape gardens, developed from 1890 onwards. There is a formal terraced rose garden, fine views to the woodland, numerous rhododendrons, a raised Dutch garden, notable patterned beds full of bright flowers and unusual half and half balled yews of golden and dark green. Open Apr to end June daily 1000-1800. Peak month May. 🅿WC 🖶

Hutton-in-the-Forest The Lord Inglewood, Penrith, Cumbria (tel Skelton [085 34] 207). 3 m N of Penrith on M6, turn NW at Jctn 41 onto B5305. NY 4635 (OS 90). A pele tower house enclosed by woodland on three sides. Terraces date from the 17th century, with roses, rhodo-dendrons and massive clipped yews; the pleasure grounds run down to the 5-acre (2-ha) ornamental lake, and there are fine specimen trees as well as two other lakes. Open daily through year, dawn to dusk. Peak seasons spring and autumn. 🅿WC 🖶 D 💠 🎋 (car park only) ♨✿ ★ 🏛 ♿

Burton Constable Country Park J.R. Chichester Constable Esq., near Hull, Humberside (tel Skirlaugh [0401] 62400). 4 m NE of Kingston upon Hull on B1238, turn N at Sproatley. TA 1836 (OS 107). Capability Brown's characteristic work can be seen in the 4 acres (1·6 ha) of lawns and gardens, with clipped yews and statuary leading the eye to the parkland beyond. Around the house are courtyards, a flower-lined walk leading to the 1780 orangery, a full herbaceous border, and 22 acres (9 ha) of lakes. Open Good Fri to end Sept, S, Su, Bank Hol M; also T, W, and F in Aug, 1200-1700. Peak season summer. 🅿WC 🖶 💠🎋♨ ★

Beningbrough Hall The National Trust, Shipton-by-Beningbrough, York, North Yorkshire (tel York

[0904] 470666). 5 m NW of York on A19, turn W at Shipton. SE 5158 (OS 105). Dating from the 18th century, and with the wilderness and two privy gardens restored in the old style, the garden also includes well-filled double herbaceous borders, a 19th-century American garden, and a Victorian conservatory. Open Apr to end Oct daily (exc M and F but inc Bank Hols) 1200-1800. ▊WC ⊖ (1 m walk) ⊟ ▛ 卄 ★

Broughton Hall H.R. Tempest Esq., Skipton, North Yorkshire (tel Skipton [0756] 2267). 3½ m W of Skipton on A59. SD 9450 (OS 103). One of the best examples of William Andrew Nesfield's work in the 1850s, with conservatory and courtyard, Italianate pavilion or open gazebo with a magnificent scroll and feather parterre, fairy walk and grove woodland, and mature parkland through which the canalised Broughton Beck runs. Open once a year under NGS; parties at other times by appt. Peak season summer. ▊WC ⊖ D ▩ 🕭 (parties by appt)

Arthington Hall C.E.W. Sheepshanks Esq., Otley, West Yorkshire (tel Arthington [0532] 842115). 5 m E of Otley on A659, turn N at Arthington. SE 2745 (OS 104). A comprehensive collection of maples, as well as flowering trees and shrubs, is the outstanding feature of this 6-acre (2·4-ha) garden. There are also two 18th-century walled gardens, a long herbaceous border, a half-mile (0·8 km) beech walk, and good views of the countryside. Open once a year in July; other times by appt. ⊟ (by appt) ▛ (open days)

Scotland

Dawyck Arboretum Dept of Agriculture & Fisheries for Scotland, near Peebles, Borders. 4½ m W of Peebles on A72, turn SW onto B712, after 5 m turn S at Bellspool. NT 1635 (OS 72). Gifted to the nation in 1978 and administered by the Royal Botanic Garden, Edinburgh, Dawyck contains many mature conifers, including fine

specimens of firs, pines, Western hemlock, spruce and larch, which provide shelter and shade for many species of flowering shrubs, especially rhododendrons. Open Apr to end Sept daily 1000-1700. Peak months Apr to June, autumn. ▊WC ⊟ ✻

Kailzie Garden Mrs Angela Richards, The Garden House, Peebles, Borders (tel Peebles [0721] 22054). 2 m E of Peebles on B7062. NT 2838 (OS 73). The large walled garden has been created largely in the last 15 years. About half is devoted to interesting shrubs and trees; the rest has herbaceous borders, a rose garden and Regency-style conservatory. The surrounding woodland is particularly attractive in the early part of the year. Open mid-March to mid-Oct daily 1030-1730. Peak months March to July. ▊WC D ▛ ⊟ ▩ ✻ ★

Manderston Mr and Mrs Adrian Palmer, Duns, Berwickshire, Borders (tel Duns [0361] 83450). 2 m E of Duns on A6105. NT 8154 (OS 74). Four distinct attractions are to be found here: formal parterres at the south front; an ornate Victorian garden; a remarkable landscape of lake and surrounds; and a recent woodland garden with trees, shrubs and rhododendrons. There is also a magnificent marble dairy, several glasshouses, and ornaments obtained from Lord Duveen. Open mid-May to late Sept Su, Th, Bank Hols, also T in Aug, 1400-1730. ▊WC ⊖ ⊟ D ▛ ⊟ ▩ ✻ ★

Barnhourie Mill Esther M. Horwood-King and Mavis R. Paton, Colvend, by Dalbeattie, Kirkcudbrightshire, Dumfries and Galloway (tel Southwick [038 778] 269). 5 m S of Dalbeattie at Colvend on A710. NX 8654 (OS 84). A fascinating collection of plants in a highly successful garden of 7 acres (3 ha) created since 1962, with dwarf species of rhododendron a speciality, and emphasis on spring plants and autumn colour. Open once a year under Scotland's Garden Scheme and by appt. Peak months Apr, May, Sept and Oct. ▊ ⊟ D ▛

Dundonnell Messrs Alan and Neil Roger, by Garve, Ross and Cromarty, Highland (tel Dundonnell [085 483] 206). 12 m SE of Ullapool on A835, turn W for 12 m on A832 then E to Dundonnell House. NH 1185 (OS 19). A surprising garden for Scotland: a formal garden with an extensive aviary and a fine collection of bonsai; the design charming and with an interesting collection of plants in the various specialised areas of the garden. Open several times each year under Scotland's Garden Scheme. WC ⌂ (by appt) ☛ ✿

An Cala Mrs H.L. Blakeney, Isle of Seil, Argyll, Strathclyde. 7½ m S of Oban on A816, turn SW onto B844 for 8¾ m to Easdale. NM 7317 (OS 55). A charming small garden created within the last 50 years, and in spite of the inevitable salt-laden winds containing a wide selection of plants that thrive in the otherwise relatively mild climate, including *Rhododendron rhabdotum*, acer, hydrangea, camellias, rock garden plants, and roses sheltering near the house. Open Apr to end Sept M and Th 1400-1800. Peak months May, June. ▣ ⊖ ⌂ D ☴ ⚔

Ardanaseig Mr and Mrs J.M. Brown, Kilchrenan, by Taynuilt, Argyll, Strathclyde (tel Kilchrenan [086 63] 216). 1 m E of Taynuilt on A85 turn S onto B845 for 8 m, turn E at Kilchrenan. NN 0824 (OS 50). The high rainfall in the west of Scotland produces a very natural effect, particularly in this garden, with its mossy-barked trees with ferns and lichen-covered stems. The garden rises through wooded slopes from the shore of Loch Awe to a 1-acre (0·4-ha) walled garden, rich in plants on the borderline of hardiness accompanying fine rhododendrons and specimen trees. Open Easter to end Oct daily 1000-1800. Peak months May to June. ▣ WC ⌂ (no coaches) D ☛ ☴ (car park) ✿ ★

Auchincruive Prof. H.J. Gooding, Dept of Horticulture and Beekeeping, the West of Scotland Agricultural College, Ayr, Strathclyde (tel Ayr [0292] 520331 ext. 312). 3 m E of Ayr on A758. NS 3823 (OS 70). A garden of historical interest is combined with the needs of students of horticulture – retaining the past and helping to create gardeners for the future. Both the garden and the modest but interesting arboretum have been retained, and there is a good herbaceous border. Open once a year under Scotland's Gardens Scheme; other times by appt. Peak times July to Sept. ▣ WC ⊖ ☛ (by appt) ✿ (open days)

Battleby Countryside Commission for Scotland, Redgorton, Perth, Tayside (tel Redgorton [0738] 27921). 4 m N of Perth on A9, turn W onto B8063 for ½ m. NO 0829 (OS 58). The house and garden were bought by the Countryside Commission for Scotland in 1970, securing the future of an outstanding collection of trees and shrubs in this garden, much of it created by the last owner, Sir Alexander Cross. Open once a year under Scotland's Gardens Scheme; parties at other times by appt. Peak months May, June, Sept and Oct. ▣ WC ⌂ ✿ (open days only) ⚔

Glendoick P.A. Cox Esq., Perth, Tayside (tel Glencarse [073 886] 205). 8 m E of Perth on A85. NO 2022 (OS 58). Situated in the Carse of Gowrie, which has been called the 'Garden of Scotland', in beautiful countryside and on rich, fertile soil, Glendoick is the result of two generations of gardeners fascinated by rhododendrons; in the woodland garden there are also numerous other interesting woody plants, and the garden boasts an impressive range of eucalyptus. Open once a year under Scotland's Gardens Scheme; other times by appt. Peak months May to early June. ▣ WC ⊖ ⌂ (by appt) ☛ ☴ ✿ (th'out year) ⚘ ★

Index